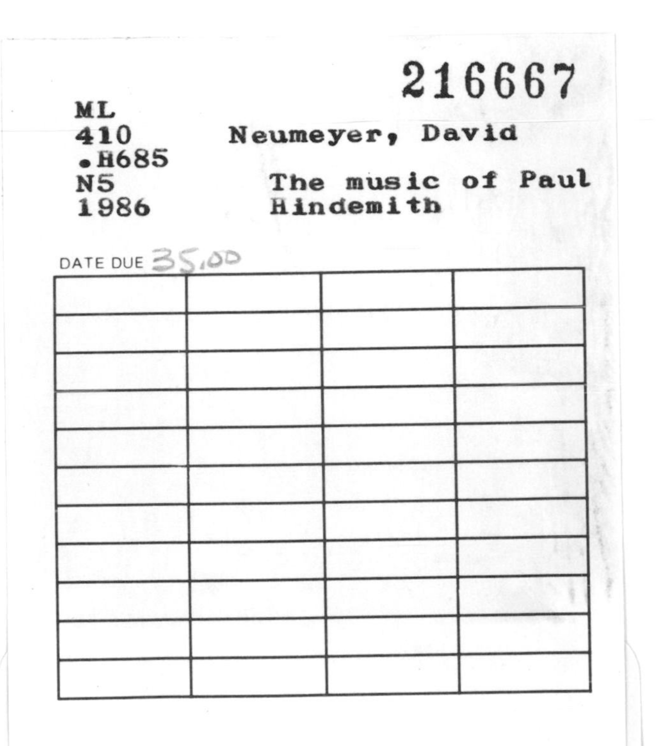

COMPOSERS OF THE TWENTIETH CENTURY

ALLEN FORTE, *General Editor*

THE MUSIC OF PAUL HINDEMITH

DAVID NEUMEYER

Yale University Press
New Haven and London

In memoriam
Raymond L. Neumeyer (1918–1982)
and
Stuart McCallum (1912–1981)

Typeset in the Baskerville types.
Printed in the United States of America by
Vail-Ballou Press, Binghamton, N.Y.

Library of Congress Cataloging-in-Publication Data

Neumeyer, David.
The music of Paul Hindemith.

(Composers of the twentieth century)
"The works of Hindemith, a chronological listing": p.
"Bibliographical note": p.
Includes index.
1. Hindemith, Paul, 1895–1963—Criticism and interpretation. I. Title. II. Series.
ML410.H685N5 1986 780'.92'4 85-14495
ISBN 0-300-03287-0

The paper in this book meets the guidelines for permanence and durability of the Committee on Production Guidelines for Book Longevity of the Council on Library Resources

10 9 8 7 6 5 4 3 2 1

CONTENTS

ACKNOWLEDGMENTS

Thanks are due to the following persons for help with the substance of my Hindemith studies over the past decade. Howard Boatwright gave the second draft of this study an exceptionally careful reading and provided extensive critical notes, some of which I have had the wisdom to incorporate in the final draft. Certain of his comments, especially those which differ from my own point of view, are reproduced in the notes. Dieter Rexroth and Giselher Schubert, of the Paul-Hindemith-Institut, Frankfurt, provided access to Hindemith documents and cordial and efficient help during two research visits. Luther Noss, curator of the Yale Hindemith Collection, prepared the annotated list of works appended to this volume. Series editor Allen Forte gave steadfast encouragement during the stages of drafting and redrafting. Lewis Rowell and Allen Winold read the first draft and offered useful suggestions for improvement. Eckhart Richter read the final draft of chapters 1–3, though the publication schedule did not permit me to make use of his comments. Douglass Green, Bernhard Heiden, Donald Johns, Lee Rothfarb, John Rothgeb, Susan Tepping, Keith Wilson, and the late Richard P. DeLone and Henry W. Kaufmann provided specific items of information. Students in a doctoral seminar at Indiana University, summer 1984—Lisa Derry, Sarah Lewis, Rudy Marcozzi, Ronald Rodman, and Thomas Sterner—helped me find weaknesses in organization and terminology in the chapter on analytic method and made their own contributions to Hindemith research. Finally, my thanks go to Mr. and Mrs. Robert Haag of Minneapolis and Mrs. Stuart McCallum of Sun City, Arizona, for generously providing space on their Great Lakes properties where I could work undisturbed during the drafting of portions of this study.

Grants from the Deutscher Akademischer Austauschdienst, Indiana University, and Kansas State University have supported aspects of my Hindemith research. Permission to quote from the published works of Hindemith came from B. Schott's Söhne, Mainz, through their American representatives, European American Music Distributors. Permission to quote from unpublished documents came from the Fondation Hindemith, Blonay, Vaud, Switzerland, through the Paul-Hindemith-Institut, Frankfurt.

Some of the material of the introduction and chapter 6 came from my program notes for a recital series, *Paul Hindemith: The Viola Legacy,* featuring Samuel Rhodes, sponsored by the Carnegie Hall Association (1985). Some of the material of chapter 10 came from my article "The Genesis and Structure of Hindemith's *Ludus Tonalis,*" *Hindemith-Jahrbuch* 7 (1978): 72–103.

INTRODUCTION

Igor Stravinsky once referred to three neoclassic trends in twentieth-century music: his own, Arnold Schoenberg's, and Paul Hindemith's.[1] This comment needs to be taken advisedly on several counts, not the least being that in another interview Stravinsky admitted his "shameful ignorance" of Hindemith's music.[2] Still, it is a reminder of the remarkable early success which Hindemith enjoyed. Stravinsky and Schoenberg were both more than ten years older and had established their careers before the First World War while Hindemith was still a conservatory student. But by 1922, at the age of twenty-seven, Hindemith was already a well-known composer, and five years later he was appointed professor of composition in the Berlin Musikhochschule, one of the best academic positions in Germany.

Part of his success in the twenties was undoubtedly due to his ability as a performer, a skill he combined with vigorous advocacy of contemporary music of all kinds. It is no overstatement to assert that the combination of performer and composer was at the heart of his musicianship. Alfred Einstein's famous assessment of Hindemith as the natural musician "who produces music as a tree bears fruit" may easily and appropriately be extended to all his music making, not just composition.[3] Being a creative performing musician was not anomalous or an unresolvable paradox, but an essential part of his makeup, as it was to a long line of masters from J. S. Bach and Mozart, to Beethoven and Liszt, to Rachmaninoff and Bartók.

Stravinsky's remark also points to the pervasiveness of an active interplay between musical tradition and the avant-garde in the period between the two world wars. As many writers have noted, however, the variety of

1. Igor Stravinsky and Robert Craft, *Memories and Conversations* (New York: Doubleday, 1960), 122. I am indebted to Douglass Green for bringing this comment to my attention. See also his article "Cantus Firmus Techniques in the Concertos and Operas of Alban Berg" in Rudolf Klein, ed., *Alban Berg Symposium Wien 1980: Tagungsbericht* (*Alban Berg Studien,* vol. 2 [Vienna: Universal, 1981]), 56–68.

2. Igor Stravinsky and Robert Craft, *Dialogues and a Diary* (London: Faber and Faber, 1968), 103.

3. Alfred Einstein, "Paul Hindemith," *Modern Music* 3 (1927): 21.

the results can only very loosely be contained by the word *neoclassicism*. The "return to . . ." movement of the twenties was part of a general rejection of the old romantic and expressionistic culture that was held responsible for World War I. More specifically, it was a rejection of the later romantic insistence on continuous evolution, a doctrine which can still be seen clearly in the writings of Schoenberg and others. The "return to" meant looking back beyond romanticism, beyond the nineteenth century, in search of artistic ideals or compositional models. Darius Milhaud, one of the composers of the Parisian group *les Six*, described the motivation as follows: "What musicians asked for now was a clearer, sturdier, more precise type of art that should not yet have lost its qualities of human sympathy and sensitivity. . . . After all the vapors of impressionism, would not this simple, clear art renewing the tradition of Mozart and Scarlatti represent the next phase in the development of our music?"[4] The term *neoclassicism* conveys at best only a partial sense of the ways in which this crisis of tradition and modernity was played out in the twenties and thirties. Indeed, perhaps the best way to regard the "return to . . ." movement is as the final chapter in nineteenth-century historicism, as characteristic a feature of that era as its doctrine of progress.

We may treat similarly the term *neue Sachlichkeit* (New Objectivity), the German equivalent of the French neoclassicism of Stravinsky and the composers of *les Six* which Hindemith took up deliberately in early 1923, and of which he is the principal representative. He was put forward by his apologists as the *neue Typus*, the antiromantic urban composer who thrived on clarity, concision, and linear energy rather than on the late romantics' diffuse forms, exaggerated emotion, and tortured harmonic logic.[5] The dichotomy was useful as fuel for polemic, but it obscured the fact that in an important sense Hindemith was also a true inheritor of the mantle of Brahms, the romantic conservative.[6] The "return to" brand of neo-

4. Darius Milhaud, *Notes without Music*, trans. Donal Evans, ed. Rollo Myers (New York: Alfred A. Knopf, 1953), 95.

5. Hindemith as the *neue Typus* is the protagonist of Heinrich Strobel's biography, *Paul Hindemith* (Mainz: Schott, 1930; 3d ed., 1948). An especially perceptive reading of the relationship between neoclassicism and expressionism in Hindemith's early music may be found in Giselher Schubert, *Hindemith*, Rowohlts Bildmonographien, no. 299 (Reinbek bei Hamburg: Rowohlt, 1981), 48–50.

6. A reasonable case could be made for Brahms as one of the most important influences on Hindemith, but it is also important to stress the wide range of Hindemith's sources: he was "a mid-twentieth-century representative of the German cosmopolitan line of Schumann, Brahms, and Reger; additional influences in his work came from Debussy as well as from Bach, Handel, Schütz, and the German sixteenth-century Lied composers" (Donald J. Grout, *A History of Western Music*, rev. ed. [New York: W. W. Norton, 1973], 687). Though it does violence to

classicism lay very much on the surface of Stravinsky's music, as in *Pulcinella* or the Octet. It was at best only an awkward appendage to a few works by Schoenberg; the Suite for Piano, Op. 25, is an example. But for Hindemith the object was always synthesis, reconciliation of past and present.

The problem he faced, however, was more complex than Brahms's looking over his shoulder at Beethoven. In common with most composers in this century, Hindemith's methods were eclectic, taking advantage of the extraordinarily increased opportunities to learn about, hear, and play music of all periods and nations afforded by the publication of historical music and such technological advances as radio and phonograph. The composers who made the most of these possibilities were those who could confront different types of music and turn their experience into a convincing, consistent personal voice. Hindemith achieved such a stylistic synthesis in the opera *Mathis der Maler* (1933–35), which drew together elements of the Western musical tradition from the medieval era to the present, by no means excluding the nineteenth century. The refinement and further exploration of that synthesis occupied him to the end of his life.

The inward journey his music describes is necessarily subtle and complex and is revealed in ways that the casual listener may often miss. Though my principal task is to chart this course of development in terms of technical features of his music, a secondary task—necessary to the first—is to fill an important gap in Hindemith research: an adequate interpretation of his compositional theory, including the nature and extent of its connection to his practice.[7] Hindemith is hardly alone among twentieth-century composers in being associated with a self-produced theoretical framework for his music, but he is the only major composer who attempted to make that framework comprehensive, general, and capable of acting as much more than a handy tool chest of compositional devices. Because he linked the theory to analysis and criticism, an assessment of it is necessary in any as-

---

the metaphor, I should also make it clear that I do not claim that Hindemith was the *only* inheritor of Brahms's mantle.

7. Two previous studies which have taken up this question with problematic results are Victor Landau, "Paul Hindemith: A Case Study in Theory and Practice," *Music Review* 21 (1960): 38–54; and Eberhart Zwink, *Paul Hindemiths "Unterweisung im Tonsatz" als der Konsequenz der Entwicklung seiner Kompositionstechnik* (Göppingen: Alfred Kümmerle, 1974). See also the comments in Andres Briner, *Paul Hindemith* (Mainz: Schott, and Zurich: Atlantis, 1971), 305–07; the review of Zwink by Peter Cahn, "Hindemith aus der Sicht statistischer Analyse," *Hindemith-Jahrbuch/Annales-Hindemith* 4 (Mainz: Schott, 1974): 140–48 (hereafter cited as *HJB*); and further comments on Zwink by Bernhard Billeter, "Die kompositorische Entwicklung Hindemiths am Beispiel seiner Klavierwerke," *HJB* 6 (1977): 104–21.

sessment of his music. I will therefore propose a new view of the *Craft of Musical Composition*[8] and allied works and, based on my reading, an analytic method suited to Hindemith's music.

BIOGRAPHICAL FRAMEWORK

The bare framework of facts about Hindemith's career, his development in compositional style and technique, is easy enough to set forth. By way of orientation to the subject, I have given a very condensed list of those facts in the section below.

To 1917 (and war service): Juvenilia, primarily chamber music on German classical and romantic models; Cello Concerto, Op. 3 (1916).

1918–22: These years combine eclectic experimentation after Debussy, Schreker, Busoni, Reger, Schoenberg, Stravinsky, and Bartók, with activity designed to make his name known as a composer: involvement as composer, performer, and (later) one of the directors of the Donaueschingen modern music festivals (which with the festivals of the ISCM [International Society for Contemporary Music] were the leading such fora in Europe for contemporary music in the 1920s); the founding of the Amar quartet, which specialized in new music; and the premieres of three scandalous one-act operas *(Mörder, Hoffnung der Frauen; Sancta Susanna;* and *Das Nusch-nuschi).*

1923–27: Early in 1923, during the composition of the song cycle *Das Marienleben,* Op. 27, he turned abruptly to the linear-contrapuntal manner of the New Objectivity (neue Sachlichkeit). This shift is especially exemplified by the *Kammermusiken* series (Opp. 24, 36, 46) and the opera *Cardillac,* Op. 39. In 1927, Franz Schreker appointed him professor of composition in the Berlin Musikhochschule.

8. Paul Hindemith, *The Craft of Musical Composition, Vol. 1: Theoretical Part,* trans. Arthur Mendel (New York: Associated Music, 1942; rev. ed., 1945). Title of German original, *Unterweisung im Tonsatz, Band 1: Theoretischer Teil* (Mainz: Schott, 1937; rev. ed., 1940). *Vol. 2: Exercises in Two-Part Writing* (New York: Associated Music, 1941). Title of German original, *Unterweisung im Tonsatz, Band 2: Übungsbuch für den zweistimmigen Satz* (Mainz: Schott, 1939). Unless indicated otherwise, citations from vols. 1 and 2 are from the translations. *Vol. 3: Übungsbuch für den dreistimmigen Satz,* ed. Andres Briner, P. Daniel Meier, and Alfred Rubeli (Mainz: Schott, 1970); trans. in part by unnamed Yale University students in the mid-1940s (unpublished photolithographic copy in the Yale Hindemith Collection). *Vol. 4: Übungsbuch für den vierstimmigen Satz* (unpublished; only one chapter, "Übung 21," extant; photolithographic copy in the Yale Hindemith Collection). Citations from vols. 3 and 4 are from the German texts. The four volumes are cited hereafter as *Craft I, II, III, and IV.*

1927–32: There are three strands in this period, two showing the influence of professional colleagues in Berlin, the third distinctly Hindemith's own: (1) experimentation with mechanical and electrical instruments, as well as ancient instruments; (2) involvement with the Jugendmusikbewegung, a musical laymen's organization that sought, among other things, to promote amateur performance of German music of the early and prebaroque eras and the integration of some of its stylistic aspects into new music composition; (3) the beginnings of a synthesis of the *Jugendmusik*-inspired style with his New Objective manner. This becomes clear in the opera *Neues vom Tage* and the three *Konzertmusiken,* Opp. 48–50, but is already evident in the last of the *Kammermusiken,* the Organ Concerto, Op. 46, no. 2. It is in connection with the *Sing- und Spielmusik* that the term *Gebrauchsmusik* (music for use) so often associated with Hindemith first appears. His promotion of the ideals of the Youth Music Movement, a collaboration with Bertolt Brecht in 1929, and finally the composition of the libretto for *Mathis der Maler* are the closest Hindemith came to direct involvement in the great, sharply polarized political-social questions of these years, though the conception of a grand musical community of laymen and professionals continued to inform his work throughout his life.

1932–42: This is the decade of *Mathis,* a time in which Hindemith's personal circumstances became unsettled. Performances of his music were banned in Germany, he lost his teaching position, emigrated to Switzerland in 1938 and then to the United States in 1940, where he took a new academic position at Yale University. But at the same time he fully achieved the synthesis of technique and style he had been working toward, and a period of free and masterful composition followed: *Mathis der Maler* and the solo and orchestral works closely related to it (including *Der Schwanendreher* [1935], *Trauermusik* [1936], and the several solo sonatas after the Sonata in E for Violin [1935]). He also worked out the first of a series of revisions of earlier pieces: *Five Songs on Old Texts* (original, Op. 33 [1924]; revised 1933) and *Marienleben* (Op. 27 [1922–23]; revised 1936–37, but not completed until 1945; published 1948). Another major task was the formulation of a compositional theory and pedagogy in *The Craft of Musical Composition* 1 (1937) and 2 (1939).

1942–52: With the *Ludus Tonalis* (1942) came even greater stylistic differentiation and refinement of technique, but also the first evidence of a tendency toward abstraction. In many respects, this was the best decade of Hindemith's career—his circumstances were tranquil, and he produced a continuing series of varied, mature compositions. He wrote a number of textbooks, including the third volume of *The Craft of Musical Composition* (not published until 1970), as well as a kind of compositional confessional document, *A Composer's World* (1952; based on the Norton lectures at Harvard, 1948–49).

1952–56: A relatively dry period—revision of *Cardillac,* but few new compositions. Hindemith worked sporadically on the opera *Die Harmonie der Welt,* which was completed in 1957. Documents give some evidence of a short-lived compositional crisis provoked by his alienation from the important segment of the rising generation of German composers represented by the Darmstadt school. He moved to Switzerland in 1953, taught at the University of Zurich till 1957, and was increasingly active as a conductor.

1956–63: Hindemith retired from university teaching but continued conducting until his death. He produced few compositions (by earlier standards): some large works including the *Pittsburgh Symphony* (1958) and his second Organ Concerto (1962), both commissioned; an exquisite one-act opera on a libretto by Thornton Wilder, *The Long Christmas Dinner;* a set of madrigals; and nine of thirteen Latin solo motets. Throughout this period, he attempted to broaden his stylistic base by a limited, very personal accommodation with the mannerisms of post-Webern serialism. His last work was a Mass for mixed chorus a cappella, premiered under his direction little more than a month before his death in December 1963.

The reader will find a short and highly readable account of Hindemith's development with reference to specific compositions and writings in Ian Kemp's *Paul Hindemith.* Kemp has also written the "Hindemith" entry for the *New Groves Dictionary of Music and Musicians.* A study that makes considerable use of letters and other documents but avoids analysis of the music is Geoffrey Skelton's *Paul Hindemith: The Man behind the Music.* The standard biography, Andres Briner's *Paul Hindemith,* published originally in German, is soon to be published in an updated English translation.[9] The reader who commands German will find three pictorial biographies helpful: *Paul Hindemith: Zeugnis in Bildern, Paul Hindemith: Die letzten Jahren,* and Giselher Schubert's Rowohlt monograph.[10] Reports on Hindemith scholarship have been appearing in the numbers of the *Hindemith-Jahrbuch/Annales-Hindemith,* which began publication in 1971.[11] An excellent summary of the views of German scholars in the past decade can be found (along with more pictorial documents) in the program book of the Nordrhein-Westfalen Hindemith festival (1980–81).[12]

9. Ian Kemp, *Paul Hindemith* (London: Oxford University Press, 1970); Stanley Sadie, ed., *The New Groves Dictionary of Music and Musicians* (London: Macmillan, 1980), s. v. "Hindemith, Paul"; Geoffrey Skelton, *Paul Hindemith: The Man behind the Music* (New York: Crescendo, 1975). The translation of Briner's biography was announced in 1984 but has not appeared as of this writing (March 1985).

10. *Paul Hindemith: Zeugnis in Bildern,* 2d ed. (Mainz: Schott, 1961); *Paul Hindemith: Die letzten Jahren* (Mainz: Schott, 1965); Giselher Schubert, *Hindemith.*

11. Twelve volumes of the *Jahrbuch* were published between 1971 and 1983.

12. Dieter Rexroth, ed., *Hindemith-Zyklus Nordrhein-Westfalen 1980–81* (Wuppertal: Kulturamt der Stadt, 1980).

AN ANALOGY TO BACH

In writing a critical appreciation of Hindemith, I feel rather as Kirnberger or Forkel must have felt in promoting the work of J. S. Bach near the end of the eighteenth century. Hindemith is doubly out of fashion now, as Bach was then. Even at the height of Hindemith's reputation and influence, when "the first pieces of his on the radio in 1948–49 were for us indescribable discoveries," as Karlheinz Stockhausen recalls,[13] stylistic changes in serious and commercial music were beginning that quickly left Hindemith behind. By the time of his death, a generation of composers who based their work on the post-Webern serialism of the 1940s was already active. These composers were not only knowledgeable about electronic music and jazz, but were also willing to exploit that knowledge. To them Hindemith could only have been as old hat as Bach was "old peruke" to his own sons.[14] Furthermore, Hindemith had the same unsettling tendency to infect his music with the qualities of the "learned mathematician," as Scheibe labeled Bach: abstract symbolism, an apparent lack of interest in instrumental color, and an off-putting tone of didacticism. Like Bach in the 1780s, Hindemith's reputation is covered with clichés fair and false which have clung to him more tenaciously than to any of his contemporaries.

The Hindemith-Bach analogy, like any, becomes problematic if pushed too far. (It would be absurd, for example, to find in the severe, scientistic generation of the fifties an equivalent to the rococo!) But the analogy is not wholly idle. Hindemith himself invoked it in a Bach bicentennial address in Hamburg in 1950,[15] at a time when he must have begun to realize that, by refusing to return to Germany to live after World War II, he had also forfeited his leadership among young German composers.

Hindemith is not the only composer in the first half of this century whose work is gradually being rescued from the complexities and confusion of the era in which he lived. The rapid pace of events, the virulence and surprising persistence of strongly polarized polemic, the wide range of national and international influences, unprecedented ease of communication, and the resulting multiplicity of crosscurrents in the political and social spheres all had their counterparts in the high arts, science, and technology. Though the era's lode points, the two World Wars, are all too clear, the paths to and from them are many and often still obscure.

13. Schubert, *Hindemith*, 108.

14. Hindemith mentions this remark of J. C. Bach in his *Johann Sebastian Bach: Heritage and Obligation* (New Haven: Yale University Press, 1952), 12.

15. Hindemith, *Bach*, is a revised version of the lecture. The autobiographical character of this document has been noted by most writers on Hindemith's later career.

In music criticism, as in art criticism in general, it is a commonplace that the significant complexes of ideas cluster about *historicism* and *modernism.* But from these complexes extraordinary paradoxes arise. The musical avant-garde of the early 1920s was an inchoate collection of atonalists, "young classicists" (after Busoni), vitalists, folklorists, and some pre–World War I expressionists. The dominant creed was the modernism of literature, painting, and sculpture. (As C. S. Lewis put it, "counter-romanticism makes strange bedfellows."[16]) Yet this modernism, paraded about as a truly revolutionary doctrine, was fundamentally an extreme extension of postures of the nineteenth-century romantics, a romantic modernism that held dear the old, convenient polarities: "the alienated artist against the complacent bourgeois, the avant garde against the academy, the outsider against the establishment." The modernist rejected precisely the most characteristic images of culture and society in the 1920s: "the machine, the metropolis, the mass man in mass culture."[17]

The resulting ironies are clear and numerous. It was not the section of the avant-garde most directly associated with the older generation—the expressionists, like Schoenberg—that made the first substantial inroads into the fields of film music, mechanical music, or a rapprochement with commercial music (the new jazz), but the neoclassicists, the historicists who were supposed to be following Busoni's advice and deliberately looking well back into the past for innovation.[18] Nevertheless, the expressionists succeeded in posing the most radical new compositional techniques, like Schoenberg's dodecaphonic method.

In music criticism, August Halm and Heinrich Schenker turned the modernists' arguments against modernity.[19] Both opposed organic unity

16. C. S. Lewis, *The Pilgrim's Regress* (London: Geoffrey Bles, 1933; reprint, Grand Rapids: Eerdmans, 1958), 98.

17. Peter Gay, *Freud, Jews and Other Germans* (London: Oxford University Press, 1978), 232.

18. On Hindemith and the several movements of the early 1920s, see the essay collection *Erprobungen und Erfahrungen: Zu Paul Hindemith's Schaffen in den Zwanziger Jahren,* ed. Dieter Rexroth, *Frankfurter Studien,* no. 2 (Mainz: Schott, 1978). Also, Rudolf Stephan, "Über Paul Hindemith," *HJB* 4 (1974): 45–62; Dieter Rexroth, "Tradition und Reflexion beim frühen Hindemith," *HJB* 2 (1972): 91–113; "Zu den *Kammermusiken* von Paul Hindemith," *HJB* 6 (1977): 47–64.

19. The most accessible of Halm's criticism is collected in *Von Form und Sinn der Musik,* ed. Siegfried Schmalzriedt (Wiesbaden: Breitkopf & Härtel, 1978). Schenker's antimodern criticism may be found scattered throughout his writings, but particularly in the later works, including *Das Meisterwerk in der Musik,* 3 vols. (Munich: Drei Masken Verlag, 1925–1930); and *Der freie Satz, Neue musikalische Theorien und Phantasien,* vol. 3 (Vienna: Universal, 1935), trans. as *Free Composition* by Ernst Oster (New York: Longman, 1979).

(the artwork as biological system) to the mechanical.[20] The alienated artist became the isolated genius whose ideas were secrets hidden from the masses of lesser intellects. For Schenker, these secrets were knowledge of the principles of composing-out from the natural triad and prolongation of strict counterpoint as well as possession of the ability to improvise out of the background (Ursatz). For Halm, the secret of genius was the ability to achieve the final synthesis of compositional craft and will (in Schopenhauer's sense). The result is an inversion of the polarity avant-garde against the academy. Schenker plainly saw the academy in his contemporaries among music historians and theorists, and he repeatedly vilified those who he felt should have known better, who should have been able to grasp the nature of genius, but who were blind to it. The so-called avant-garde, on the other hand, was filled with radical know-nothings and nihilistic madmen. Schenker and Halm disagreed on who was Zeus in music's pantheon (Halm favored Bruckner, Schenker Beethoven), but both were in agreement on their principal task: the preservation of an older aesthetic culture free from the political and materialistic distortions so bitterly obvious in the twenties. The true person of the present was the one who could appreciate genius; not the avant-garde versus the academy, but the true musician versus the academy, the modernist avant-garde being outside the argument altogether. That the practical result of their views must be stylistic and technical stasis did not seem to concern them. As Schenker stated:

> A theory teacher writes: "If Beethoven were composing today, his tonal language would more closely resemble Hindemith than Clementi." The names of Beethoven, Hindemith, and Clementi clash rudely here! It might be . . . but the solution to this problem is really very simple. If we assume that Beethoven were writing "today" like Hindemith, then he would be just as bad as Hindemith. If there were a composer alive of Beethoven's abilities, rest assured, he would compose like Beethoven![21]

The present century has been an era of great diversity and sharp contrasts, an era which, at least until the Second World War, drew forward many of the paradoxes and contradictions of the nineteenth century. I have dwelt on these points in order to emphasize a perception underlying recent Hindemith criticism. As Ludwig Finscher writes, Hindemith's work is "at once more and less than the [critical] ideologies would have it. Cliché images are little help in grasping the whole picture, complex and contradictory as it is." What Peter Gay says of Brahms may as appropriately be

20. Schenker's mystical formulation of this appears in the introductory material to *Free Composition*. The biological analogy apparently never attracted Hindemith, who favored the physical and architectural images he derived from Hans Kayser.

21. Schenker, *Meisterwerk I*, 219.

said of Hindemith: "The lesson of his reputation is the urgent need to restore our sense of complexity in Modernism."[22] The various Hindemiths of music criticism over the years have been mostly cardboard figures—the Dadaist-for-a-day of the early twenties, the unreflective *Musikant* or *Spielmann,* the dogmatic natural theorist, the tonal reactionary, and the bitter and isolated retiree. Such characterizations are in the same league as those that make of Schoenberg nothing but a dodecaphonic radical, Stravinsky a suave pandiatonicist changing styles like hats, or Bartók a Hungarian folk melodist. All are too simple to be true.

Hindemith especially needs to be rescued from the residue of the tonal-dodecaphonic debate of the late forties and fifties. Certainly he was partly responsible for the outcome: his *Craft of Musical Composition* and later publications promoted a physically based theory of music with the major triad at its center, and he vigorously rejected deliberate atonality or polytonality and serial techniques. His criticism of the last in particular has caused both consternation and confusion.[23] Hindemith plainly did not connect his assessment of the fundamental shortcomings of serial techniques with his opinion of the "classic" music written with their aid. For example, in his final act as a university teacher he gave a series of lectures on Schoenberg's string quartets at the University of Zurich in 1957; in an earlier lecture he described pieces by Webern as "complete miniature forms [which] are thoroughly consistent . . . and can be recognized as such immediately."[24] But Adorno found in Hindemith as useful a villain as he did in Stravinsky and worked out a critique centering on the Musikant and on Gebrauchsmusik, by means of which Hindemith was said to have violated modernist principles and so his place in the necessary historical evolution in attempting to obscure the distance between the composer and public. To Adorno,

22. Ludwig Finscher, "Paul Hindemith: Versuch einer Neuorientierung," *HJB* 1 (1971): 18; Gay, *Freud,* 233.

23. *Craft I,* 153–56; *Introductory Remarks for the New Version of "Das Marienleben,"* trans. Arthur Mendel (New York: Associated Music, 1948), 13; *A Composer's World: Horizons and Limitations* (Cambridge: Harvard University Press, 1952; reprint, Gloucester, Mass.: Peter Smith, 1969), 139–44; "Hören und Verstehen ungewohnter Musik," lecture at University of Zurich, December 15, 1955, published in *HJB* 3 (1973): 178–79.

24. Briner, *Hindemith,* 273–74. Rudolf Stephan discusses the influence of Schoenberg on Hindemith's music in the twenties in "Über Paul Hindemith," *HJB* 4 (1974): 45–62. See also Andres Briner, "Paul Hindemith und Arnold Schoenberg," *HJB* 4 (1974): 149–51; Hans Heinz Stuckenschmidt, "Paul Hindemiths Aufbruch und Heimkehr," *HJB* 4 (1974): 18, 26–7; and my Ph.D. diss., "Counterpoint and Pitch Structure in the Early Music of Hindemith" (Yale University, 1976), 218–21. The comment about the Webern pieces is in Hindemith, "Hören und Verstehen," 185.

Hindemith was bourgeois and unimaginative (= not alienated), not profound (= not a genius), a dogmatic theorist (= academic).[25] The revisions of several of his earlier compositions worked out in the 1940s and early 1950s became the hapless victims of this critical battle. Hindemith fired the first shot with the "Introductory Remarks" to the revised *Marienleben* cycle (1948), in which he repeated his antiserial arguments and set up a spurious dichotomy between his earlier and later work.

The critical attitude toward Hindemith that prevailed about the time of his death can be summarized as follows: the wild-eyed radical of the early twenties who seemed to alternate between morally irresponsible expressionism and Dadaist absurdity eventually became the benign exponent of Gebrauchsmusik, turned dogmatic when he acquired a theory, and finally became bitter when he could not convert everyone to his point of view. Fortunately, in the past decade the situation has begun to change, and the picture that is gradually emerging is much richer. Even in Hindemith's very eclectic and often simply modish early music, Dieter Rexroth has found evidence of sober historical reflection, which would have contradicted the Musikant cliché before it was formed.[26] By 1925 Hindemith knew the most current theoretical writings of Schenker and Kurth, and he could write to the former:

> I can say to you that I am an enthusiastic and delighted reader of your books. Delighted because . . . in them the foundations of musical creation are revealed, which—as you so rightly say again and again—have always been and will always be valid. And for our present-day music they are just as important as for any in the past. That I, before I had read a sentence of your writings, sought consistently to fulfill these fundamental requirements—please do not laugh yet—do believe true of me. These attempts have in part failed, to be sure; in many pieces they are probably not clear, in others they are perhaps hidden in a waste of superficialities. (It takes a long while before one has come so far as to be able to express correctly what one wishes to say.)[27]

25. Theodor W. Adorno, "Ad vocem Hindemith, eine Documentation," in *Impromptus* (Frankfurt: Suhrkamp, 1968), 51–87. See also Rudolf Stephan, "Adorno und Hindemith: Zum Verständnis einer schwierigen Beziehung," *HJB* 7 (1978): 25–31; Briner, "Hindemith und Adornos Kritik des Musikanten: Oder, von sozialer und soziologischer Haltung," *HJB* 1 (1971): 26–41.

26. Dieter Rexroth, "Tradition und Reflexion," 91–113.

27. Dieter Rexroth, ed., *Paul Hindemith: Briefe* (Frankfurt: Fischer, 1982), 122–23. The translation is mine. Hindemith's letter, which is dated Frankfurt, October 25, 1926, was written in response to the comment in Schenker's *Das Meisterwerk in der Musik*, volume 1, cited above. The version of Hindemith's letter published by Rexroth is actually a draft; John Rothgeb shared a copy of the final letter, in which only a few small changes were made. Schenker replied on November

More recent scholarship offers a view of Hindemith's career and music that supplants both the "young-brash-atonal" versus "old-dull-tonal" polarity of the old criticism and the constructivist, counter-romantic *neue Typus* of Strobel and Mersmann.[28] This is hardly to claim unanimity among Hindemith scholars or to suggest that the old criticism is wholly dead. In Arnold Whittall's *Music since the First World War,* for instance, the schizophrenic Hindemith appears once more as brash, atonal, vigorous in his earlier years, but suffering a change of heart about the time of *Mathis* and promptly becoming careful, tonal, and anemic: "Dull, leisurely, lyric flow is the predominant quality and one longs for a touch of the old eccentricity or vulgarity." There is even the patrionizing sympathy for the old man evident in some earlier literature: "It is infinitely sad that Hindemith's later music gives no more than an occasional flicker of a positive conservatism which could have balanced the youthful excesses of the 1920s."[29]

A COMMON THREAD

If the Hindemith-Bach analogy is dependent on an unpredictable future and the atonal-tonal or progressive-conservative dichotomy is insufficient, then what are the common elements in Hindemith's artistic journey from the New Objectivity through the Jugendmusikbewegung and *Mathis der Maler* to "Ite, angeli veloces," *Harmonie der Welt,* and the Mass? The central theme is exactly that consistent development which the old criticism denied him. Hindemith began with the juxtaposition of counter-romanticism to expressionism, advanced to a synthesis of that juxtaposition with attributes of nineteenth-century style, and finally, through years of refinement,

12. To Hindemith's point about Schenker's idea and the musician's understanding, Schenker said: "Your 'good musician' always waits till someone else's opinion is published and then wants to make everyone believe that he knew the same thing (really beforehand). Why didn't he discover his own opinion earlier?" To Hindemith's assertion that Schenker's theories also have validity for contemporary music: "You had the kindness to express [the thought] that my ideas on past music hold true for present-day music as well. I myself do *not* find this [to be the case]. I think that you would do better to have the courage to declare that contemporary music is wholly new than to attempt to anchor it still in the past." The final line of Schenker's letter makes the gulf between the two men plain indeed: "It is certainly true that your music is no longer connected with that of the masters. You do not admit it, so I must unequivocally state it."

28. Heinrich Strobel, *Paul Hindemith*; Hans Mersmann, *Die moderne Musik seit der Romantik* (Wildpark-Potsdam: Athenaion, 1928); *Die Tonsprache der neuen Musik* (Mainz: Schott, 1930). Strobel also wrote the forewords to *Zeugnis in Bildern* and *Paul Hindemith: Werkverzeichnis* (Mainz: Schott, 1969).

29. Arnold Whittall, *Music since the First World War* (London: J. M. Dent, 1977), 74, 75.

tended at times to carry the synthesis into an idiosyncratic, abstract world of musical symbolism. In the first stage is the neue Typus; in the second, *Mathis* and music allied to it; in the last, *Melancholie des Vermögens*—the melancholy of success Hindemith himself ascribed to Bach.[30]

The New Objectivity was frankly antiromantic, a rejection of pre–World War expressionism and an affirmation of a new urban culture—society as a city-machine. The New Objective composers substituted linear, kinetic energy and deliberate formal constructivism for the nineteenth century's psychological development (motivic working and endless melody), functional harmony, and sensuous orchestral timbres. To counteract the self-serious subjectivism of the expressionists in particular, the music of the twenties was brittle, witty, sometimes vulgar, and often politically engaged. Even music using expressionistic techniques was more "spatial" than emotional, resulting in a "constructed subjectivism." Excellent examples in Hindemith's work are the slow movement of the *Kammermusik* No. 1, Op. 24, no. 1, the slow movement of the Sonata for Viola, Op. 25, no. 4, and the Passion songs from *Das Marienleben,* "Vor der Passion" and "Pietà." These pieces, all from 1922, combine pure form with intensity in much the same way as the early Bauhaus paintings of Klee and Kandinsky.

In the first extended study of Hindemith's music (1925), Franz Willms claimed that the consistent thread in his development was "emphasis on the melodic and a striving for formal clarity."[31] In traditional major-minor tonal music, the essential dialectic was between the forces of melody and harmony. In the new music of the twenties this opposition was replaced by melody and form. The melodic line has energy, motion, rhythmic drive, motivic "thought"; form shapes and controls. This is closely related to contemporary emphases in the visual arts. Klee's famous phrase "taking a line for a walk" shows the conception of line as energy and as thought. The return to simple geometric forms shows the clear shaping and control of that linear energy.

Willms takes for granted the pervasive influence of Ernst Kurth, an influence seriously underrated in much current literature on music of the twenties. Composers after the First World War took their justification for "linear counterpoint" and "functionless harmony" from two of Kurth's books, *Die Grundlagen des linearen Kontrapunkts* and *Romantische Harmonik.*[32] (I leave aside the question whether the reading was a fair one.)

30. *Bach,* 39. In the English translation, Hindemith uses the phrase "melancholy of capacity." See also Schubert, *Hindemith,* 112.

31. Franz Willms, "Paul Hindemith: Ein Versuch," in *Von Neuer Musik,* ed. H. Grues, E. Kruttge, and E. Thalheimer (Cologne: F. J. Marcan, 1925), 115–16.

32. Ernst Kurth, *Die Grundlagen des linearen Kontrapunkts: Bachs melodische Polyphonie* (Bern: Paul Haupt, 1917); *Romantische Harmonik und ihre Krise in Wagners "Tristan"* (Bern: Paul Haupt, 1920). See also Rudolf Stephan, "Zur Musik der Zwanzigerjahre," in Dieter Rexroth, ed., *Erprobungen und Erfahrungen,* 11–12.

For Willms, "With Hindemith the purely kinetic character of melody . . . stands in the foreground."[33] A functionally indifferent harmony focuses attention on these purely melodic forces of linear energy, motive, and rhythm. Kurth also opened the door to functionless harmony with his assertion that the intrusion of melodic elements into the harmonic structure broke apart, separated, the elements of that structure, so that harmonic logic was often reduced to a few *harmonische Hauptstützpünkte* (harmonic pillars), which appear occasionally in order to hold up some kind of larger harmonic-tonal logic. To replace the form-creating power of harmony, form was now constructed, either as the psychological flow of motivic development and variation or by clearly articulated (often borrowed) designs.

Hindemith was never so radical a Kurthian as, say, Ernst Krenek. By the time he turned to the New Objective manner in early 1923, Hindemith had achieved a synthesis of kinetic energy and tonal framework that served him well for a long time, though it was more than two years later before he achieved a similar synthesis of surface stylistic elements in the opera *Cardillac* (1925–26). By reclaiming the tonal framework, Hindemith did intuitively what in the late thirties and forties he would do deliberately: balance and equalize the three forces of melody, harmony, and rhythm (form).

When Hindemith wrote his Sing- und Spielmusik in the late twenties, he found himself in a very different milieu, away from a brash, cynical cocktail-party modernism, in a circle of earnest, historically-minded amateurs. But the intellectual change that brought him there was not so great as it might seem. He had already been looking for an accommodation between past and present that would give a better moral foundation to his work, as the final sentences of his letter to Schenker make explicit: "Try to have the calm that permits one not to denigrate one's fellow men. . . . The calm and the boundless love for music that have brought me to undertake everything that I have—even this perhaps pointless letter—can serve to put misunderstandings out of the way, make rough places plain, and further work with, not against, one another."[34]

The obvious historicism of the Jugendmusikbewegung can obscure the strong and antiromantic elements present there as well, namely the rejection of the virtuoso, of the hegemony of professional music making, and of the medieval-Renaissance dichotomy central to the nineteenth-century debate between romantics and liberals. Closely bound to this is the repudiation of the progress argument, the insistence on an inevitable, unbroken chain of historical evolution. A positive interaction with older music and appreciation of its vitality challenged the notion that the main function of historical music is to prepare for the present. In *A Composer's World*

33. Willms, "Hindemith: Ein Versuch," 83–84.
34. Rexroth, *Hindemith: Briefe*, 124. My translation.

Hindemith says bluntly, "The evolutionist theory of music's unceasing development toward higher goals is untenable."[35] The composers of the New Objectivity "progressed" by antithesis, but those who guided the Jugendmusikbewegung rejected the dialectic altogether.

The complex interplay of these ideas and their reconciliation is an underlying theme in the libretto to *Mathis der Maler*[36] and makes possible the special style and technique of its music. A decade later Hindemith wrote a short poem called "The Posthorn (Dialogue)" as an epigraph to the final movement of the Sonata for Alto Horn (or Alto Saxophone [1943]). The Horn, a powerful symbol in German tradition, speaks first:

> Is not the sounding of a horn to our busy souls
> . . . .
> like a sonorous visit from those ages
> which counted speed by straining horses' gallop,
> and not by lightning prisoned up in cables;
> . . . .
> The cornucopia's gift calls forth in us
> a pallid yearning, melancholy longing.

The pianist counters this simple nostalgia with a play on "old" and "new" that is often quoted as a summary of Hindemith's musical and philosophical outlook:

> The old is not good just because it's past,
> nor is the new supreme because we live with it,
> and never yet a man felt greater joy
> than he could bear or comprehend.
> Your task it is, amid confusion, rush, and noise
> to grasp the lasting, calm, and meaningful,
> and finding it anew, to hold and treasure it.

By using the music of all eras as models, he hoped to step outside the evolutionary treadmill, but by retaining certain techniques, even certain attitudes, of the previous century, not reject his place in the present. Hindemith's *Bewahrertum*[37]—his conservatism—was positive in a way that the

35. P. 134.

36. The sharp polarization of opinion and the mixture of arts criticism and politics is very characteristic of the period. Hindemith, for example, concentrated in the major operas on the question of the artist's social responsibility. See Dieter Rexroth, "Das Künstlerproblem bei Hindemith," *HJB* 3 (1973): 63–79; and "Zum Stellenwert der Oper *Cardillac* im Schaffen Hindemiths," in *Erprobungen und Erfahrungen*, 56–59; also James D'Angelo, "Tonality and its Symbolic Associations in Paul Hindemith's Opera *Die Harmonie der Welt*" (Ph.D. diss., New York University, 1983).

37. The last phrase of the German version of this poem is "neu zu bewahren."

New Objective counter-romanticism could not be: it was a successful, very personal synthesis of ideas and attitudes that, as social-cultural synthesis, had failed in the Weimar Republic. The demise of the Weimar Republic and the loss of the world to which his artistic synthesis referred was an important part of Hindemith's later melancholy. But equally important was the threat he felt by the late forties to his attempts to generalize his notion of world community over nationalism, community action over professional oligarchy, and a balance between progress and preservation.[38]

In 1950, shortly before he gave his Bach bicentennial lecture in Hamburg, Hindemith wrote the foreword to a collection of fourteenth-century French secular music compiled by Willi Apel.[39] The second paragraph of this foreword is not only an affecting critical appreciation of this music by a person deeply involved with it as a performer, but is also a mature expression of his musical and personal ideals:

> The modern musician's problems, of which there are so many, will lose some of their puzzling oppression if compared with those of our early predecessors. . . . It is rewarding to see those masters struggle successfully with technical devices similar to those that we have to reconquer after periods in which the appreciation of quantity, exaggeration, and search for originality in sound was the most important drive in the composer's mind. They knew how to emphasize, on a fundament of wisely restricted harmony, the melodic and rhythmic share of a sounding structure. Their distribution of tonal weight, their cantilever technique of spanning breath-takingly long passages between tonal pillars hardly finds it equal. Their unselfish and uninhibited way of addressing the audience and satisfying the performer; the perfect adequacy of poetic and musical form; the admirable balance of a composition's technical effort and its sensuous appeal—these are only a few of the outstanding solutions they found in their works. One could go on pointing out surprising and exciting features in those miraculous microcosms of sound, but these few hints will suffice to make us aware of the creative power that keeps those structures in motion and of the human quality that guided their creators.

POSTSCRIPT TO PERFORMERS

The practical musician looking for clues on how to perform Hindemith's music will receive little help from the "Performers" chapter of *A Composer's*

38. Hindemith even uses ecological imagery in "Hören und Verstehen," 176; and in "Sterbende Gewässer," in *Reden und Gedenkworte (Orden pour le Mérite für Wissenschaften und Künste)* 6 (1963–64): 47–75.

39. Willi Apel, ed., *French Secular Music of the Late Fourteenth Century* (Cambridge, Mass.: Medieval Academy of America, 1950).

World. Instead, he will find deprecation and even insults not wholly uncharacteristic of that sometimes visionary, sometimes cranky document. Mixed in with Hindemith's noble if fastidious view of a world in which music serves moral improvement (its true role is not its "sensous exterior") is a somewhat incongruous defense of the composer's birthright. He goes so far as to say: "That music for its realization has to count on the performing musician is an inherent weakness, although it cannot be denied that the multiplied tensions between composer and listener, added in the course of a composition's performance, are a source of further intellectual and emotional sensations which may heighten our enjoyment."[40]

Hindemith's relation to the performer, despite his own virtuoso skills, is not a simple one. He had every reason to want to protect his music from the extremes of "over-individualistic exhibitionism on the one side and the dullest metric-dynamic motorism on the other".[41] Yet though he articulated his position on the matter, he seems by action to have contradicted it. For example, he is reputed to have said that he did not supply extensive performance instructions in his compositions because any good performer would know what to do with the music anyway.[42] Nor can one always trust what is there: once when Keith Wilson of Yale was preparing an ensemble to perform the difficult Wind Septet (1949), Hindemith audited a rehearsal, then took over the baton for another reading and changed a substantial number of performance directions in the process, including all the indicated tempi.[43]

I suggest that Hindemith should often be treated like a baroque composer—not in the sense that one should add ornamenting diminutions (certainly not!), but in the sense that one must be free to emphasize the best musical qualities of his pieces. A successful performance will display analytic and proportional sense, show a grasp of hierarchies, and illuminate a sense of drama, of action, within an essentially tranquil framework. Nothing has done Hindemith more harm than the supposedly neoclassical renderings with which his sonatas especially have had to contend (and not just from immature performers—Glenn Gould's recordings of the three piano sonatas (1936) is a case in point).[44] Such performances exchange the vigor, interest, and lyricism of detail within a broadly proportioned, readily understandable formal frame for placidness, aridity, and a sad predictability that is entirely at odds with Hindemith's conception of music.

Hindemith's severer critics were profoundly wrong in claiming that

40. *A Composer's World*, 154.

41. Foreword to Apel, *French Secular Music*.

42. I am indebted to Luther Noss for this information.

43. Interview with Keith Wilson, New Haven, Conn., October, 1979.

44. *Paul Hindemith: Three Piano Sonatas*, Glenn Gould, Columbia M 32350 (copyright 1973).

the *Craft* theory turned his work into academic exercise. Instead the constraints of the compositional habits developed from his theoretical basis freed and renewed his creative impulses and enriched his music just as Hungarian folk music did for Bartók and Kodály, or as the atonal syntax and later the twelve-tone method did for Schoenberg and those associated with him. The insight, imagination, and self-criticism Hindemith brought to his own music was increased by the compositional guidelines of the *Craft* theory, especially in its mature stages. Anyone who knows the series of masterworks produced between 1934 and 1939—among them *Mathis, Der Schwanendreher, Trauermusik,* the three piano sonatas, *Nobilissima Visione,* and the six chansons—will grasp this point readily.

If these comments seem to clash with published reports of Hindemith's performance style, I do not believe that they are inconsistent with his recorded performances from the 1950s or with the ideals of his music.[45] A few cautionary remarks should be added, however, about his early music. In pieces written before Op. 43, the performer or conductor must have a keen sense of the different stylistic idioms of the first quarter of the century, for this music is as stylistically eclectic as it can be technically inconsistent. The Viola Sonata, Op. 11, no. 4, is Hindemith's homage to Debussy, and it would plainly be the gravest error to give it a too architectural or Regerian quality or to put too brittle an edge on its occasional Pierrotesque whimsies. On the other hand, the Sonata for Viola Solo, Op. 11, no. 5, is a unique synthesis of Debussy and Reger (or Reger-Bach), and the character of the performance must be adjusted accordingly. The piece must not be given the frankly New Objective tone of its companion, Op. 25, no. 1. Likewise, the Cello Concerto, Op. 3, and the cello pieces of Op. 8 should clearly reveal their antecedents in Strauss. But the Cello Sonata, Op. 11, no. 3, has to be as sharp as possible, at once as architectural, rhythmically intense, and psychologically detached as the New Objective transmutation of *brutalismé* that it is. The same may be said of most of the Suite "1922," Op. 26, though it is tempered by parody. The wind quintet *Kleine Kammermusik,* Op. 24, no. 2, is a delightful combination of Mozart and the gentlest side of the New Objective manner—the best preview in the early music of an important facet of Hindemith's later style.

These examples should indicate the requirements of Hindemith's early music: a knowledge of the period and the ability to render subtle stylistic differentiations. The later music demands a considerably broader historical knowledge, and a combination of formal repose and lively detail.

45. Dietrich Bauer, "Paul Hindemith als Bratschist," *HJB* 6 (1977): 146–47; Skelton, *Hindemith*, 98. I refer to his performances in the EMI series "*Paul Hindemith Conducts His Own Works*" (Angel nos. 35489–35491).

PART I
PRELIMINARIES: ON THEORY, COMPOSITION, AND ANALYSIS

ONE
HINDEMITH'S COMPOSITIONAL THEORY

Hindemith's writings on music theory are all of a piece, parts of a system of comprehensive training for student composers—a system he unfortunately left incomplete.[1] The first volume of *The Craft of Musical Composition* (1937) provides the strictly theoretical foundations; the second volume (1939) gives the first part of the practical curriculum, two-part writing. In the late forties, Hindemith intended to consolidate these two volumes into one, using the format of the third volume (on three-part writing), which was completed in the forties or early fifties but published posthumously in 1970. Some rejected materials for the third volume are extant, as is a single unpublished chapter for a projected fourth volume on four-part writing.[2] This surviving chapter shows that the harmonic materials covered in the fourth volume would have been very much like those of *Traditional Harmony,* volume 1 (1943), although the pedagogical approach would certainly have been quite different, following the exercises on a cantus firmus in *Craft II* and *III* with wider possibilities for harmony, rather than figured-bass exercises and strictly traditional harmonic progressions. Volume 2 of *Traditional Harmony* (1948), despite a disclaimer in the foreword, probably gives a good idea of what the exercises in the later chapters of *Craft IV* would have been like.[3] Hindemith used a method nearly identical to the one he described in chapter 6 of *Traditional Harmony II* in composition

1. That Hindemith was concerned primarily with student composers and their teachers is plain from *Craft I*, 3–13.

2. A photolithographic copy of this chapter (no. 21) is in the Yale Hindemith Collection. A fragmentary ch. 19 (rejected) is reproduced in Andres Briner, *Paul Hindemith*, 323–38. Hindemith also makes several references in *Craft III* to later chapters whose topics fall outside any addressed in that volume.

3. Hindemith, *Traditional Harmony*, vol. 2 (New York: Associated Music, 1949), iii (hereafter cited as *Traditional Harmony II*). See also Andres Briner, P. Daniel Meier, and Alfred Rubeli, foreword to *Craft III*, 7; and Briner, *Hindemith*, 318.

courses and seminars at Yale University and the University of Zurich between 1948 and 1953.[4]

Example 1.1 shows the new harmonies introduced in the four-part chapter (excluding four-note chords created by doubling). If the plan of *Craft III* were followed, presumably these would have been the harmonic material for most of *Craft IV*. If so, a clear pattern emerges for the introduction of new sonorities in the *Craft* pedagogy. In *Craft III,* Hindemith concentrated on chords belonging to Group I in the table of relative chord values given at the end of *Craft I*: major and minor triads.[5] Three-voice chords with the tritone—chosen from Group II—appear only in the last two chapters (19 and 20). In *Craft IV,* Hindemith would have introduced all the chords from Groups II and III which belong to traditional harmonic practice. Either at the end of *Craft IV* or, more likely, in a *Craft V,* he could have introduced the remaining sonorities of Groups II and III and at least some of those in Group IV, chords associated with contemporary practice.

Example 1.1: *Übung 21* (*Craft IV*), new sonorities

The sequence of the entire curriculum can be summarized as follows: *Elementary Training for Musicians* (1946), which provides instruction in music fundamentals; the projected combined *Craft I* and *II; Craft III; Craft IV* (incorporating materials from *Traditional Harmony I* and *II*); *Craft V*. One other work, *A Composer's World* (1952), discusses a number of theoretical issues from the same point of view as *Craft III,* but in the main it offers an outline of the philosophical basis of Hindemith's work.

One of the assumptions on which this book is based is that there are clear differences in attitude and approach between the books written in the 1930s and those written afterward. It is mainly on the latter, in particular *Craft III* and *Traditional Harmony II,* that the analytic method presented in chapter 3 is based. Because Hindemith's theory is still generally understood in terms of the books from the thirties, the point of view which I adopt here differs in a number of important respects from most previous literature on the subject.

4. Briner, *Hindemith,* 340; Eckhart Richter, "A Glimpse into the Workshop of Paul Hindemith," *HJB* 6 (1977): 126–39; Hans Ludwig Schilling, *Paul Hindemiths "Cardillac"* (Würzburg: Konrad Triltsch, 1962), 41–48; Skelton, *Hindemith,* 96–98. See also ch. 3, below.

5. *Craft I,* table following p. 223. Explanation of the table is found in the same volume on pp. 95–96, 100–106.

CRAFT I AND *II*

The *Craft* is often cited for its problematic acoustical system or its speculative tonal cosmology, but its roots are in problems of practical music. When Hindemith took his first academic appointment at the Berlin Musikhochschule in 1927, he came to it without benefit of degree, on the strength of his exceptional reputation as a composer and performer of new music. As he later admitted, he felt forced in self-defense to develop some manner of theoretical framework from which to teach composition so that he could cope with students' questions as they sought to do more than imitate their teacher's style intuitively.[6]

> Anyone who has not sidestepped this unending struggle with the Why of things, and, at the risk of laying himself bare before his pupils, has taken each new question as a stimulus to deeper and more searching study . . . will understand why I feel called upon to devote to the writing of a theoretical work the time and trouble I would rather spend in composing living music.[7]

This may be slightly misleading, since Hindemith's letter to Schenker, among other documents, shows that he was looking for a compositional order for himself as well. That aim was unquestionably a factor in writing the *Craft,* but it would be a mistake to assume that Hindemith was mainly addressing his peers or making some sort of compositional confession.[8]

Peter Cahn has shown that Hindemith had a remarkably clear and developed sense of his views on theory pedagogy as early as the beginning of 1927, even before he moved to Berlin.[9] Comments included in a curriculum plan for a proposed Staatliche Musikhochschule in Frankfurt indicate that Hindemith regarded music-theoretical studies as essential to the education not only of composers but of performers as well:

> The separation of theoretical training [from instrumental performance and ensemble-playing] is definitely one of the most pernicious aspects of

6. Briner, *Hindemith,* 314–15; Skelton, *Hindemith,* 86–87. On his theory as apologia for new music, see Giselher Schubert, "Vorgeschichte und Entstehung der 'Unterweisung im Tonsatz: Theoretischer Teil,' " *HJB* 9 (1980): 18–22.

7. *Craft I,* 8.

8. "Hindemith hat eben gerade nicht eine Darstellung seiner eigenen Kompositionstechnik gegeben" (Peter Cahn, review of Zwink, "Hindemith aus der Sicht statistischer Analyse," 147). The interplay of the pedagogical and confessional, which has been one of the major stumbling blocks in the critical literature on the *Craft* theory, eventually also became a problem for Hindemith himself.

9. Peter Cahn, "Ein unbekanntes musikpädagogisches Dokument von 1927: Hindemiths Konzeption einer Musikhochschule," *HJB* 6 (1977): 148–72.

> our modern curriculum. . . . These subjects must be so combined that they draw together toward a common focus. . . . The framework of this pedagogy is made up of all types of ensemble performance, carried out at once theoretically and practically. . . . At the same time practical mastery is gained, theoretical illumination of the material should occur. For without an intellectual grasp of the structure of compositions, thoughtful interpretation and the training of musical thinking are impossible. . . . To date, all music students concentrate overwhelmingly on instrumental performance studies and so are trained to be more or less capable virtuosi, not [complete] musicians.[10]

Hindemith knew the current theoretical literature at the time he moved to Berlin, but as he became increasingly concerned with working out his own compositional pedagogy he read more widely, exploring works from all periods. He taught himself Latin expressly to read medieval and Renaissance treatises. He read (or already knew) the principal works of Rameau, Fux, Tartini, Kirnberger, and contemporary studies (after 1850) in music theory, music psychology, and acoustics: Hauptmann, Helmholtz, Riemann, Stumpf, Schenker, Halm, Schoenberg, Kurth, and others. By this means he acquired an extensive knowledge of music theory, its history, and related subjects which served him in good stead throughout his teaching career.

In 1933 (during the period in which *Mathis der Maler* was conceived and written), he produced a draft for a book to be called "Die Lehre der Erfindung and Gestaltung in der Instrumentalmusik," which had been requested for a series of music handbooks to be edited by Josef Müller-Blattau. Hindemith's title for the manuscript was simply "Komposition und Kompositionslehre."[11] Three drafts of this work were produced between 1933 and early 1935, but the publisher, Athenaion, was unwilling to bring the book out for fear of political repercussions.[12] "Komposition und Kompositionslehre" offers Hindemith's reflections on his experience in teaching composition in Berlin and includes the outline of a new pedagogical method. The eight chapters are entitled:

1. Invention and form (Erfindung und Gestaltung)
2. The music of the last decades
3. Teacher and student
4. Harmony and counterpoint
5. Curriculum I

10. Ibid., 162–63. The document is signed by Licco Amar, but the ideas and much of the language are Hindemith's.

11. Schubert, "Vorgeschichte," 27–28; Alfred Rubeli, *Hindemiths A Cappella Werke, Frankfurter Studien*, vol. 1 (Mainz: Schott, 1975), 75. Schubert quotes from the drafts on pp. 30–37, Rubeli on pp. 75–78; Briner, *Hindemith*, 316–17.

12. Schubert, "Vorgeschichte," 28–29.

6. Curriculum II
7. Curriculum III
8. Again, invention and form.[13]

A substantial amount of this material found its way into the first drafts of *Craft I,* and the three curriculum chapters became the basis for *Craft II.*

The writing of "Komposition und Kompositionslehre" was an important preparatory exercise for *Craft I,* which Hindemith began at the end of 1935, shortly after he must have realized that the Athenaion handbook was not going to be published. Four complete drafts of *Craft I* were produced between December 1935 and early 1937. The first edition was published by Schott in mid-1937. Plans for a simultaneous publication in English translation (with an introduction by Tovey) fell through;[14] the English translation, based on the second German edition (1940), appeared in the United States in 1942. The second volume was begun in September 1938 and completed in February 1939, on board ship to the United States.[15]

The central theoretical issue Hindemith faced has been aptly described by Humphrey Searle: "The problem which Hindemith attempts to solve . . . is that of the free use of all the twelve tones of the chromatic scale within a tonal framework."[16] Hindemith wanted to reverse the priorities of traditional theories of harmony and melody: where chromatic tones and chords had been understood as special cases (by embellishment or alteration) which could be referred or reduced to underlying diatonic patterns, he understood the diatonic as a special case of the fully chromatic. By this device he hoped both to open up a whole range of possibilities for musical structures and to account for the procedures of music of all styles.

Hindemith intended to retire at seventy and devote his energies to the revision and completion of the *Craft* series.[17] The only extant document is an outline from 1951 for the consolidation of *Craft I* and *II.*[18] The new *Craft*

13. Rubeli, *Hindemiths A Cappella Werke,* 75.

14. Skelton, *Hindemith,* 142. Nadia Boulanger's projected translation into French never appeared (139–40).

15. Luther Noss, "Hindemith's Concert Tours in the United States: 1937, 1938, 1939," *HJB* 7 (1978): 126.

16. Humphrey Searle, *Twentieth Century Counterpoint,* 2d ed. (London: Ernest Benn, 1955), 55.

17. Rubeli, *Hindemiths A Cappella Werke,* 84.

18. The outline is in the Yale Hindemith Collection. The revision's eleven chapters were given provisional titles which show that the topics and ordering were to be much like *Craft II*:

1. Construction of basic linear patterns
2. Basic two-part exercises
3. Elaboration of the two-voiced exercises written in chap. 2
4. Application of other melodic formulae

I would still have contained eleven chapters covering for the most part the same material, but the three sections of each original chapter ("Work-Material," "Work-Procedure," and "Model Examples") would have been expanded to six:

1. Problem
2. Material
3. Theory
4. Procedure
5. Model Examples
6. Historical Examples.

The theory section would have allowed sufficient material to be salvaged from *Craft I* to provide a theoretical underpinning for the entire series without seeming to make too great a point of it. This outline confirms what *Craft III* suggests: that the most practical aspect of the *Craft*—its compositional pedagogy—was Hindemith's major concern from the start, not converting professional composers to his own style or laying down the details of his own method of writing. The outline also shows that *Craft I* and *II* as they are cannot be considered the final, fully developed expression of Hindemith's ideas.

CRAFT III

Craft III is intimately associated with Hindemith's teaching at Yale in the 1940s and at the University of Zurich in the early 1950s; much of its material was developed in connection with classroom work. Here are two comments from letters to this point: "The *Craft* volume is officially resting at the

5. Principles of melodic construction
6. Use of other melodic formulae
7. Tonal coherence, its properties, how to achieve it
8. To analyze and establish tonal order in melodies
9. Elaboration of the model; additions to melodic formulae
10. Free two-voice setting I
11. Free two-voice setting II

Section C (Theory) of chapter 1 has the following list: (1) origin of melodic intervals, feeling for purity; (2) natural facts = overtones, combination tones; (3) measurement of sizes, monochord, ratios, cents; (4) are scales necessary? difference between diatonic scales and chromatic scale (precomposed melodies; tonal implications; neutrality). Section C of chapter 2 has this list: (1) melody and harmony as projections of musical time and musical space (rhythm), derived from feeling for actual space and actual time, memory—relativity of musical time: effects add up to spatial concepts; (2) evaluation of intervals (harmonic values).

moment, but almost every day I am collecting new tidbits for it" (from teaching).[19] And "that brings us to the theory book. Its new version is about one-third completed and already is doing excellent service in teaching. The remainder will be added slowly but surely, so that you should be able to count on its completion in the foreseeable future."[20]

According to Howard Boatwright, *Craft III* was begun even before Hindemith came to live in the United States in 1940 (shortly after he completed the second volume).[21] In any case, material from the new volume was used in classes at Yale at least as early as 1943.[22] The Yale Hindemith Collection has copies of an English version of chapters 12–16 (the first five chapters of *Craft III*) which were used in Hindemith's class in 1945–46 and a German version of chapters 16–20. Whether the original contained only chapters 12–16 or included some form of the later chapters cannot be determined with certainty. At any rate, a first version of the whole (chapters 12–20) was in existence no later than 1945. That a manuscript version of at least part of *Craft III* was probably written shortly after *Craft II* explains why *Traditional Harmony I* (1943) can be regarded as a prototype for the unfinished *Craft IV:* Hindemith had already worked out the main lines of the three-part instruction and could leap ahead to the four-part material without difficulty.[23]

19. Hindemith to Willy Strecker, 3 Dec. 1947.

20. Hindemith to Willy Strecker, 20 Jan. 1947.

21. Howard Boatwright, "Paul Hindemith as a Teacher," *Musical Quarterly* 50 (1964): 281.

22. Charles Schackford, review of *Craft III, Journal of Music Theory* 16 (1972): 238.

23. On the basis of the evidence of *Craft IV,* ch. 21, I think this assertion sound, but it is fair to report that Howard Boatwright disagrees (notes on a draft of this book, Feb. 1984): "*Traditional Harmony I* was not connected in any way to the *Craft* (see the *Traditional Harmony* preface). It came about through Hindemith's dissatisfaction with the previous harmony training of his students, and it was also to train them in what they would have to do in their future jobs—teach harmony. In our Tuesday afternoon class called "The Teaching of Theory," we (Hindemith's majors) were in Room 2 with perhaps 20 or 30 non-majors from the School of Music and the college. We did exercises ourselves for Hindemith, and helped and corrected the exercises of the other students. . . . Hindemith used to say that *Craft IV* would deal with more than three parts, and also with free textures (piano style), getting away from the strict linear approach of *Craft II & III.* His whole view of *Traditional Harmony I* was that it was a conscious step backwards (again, see the preface). Of course, four or more notes means seventh chords will occur, and perhaps the first ones treated in *Craft IV* might have been the familiar shapes from *Traditional Harmony.* But the resemblance was only a coincidence, since in this theory (and not in *Traditional Harmony,*) a chord was any combination of intervals, and not a preexisting unit, as it was from Rameau on. In my class notes I have one

Hindemith apparently completed an expanded revision of the manuscript at Zurich in the early 1950s,[24] but several references to revisions in letters from the late forties contradict one another. On July 18, 1949, Hindemith wrote: "I now have about 200 pages of the new chapters (12–20) finished—that is about half of it."[25] Unless this refers to typing the manuscript, the notation in his daybook four days earlier, "*Craft III*—finished,"[26] is inexplicable. Nevertheless, it is likely that the greater part of the revision and extension of the manuscript was done in 1949, and perhaps a draft was completed in July of that year. We can surmise that Hindemith held back the final manuscript because of his plans to revise *Craft I* and *II* and write a *Craft IV* based on the material of *Traditional Harmony.*

The decision to condense *Craft I* and *II* into a single volume, the completion of the *Craft III* manuscript, and the writing of *A Composer's World* and *Traditional Harmony II* all belong to the same short period (1947–51), revealing these years as critical in the development of Hindemith's mature theory. The "Introductory Remarks" to the revised *Marienleben* (1948) offer a concise summary of the characteristics of this theory:

> The primary elements of composition (rhythm, melody, and harmony) are . . . no longer placed one upon another, like building blocks, but rather each element is determined by the vision of the complete work,

---

of those extremely simple but profound crystallizations Hindemith could produce. It was as follows:

> a. Any theory must have principles to cover three things: the supply of tones, the vertical combinations of tones, and the movement of these combinations horizontally.
>
> b. In the polyphonic period, the modes supplied the tones, vertical combinations were treated as combinations of consonant intervals, and horizontal movement was regulated by conformity of the lowest part to the mode.
>
> c. In the harmonic period, the major and minor scales supplied the tones, vertical combinations were not combinations of intervals but fixed units (chords), and the horizontal movement (chord to chord) was regulated by the movement of chord roots (*basse fondamentale*).
>
> d. In Hindemith's formulation, the chromatic scale supplies the tones, chords are again combinations of intervals (but not limited to consonances), and harmonic movement is controlled by the root progression, or if the roots are not clear, by the bass line itself.

The above is not a direct quote, of course, but it represents Hindemith's thinking as I understood it. You can see how far off it would be to suggest a connection between *Traditional Harmony I* and the projected *Craft IV.*"

24. Briner, Meier, and Rubeli, forward to *Craft III*, 8.

25. Hindemith to Willy Strecker, 18 July 1949.

26. I am indebted to Luther Noss for this information. The daybooks are in the archives of the Paul-Hindemith-Institut.

and in each the labor of composition proceeds from the large to the small, from the general to the particular, from the outline to the realization, from the continuous to the discrete. Meter is no longer allowed to place everything else under its yoke, but is relegated to its proper sphere, and basic rhythmic forms of greater extension, resting on irregular proportions, are preferred as the source material in the field of temporal relations.

Melody then does not remain confined to the explicit interval steps from each tone to the next, but is laid out in advance over longer periods, and then subdivided.

Individual harmonies are then considered important only to the extent that they take their assigned places in the unfolding of the superior harmonic principle—that of tonality.

The accompanying constructive factors of dynamics, tone-color, agogics, and so on, are placed entirely at the service of the balanced cooperation of the primary elements.[27]

The hierarchic relationship of melodic and harmonic components and of harmony and tonality are further explained in *Craft III:*

> The will toward intensified motion dominates the contrapuntal structure in all its aspects. The deeper this motion is to grasp, the greater the masses that must be moved, the slower and more rolling the motions. The slower waves of harmonies, moving at greater depth, follow the surface-rooted melodic intervals, which unite into lines. These waves move on the next lower, more forceful level of motion represented by the intratonal relations, which themselves feel beneath them the effective but stationary burden of the total tonality [Gesamttonalität], the last and most comprehensive concept of harmonic-melodic construction.[28]

These quotations show the broad shift in emphasis between Hindemith's theory in the thirties and in the forties. He did not abandon the acoustically based system expounded in *Craft I,* but reduced the orientation toward physical explanations in favor of contextual or psychological explanations, a change which helps make *Craft III* the best of his textbooks. He also won his way finally past the obstacle of harmonic function: in *Craft I* his theory of modern harmony was muddled because he treated it as an extension of a narrow view of traditional tonal harmony. In *Craft III,* though no element of consequence in *Craft I* was abandoned, corrections were made (for example, in interval reckonings and chord-root determination), and the position and function of elements were changed by a new interpretation of their interaction in a musical structure. A point made

27. Hindemith, *Introductory Remarks,* 4. Part of the first paragraph was also used in *Craft III,* 195.

28. *Craft III,* 199. I am indebted to Lee Rothfarb for corrections in the translation of this passage.

only in passing in *Craft I* [29] became the cornerstone of the theory: the balanced cooperation of the primary elements. In *Craft III* each of these has a specific function carried out at several levels of structure. Melody usually lies nearest the surface; it generates the most detail. But it can also be extended through long-range melodic connections (step-progressions of various lengths) or thematic-motivic connections. Harmony, for the most part, "moves at a greater depth" and is organized by intratonal relationships (a functional hierarchy based on Series 1) into areas of tonal focus or, at a larger level, the tonality of the whole. The range of operation is even broader for rhythm, which in its higher manifestations Hindemith equates with formal design: "Basic rhythmic forms of greater extension [are] the source material in the field of temporal relations."

> The smallest metric and rhythmic units . . . are therefore only the ultimate subdivisions and ramifications of the powerful metric and rhythmic pulsations that organize the general temporal outlines of a musical form and divide it into movements and sections, peaks and valleys of intensity, and so on down to the very smallest subordinate units.[30]

Rhythm/form penetrates most deeply into the structure; it is, so to speak, the first among equals, as the other elements depend on it for definition. The cadence, for example, is—first and foremost—a rhythmic event. "In the harmonic-tonal idioms of the cadence *every* harmonic connection . . . subordinates itself to the formal force of closure; it is—like melody—the servant of the form-organizing rhythm. Measured by purely harmonic means, a cadence is a progression like any other. What gives it its special meaning is its position in the . . . conclusion of a passage."[31]

The musical structure is, thus, dynamic but proportioned; a balance of forces but hierarchic.

Figure 1.1 is a tabular summary of important features of Hindemith's theory. Although he laid stress on the separate roles of the three primary elements in serving the "vision of the complete work," in the practical instruction of the *Craft* he routinely discussed their mutual influence and in-

29. *Craft I*, 175.

30. Hindemith, *Elementary Training for Musicians* (New York: Associated Music, 1946), 158. Once again, Hindemith makes this point in passing in *Craft I*, 110, 178. For studies of the rhythm-form theory, see Josef Horst Lederer, "Zu Hindemiths Idee einer Rhythmen- und Formenlehre," *Musikforschung* 29 (1976): 21-36; also Briner, *Hindemith*, 317–42. For more specialized studies on rhythm in Hindemith's work, see James C. Kidd, "Aspects of Mensuration in Hindemith's Clarinet Sonata," *Music Review* 38 (1977): 211–22; Norbert Schneider, "Prinzipien der rhythmischen Gestaltung in Hindemiths Oper *Mathis der Maler*," *HJB* 8 (1979): 7–48.

31. *Craft III*, 137.

teraction. The more significant of these are represented in a second table (fig. 1.2).

Hindemith also put heavy emphasis on several continua in the effects of the musical elements. The bases of these were still the Series 1 and 2 constructs of *Craft I,* which he believed to represent physical facts of sound (ex. 1.2). Series 1, derived from a manipulation of the overtone series, charts the relative strength of relationship to a tonic for all chromatic degrees. Hindemith referred to its compositional application as *intratonal relations* or *tonal amplitude.*[32] Series 2, derived from Series 1 and from a comparison of combination tones, shows (left to right) the relative harmonic force of intervals and (right to left) the relative melodic force of intervals. The strongest intervals from both directions become the *principal tonal functions*: tonic, dominant, subdominant, and the two leading tones.[33] The tritone, although actually outside the scheme, acquires special harmonic and melodic force through its association with the traditional diminished-seventh and dominant seventh chords.

The intervals of Series 2 provide the basis for determining chord roots and gradations of chord value (relative dissonance) from the sonorities of traditional harmony (triads and seventh chords) and just beyond (pentatonic and whole-tone groupings) to very complex pitch collections. The compositional application of this timbral aspect of harmony is called *harmonic fluctuation.*[34] Hindemith advised students to "acquire the habit of carefully calculating harmonic fluctuation," but in his own work he treated it in the more general way suggested by the following: "Chords of high ten-

Example 1.2: *Craft I*

32. "Tonal amplitude" is used in *Traditional Harmony II*, 41. In *Craft III*, Hindemith uses "Tonverwandschaften," "Verwandschaftsgraden," and "Verwandschaftsfunktionen," all of which I have translated as "intratonal relations." The title of ch. 17 in *Craft III* is "Inner-tonaler Ausbau" (124); in *Traditional Harmony II*, 41, he refers to a "rich inner-tonal life."

33. "Tonale Hauptfunktionen." *Craft III*, 88.

34. *Craft I*, 115ff.

(speculative):	Tonal cosmology		Psychology
(physical basis or manifestation):	Overtone series; combination tones		*Gesamtrhythmik*
(practical principles):	Series 1	Series 2	Formal design or articulation
(techniques or phenomena):	Melodic: Step-progression and melodic degree progression	Melodic: Two-voice framework	Cadence and rhythmic details of the surface
	Harmonic: Intratonal relations and harmonic degree progression	Harmonic: Chord groups (or chord values) and harmonic fluctuation	

Figure 1.1: Hindemith's compositional theory: important features

Elements	*Small-scale*	*Large-scale*
Melody and rhythm	Speed of tone successions and speed of development (succession of cells); connection of basic rhythmic units	Cadence; formal articulation of phrase, period, section; motivic development, proportions, or large-scale step-progression connections link or separate articulated sections
Harmony and rhythm	Harmonic rhythm (density); influence of duration of individual tones on chord definition; chordal division of rhythmic flow	Cadence; formal articulation of phrase, period, section; relation of function and chord position in phrase; influence of large-scale tonal design on perception of formal units (relative weights)
Harmony and melody	Degree and kind of melodic activity influences chordal definition; ↥ ↧ as strong functional degrees; chordal basis defines nonharmonic elements; melodic cells and fields (including perfect fifth and fourth as melodic entities)	Harmonic succession (function) emphasized over linear development (homophonic texture); linear development emphasized over harmonic function (polyphonic texture); ↥ ↧ as tonal areas; the possible melodic background of a succession of tonal areas

Figure 1.2: The three principal elements and their interactions

sion should not occur merely as the result of following the path of least resistance in the voice-leading; and a sudden relaxation of tension after progressions of chords of high tension is advisable only when one considers the resulting harmonic shock aesthetically justified."[35] In addition, the effects of harmonic fluctuation are often compromised by non-chord-tone figuration.

The direct compositional procedure following from Series 1 is exploitation of tonal amplitude, "the degree of tension that exists within a clearly established tonal structure between the tonic chord and every other chord that bears a relation to it."[36] Here Hindemith referred to chords, but "degrees" would be equally correct. On the one hand, tonal amplitude provides the basis for functional harmonic procedures, for chord-to-chord movements. On the other, it offers a means of relating the several tonal regions of a whole composition.

The degrees of tonal amplitude and the harmonic or melodic force of intervals also suggest a continuum of tonal definition, an idea essential to an understanding of Hindemith's stylistic development after *Craft I*. Tonality can be clearly established through strong harmonic intervals, clear chords, and closely related degrees, but it can also be weakly established or even negated through distant degrees, ambiguous or complex chords, and weak intervals. Hindemith was careful to restrict the use of "ambiguous, unstable, or quickly changing tonality . . . [to] contrast to more stable tonal areas." But he left himself an opening from which much of the music of the last decade of his life proceeded: "As the primary constructive principle of harmonic-tonal organization . . . [ambiguous or rapidly shifting tonality] is best left to a rather well-cultivated musical ear."[37]

The distinction between melodic and harmonic forces results in a textural continuum based on their relative emphasis. At the one extreme is a purely homophonic music, in which the free development of melody is completely subordinated to harmonic order; at the other is a purely polyphonic music, which subordinates harmonic concerns to the freest development of melody.[38] Any number of stages lie between.

35. *Traditional Harmony II*, 42.

36. Ibid., 41.

37. *Craft III*, 86–87.

38. Ibid., 198–201; *Craft I*, 110–11; *Craft II*, 134–35, 153. See also ch. 3, below.

TWO

STAGES OF THE COMPOSITIONAL PROCESS

In a famous passage in *A Composer's World,* Hindemith used the metaphor of a lightning bolt illuminating a landscape to describe inspiration: one must "in the flash of a single moment see the composition in its absolute entirety, with every pertinent detail in its proper place."[1] This is, of course, "the vision of the complete work" alluded to in the passage from the "Introductory Remarks" to the revised *Marienleben* quoted in chapter 1 above. Even though the process of composition must, then, proceed "from the large to the small, from the general to the particular," in fact it is even more difficult than that, because the composer, in contrast to the listener, must work "along two completely different lines. On the one hand, he must see before him as a vision an undivided whole, the complete form [Gesamtform] which is eventually to make its impression on the listener, but he must also understand how to construct this envisioned complete form out of a great number of individual parts."[2]

On this basis (and closely allied to Hindemith's classroom methods at both Yale and Zurich), *Craft III* sets forth a step-by-step procedure for composition, from the first vague conception of a work, through the crystallizing of formal and tonal plans, to the minutiae of melody and harmony:

> We begin in the indefinite, the uncertain. An approximate conception of the goal, the character, the length, the technical requirements of our piece—these are what first step into the circle of our mind's view. . . . Slowly we can give to this nebulous picture sharper contours. A clearer formal plan, the rhythmic structure, is the first thing to which we turn our attention, so that thereafter—or after much practice at the same time—the tonal foundations will appear, on which follow the harmonic plans. Then the properties of its progressions are dictated for the melodic construction, whether the melody is the only significant linear content of a homophonic piece, or whether it is one of the more-or-less equal melodic strands of a contrapuntal composition.

1. Hindemith, *A Composer's World: Horizons and Limitations*, 71.
2. *Craft III*, 147.

Whether homophonic or polyphonic, "the rhythmic (formal) and harmonic (tonal) processes must be planned beforehand in great strokes."[3] This last quotation gives the impression that the formal and tonal plans are to be equated, but it is clear from other sources that this is not the case. Eckhart Richter describes four stages in Hindemith's working method in a class at Yale in 1951:

> 1. The general determination of the character, medium, and basic purpose of the piece, as well as expressive character and even place of performance.
> 2. A master plan of formal design, including the overall shape, the number and character of sections, changes in mood and tempo, rhythmic character, texture, and degree of activity, the gauge being the amount of effort the listener must expend to comprehend.
> 3. Then "came the tonal layout in which the basic tonalities of each section and their relative degrees of tonal stability and complexity, as well as the modulations, were mapped by means of a diagram."
> 4. Specific thematic material.[4]

Hindemith converted this procedure into a guide for listening in the lecture he gave at the University of Zurich in 1955 titled "Hören und Verstehen ungewohnter Musik" (Hearing and understanding unfamiliar music).[5] In the latter portion of this lecture, he took a short excerpt from Bartók's Sixth String Quartet (mm. 36–54 of the first movement) and led the audience down what he called the "path to structural understanding."[6] The analytic examples used in the lecture are reproduced in example 2.1. Hindemith began by describing only the composite rhythmic pattern of the passage, since he considered rhythmic awareness the "most basic level of hearing and understanding" (see ex. 2.1a). There are only two points at which this *Gesamtrhythmik* pauses, and the two tetrachords formed at those points (ex. 2.1b) are regarded as the harmonic pillars (harmonische Hauptstützpünkte) of the whole passage.[7] We cannot tell anything from this about the larger workings of form, but we can see that it is rhythmic-formal articulation that admits the definition of tonality and harmony. In the third and fourth examples (2.1c–d), the principal melodic connections and some harmonies appear, with successively greater detail in the fifth and sixth examples (2.1e–f). The listener, then, always works "from the general to the specific, . . . from the outline to the realization," as Hindemith admonished the student composer to do.

3. Ibid., 196, 197.
4. Richter, "A Glimpse into the Workshop of Paul Hindemith," 126–27.
5. Published in *HJB* 3 (1973): 173–90. For comments on this lecture, see my "Counterpoint and Pitch Structure in the Early Music of Hindemith," 236–40. A partial translation is given in the same work, pp. 282–87.
6. Hindemith, "Hören und Verstehen ungewohnter Musik," 186.
7. *Craft III*, 203.

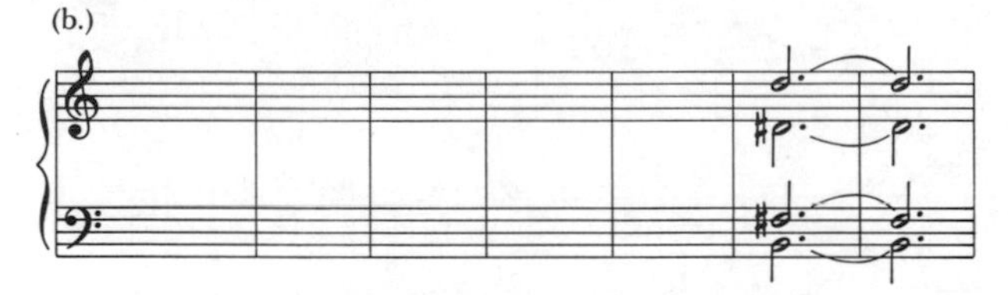

Example 2.1: Hindemith's analysis of Bartók's Sixth String Quartet, I, mm. 36–54

e.

f.

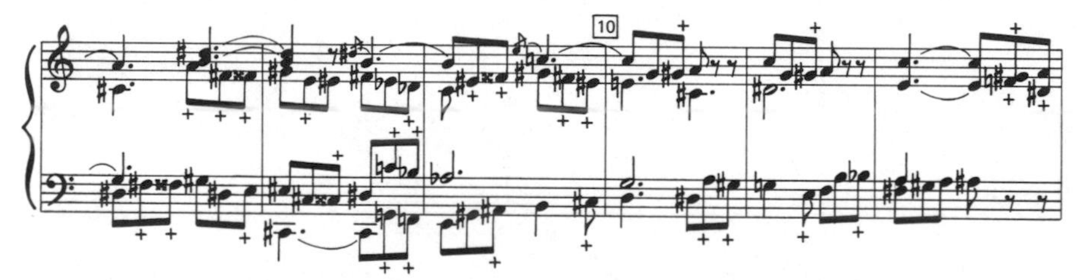

Example 2.1: *Continued*

THE FIVE STRUCTURAL STAGES

The analytic method described in Chapter 3 is based on *Craft III, Traditional Harmony II,* published descriptions of Hindemith's classroom method, and the Zurich lecture's listening guide. In this method, a composition is understood as a hierarchic structure in which five stages are distinguished. Stage I is the level of interaction of tonal design and form: the degree progression of the pillar and cadence chords with a form plan and, where appropriate, a graph of the proportional scheme. Stage II presents only the pillar chords (sometimes with the other cadence chords)—the deepest level of harmonic-tonal activity maintaining chord voicing. Stage III is an interpretation of significant melodic activity moving between and connecting the pillar chords. Stage IV shows surface harmonic activity, including chord values, chord voicing, local degree progression, and voice-leading. Stage V shows the surface melodic activity (independent of harmonic connections): step-progressions, harmonic steps and cells, and arpeggiations. An interpreted reduction of this melodic activity—or a melodic synopsis—may be used as Stage Va.

These stages correspond approximately to the second to fifth examples in the Zurich lecture. In terms of Richter's description, the master tonal and formal plans are the material of Stage I. In Stage II, tonality and harmony are linked for the first time by the construction of specific chords on the degrees in the tonal plan. Stages IV and V deal with the harmonic and melodic details of the surface. Stage III is my addition: an intermediate stage of interpretation concentrating on the broader structural features of melody and harmony.

FORM AND PROPORTION

In the summary of his mature theory quoted in chapter 1, Hindemith says that "basic rhythmic forms of greater extension, resting on irregular proportions, are preferred as the source material in the field of temporal relations." From this statement we may reasonably infer that proportional structure was an aspect of Hindemith's compositional procedure, and in fact the additional evidence of sketches, unpublished documents, and the music itself strongly supports such a conclusion.

The appeal of proportional structure (that is, the laying out of formal divisions by means of whole-number ratios or golden section divisions) was the same to Hindemith as to several other twentieth-century composers: it offered a convincing alternative to the traditional forms of sonata, rondo, and so on. Even where it was used in conjunction with such traditional forms, proportional structure provided a universal principle that could override historical or stylistic associations. And, like Webern and Bartók, among others, Hindemith saw in proportional structure a principle not only universal, but natural. At the end of the introduction to *Craft I*, he makes this position plain:

> Far-sighted composers of the Middle Ages and of modern times hold firmly to [ancient views of compositional technique] and pass them on. What did tonal materials mean to the ancients? Intervals spoke to them of the first days of the creation of the world: mysterious as Number, of the same stuff as the basic concepts of time and space, the very dimensions of the audible as of the visible world, building blocks of the universe, which, in their minds, was constructed in the same proportions as the overtone series, so that measure, music, and the cosmos inseparably merged.[8]

This quote depends very heavily on the Austrian musico-metaphysician Hans Kayser, a Keplerian and disciple of Jakob Böhme and Albert von Thimus. Hindemith read Kayser's work and corresponded with him briefly beginning in the late twenties. Undoubtedly this contact planted in Hindemith's mind the notion of an opera on the life of Kepler, a project which came to fruition more than twenty-five years later in *Die Harmonie der Welt.*[9]

In the first draft of *Craft I* (1935–36), one of many passages obviously derived from Kayser discusses number, rhythm, and form:

> [The ear] hears the pure interval as a beautiful and correct sound. This primal fact of our perceptual faculty shows us the inner relationship of number and a feeling for beauty—the inexplicable merging of mathematics and aesthetics. . . . As the present *Unterweisung* tries to proceed from so sure and deep a foundation as this undeceivable feeling of the ear for mass and value and thereby to expand greatly the technical basis of composition, so from the same fundamental facts a rhythm and form theory could be developed, which in contrast to all previous and mistaken

8. *Craft I*, 12–13.

9. See Rudolf Haase, *Paul Hindemiths harmonikale Quellen: Sein Briefwechsel mit Hans Kayser* (Vienna: Elisabeth Lafite, 1973); also, Briner, *Hindemith*, 312–13; Erich F. W. Altwein, "Zum Briefwechsel Paul Hindemith–Hans Kayser," *HJB* 3 (1973): 144–51; Schubert, "Vorgeschichte und Entstehung der *Unterweisung im Tonsatz, Theoretischer Teil*," 54–58. See also Briner's essay on *Die Harmonie der Welt* in his *Hindemith*, 260–72; and Joscelyn Godwin, "The Revival of Speculative Music," *Musical Quarterly* 68 (1982): 382–84. Haase sees a substantial influence by Kayser on Hindemith's *Craft* theory; Altwein disagrees. Schubert claims (58) that the two preliminary drafts of *Craft I* do not have material which can unequivocally be traced to Kayser, but that such material only appears in the final draft (November–December 1936) as "theoretical sublimation," a direct response to the official ban on performances of his music.

> formal-aesthetic theories could show for the first time the inner being of all sounding forms.[10]

In another passage from the published volume, Hindemith used his favorite architectural analogy to speak of rhythm and form: "Just as in architecture the big supporting and connecting members . . . determine the form and size of a building, . . . so tonal relations introduce order into the tonal mass. Rhythm determines only its temporal succession, . . . the dimensions of the parts . . . and their distance from one another."[11] The hint of denigration in this passage derives from his realization that, although he felt he could treat the theories of harmony and melody satisfactorily, he could not do the same for rhythm, and so he assigned it a secondary role. Such an attitude was no longer possible in the forties, when he had decided that the central process of musical patterning was the "balanced cooperation of the three primary elements." Unpublished documents show that Hindemith conducted a serious search for a theory of rhythm in the mid-forties and came away from it sufficiently convinced to make his statement about "basic rhythmic forms of greater extension."[12] But still he was unable to work out a theory completely: Briner reproduces a fragmentary "Übung 19" (meant for *Craft III*) which was to have provided the foundations for that theory.[13] The failure of this chapter was undoubtedly another factor in Hindemith's decision to postpone publication of *Craft III*.

The theory may not have worked primarily because Hindemith could not find a way to link the short-range manifestations of rhythm (rhythmic figures and motives) and meter with the large rhythms of formal design; nevertheless he was able to make extensive compositional use of proportional structures. I have found no evidence of such designs in the music before about 1930, though I do not rule them out. In the 1930s they occur occasionally. Given Hindemith's debt to Kayser and his interest in medieval and Renaissance music theory, it is not surprising that the "Angelic Concert" which opens *Mathis der Maler* is based on a network of golden section proportions. In the Second Piano Sonata (1936), Hindemith uses simi-

10. The first draft is bound separately and is labeled "Theoretischer Teil, Weihnachten 1935–Neujahr 1936." The quotation is from p. 34. The German text is cited in Briner, *Hindemith*, 317.

11. *Craft I*, 56.

12. The most important of these documents are a collection of note cards, which include extensive notes on Joseph Schillinger's *Mathematical Basis of the Arts* (New York: Philosophical Library, 1948), and the partial texts of two lectures given at the Cleveland Institute of Music on March 3, 1947: "Contemporary Techniques in the Conjectural Opinion of a Musician of the Future" and "Old and New Problems of Music Theory."

13. Briner, *Hindemith*, 323–38.

lar networks of proportions to recast the classic sonata and rondo designs. After 1941 or 1942, when Hindemith first used Series 1 for abstract symbolism (in the revised *Marienleben*) or as a large-scale tonal scheme (in *Ludus Tonalis*), proportional schemes occur somewhat more frequently. After 1945, when his search for a rhythmic theory was well under way, they appear very often. After 1950, he wrote little music which is not controlled by a proportional scheme.

A question that dogs any analysis making claims about large-scale proportions is: how much is conscious intent, how much intuition, how much coincidence? Moreover, as Roy Howat has put it in his excellent essay on Debussy: "Proportions can too easily become the type of study where one finds whatever one wants by looking hard enough."[14] For answers to these questions or to other possible objections, I must refer the reader to Howat's book. I do not attempt here an exhaustive study on Hindemith's use of proportional design, but in those few cases where such designs are discussed, I have relied on Howat's methodology.

HARMONY AND TONALITY

Even in *Craft I,* Hindemith regarded harmony (explicit chords on degrees in a progression) as hierarchically subordinate to tonality, which organizes the elements of a degree progression about a single tonal center (with more or less success, depending on the context). The pillar chords of *Craft III* (and their relationship to cadence) are the significant intermediaries between the harmonic surface and an abstract tonality: "If the tonality is well thought through and clearly presented by means of several harmonic pillars placed in wisely calculated positions, then the harmonic construction in-between can be somewhat looser, the tonality worked out in weak, even the weakest, form."[15]

The complex interplay of melodic and harmonic factors—the varying hierarchies established among them—is the central factor in the surface activity of the music. Hindemith made it clear that melody "rests on" (is hierarchically subordinate to) harmony, but it is equally clear that some melodic factors can be independent of harmony (both step-progressions and harmonic cells) or even take precedence over surface harmonies (longer-range step-progressions, for example), the norm in all but cadence points in polyphonic texture. No simple principle can be applied consistently to the relation of harmony and melodic activity: contexts are variable.

14. Roy Howat, *Debussy in Proportion: A Musical Analysis* (Cambridge: University of Cambridge Press, 1983), 22.
15. *Craft III*, 203.

Though traditional voiceleading rules are sometimes in force, they are by no means always valid in Hindemith's music.

Contextual factors also play a surprising role in the definition of tonality. Although Hindemith could on occasion wax metaphysical on the subjects of the triad and tonality, in the main his attitudes reflect his intense pragmatism. In *Craft III,* he says of one example that tonal definition is not well achieved because of "the great variety of [harmonic] facts involved and their rapid succession. . . . A clear expression of tonality depends not only on the physical character of its constituent harmonies, but equally on our interpretive faculties."[16] The definition of the harmonies and the clarity and force of their presentation in context should be kept in equilibrium unless some expressive purpose demands otherwise.

Unlike Schenker, Hindemith did not regard the whole tonal system as preexistent in the nature-given material of the major triad (not even in *Craft I*).[17] Instead, he believed that, once the nature-given materials were used for music, tonal contexts were created and the patterning we call tonal organization would always result. The tonal principle is unavoidable; but to pattern music most successfully, one has to do some work. "Tonality is by no means something which exists beforehand, without any help on our part. To be sure, the nature-given raw material of Series 1 exists, but from it we must ourselves fashion the tonal relationships between tones, intervals, and chords."[18]

In *Traditional Harmony II,* he defined tonality and the means by which it is best achieved in harmonic terms: "A tonality is the sum of all the harmonies that our analytic hearing can relate to a central harmony (tonic). . . . The tonic gains the upper hand over the other harmonies through cadences, favorable position in the phrase, recurrent appearance, and support by its most closely related harmonies."[19] From this Hindemith advanced another hierarchic notion about harmony which applies regardless of texture type: "Once the principal functions are established [tonic, dominants, and leading tones], the basic outlines of the tonal structure become clear, and the other functions, which simply complete and fill out the tonality, hardly ever need separate analysis."[20] Because the overriding strength of the five principal tonal functions is so great, Hindemith even suggested that chords built on these degrees should be introduced into sections of poorly defined tonality to help orient the ear.

The idea that tonality is made, not born, so to speak, allowed Hin-

16. Ibid., 85.

17. *Craft I*, 107. On the other hand, it is very easy to misread passages such as those on p. 22 (the extolling of the major triad) and pp. 152–56 (contra atonality).

18. *Craft III*, 172.

19. *Traditional Harmony II*, 39.

20. *Craft III*, 89.

demith to construct the corollary of tonal vagueness mentioned earlier. "If the [tonal] outline is unclear, obscure, or ambiguous, one can be convinced either that the composer was not capable of constructing a clearer order, or that the vagueness is a well-planned artistic device included as part of the complete compositional plan."[21] In *Traditional Harmony II,* he described the formal-tonal plan of one exercise as consisting "partly of sections in which a single tonality must appear with great definiteness, and partly of others which contrast with those stable arrangements by their tonal vagueness."[22]

Of quite another nature is the cadence. Hindemith attached great importance to the cadence as the point at which harmony and melody within a phrase or period intersect with the structural forces of tonality and form. His conception of cadence, however, is not a revival of the old notion of point of rest. To Hindemith, the cadence is first of all a force of binding, joining melodic activity firmly to the harmonic-tonal basis, and harmonic-tonal patterns to the formal structure. Any of the eleven nontonic degrees may be used as the penultimate degree in a cadence, though differing levels of harmonic strength result, of course.

> No doubt about tonal meaning can arise in cadences. . . . Here the harmonic close falls together with the formal ending.[23] The structural tendency toward an ending in a cadence subordinates all other factors to it, while in other harmonic developments what is sought is the free unfolding of rhythm, melody, and harmony.[24]

Chapter 17 of *Craft III* gives twenty-four elaborated melodies for the student to set. Each melody is the length of a short period (about eight measures in a slow tempo, up to sixteen in faster tempi). The typical harmonic-tonal disposition of each setting is explained as follows:

> [Each setting] normally . . . begins with the establishment of the tonality—the first two or three chords will serve for that purpose. Thereafter follows a series of harmonies built on a degree progression of freely chosen degrees. Among these degrees the principal tonal functions are represented according to taste and purpose. The exercise closes with one of our various cadences. None of these three tonal phases should be set sharply against its neighbour, if we want to avoid disturbing the normal progressing of the exercise with powerful harmonic jolts.[25]

21. Ibid., 175.
22. *Traditional Harmony II*, 39.
23. *Craft III*, 176.
24. *Craft I*, 143. See also Peter Cahn, "Hindemiths Kadenzen," *HJB* I (1971), 80–134; and Friedrich Neumann, "Kadenz, Melodieführung und Stimmführung in den *Six Chansons* und *Five Songs on Old Texts* von Hindemith," *HJB* VIII (1979), 49–78.
25. *Craft III*, 146.

One should, then, establish

> the main points of the tonal progression: the beginning, the cadence (on which to a great extent depends the character and strength of definition of the tonality), and some of the more prominent and significant intermediate points, such as tonic recurrences, active tonal functions, deceptive progressions, the most distant degrees, the secondary functions, etc. . . . Only thereafter do we fill in the missing elements. This manner of working is analogous not to the method of the mason . . . but to that of the sculptor: it is always a complete structure which we have before us and around which we range as we work, alternately modelling in all places.[26]

THE ANALYSES OF *CRAFT I*

At the end of *Craft I,* Hindemith presented analyses of works ranging from Gregorian chant to an extract from his own *Mathis der Maler.* These have not entered into my reckoning in any significant way, in part because those who have attacked the analytic methodology presumed to be implied by the analyses have done so with some justification. Hindemith did make some questionable judgments with respect to a number of points of detail, especially in the analyses of music from the period of major-minor common practice.[27] But this criticism has, for the most part, proceeded from a misunderstanding of his intentions. The analyses were designed, first, to demonstrate that the compositional principles expounded in the *Craft* belong to the traditions of Western music and are not gimmicks invented by Hindemith; second, to put the student composer's sundry analytic rules of thumb together in one package; third, to suggest that the cleft between historical and contemporary composition is false, and that historical compositions—even Gregorian chant—can be rich sources for the student composer.

In other words, the *Craft* does not present an analytic theory, and much mischief has been done by the assumption that it does. Hindemith intended to show the general applicability of the basic principles of his compositional theory, which he also regarded as guidelines both composer and student could use for "correction, editing, improving." He was quite careful to note that he was offering only one solution to the problems posed by the compositions examined: "Often [the reader] will arrive at different

26. Ibid., 48–49.

27. For criticism of these analyses, see Siegfried Borris, "Hindemiths harmonische Analysen," in *Festschrift für Max Schneider,* ed. W. Vetter (Leipzig: Deutscher Verlag für Musik, 1955), 295–301; Rudolf Stephan, "Zum Verständnis von Hindemiths Analysen," in *Festschrift für Siegfried Borris,* ed. Richard Jakoby and Clemens Kühn (Wilhelmshaven: Heinrichshofen's Verlag, 1982), 81–91.

results from those given here. There is no harm in that. I have in each instance chosen only one of many possibilities. Even with the closest familiarity with the objective content of a work of art, the judgements of all observers will never completely coincide."[28] Furthermore, the theoretical basis changed considerably in emphasis in the decade which separates *Craft I* from *Traditional Harmony II* and *A Composer's World.* A great and obvious difference exists between the listener's analysis in the Zurich lecture (1955), which is "analysis," and the sketches for the benefit of student composers in *Craft I.* It cannot be said to be to the credit of Hindemith's critics that they have failed to notice the difference.[29]

A similar problem exists in the relationship of the compositional pedagogy to Hindemith's own compositions. Those who have extracted rules from *Craft II* and compared them with the music to see how well Hindemith followed his own advice have at best been misled by such statements as, "The present exercises will be found to have served as foundation for all [musical] settings," for they have ignored his next statement, "they address themselves to the beginner."[30] Both Eberhard Zwink and Victor Landau have done statistical or quasi-statistical studies of the relation of *Craft* rules to Hindemith's practice, proceeding from the assumption that "Hindemith actually composed in the manner he prescribes in his textbook."[31] Andres Briner, on the other hand, insists that "Hindemith never, not even in the second half of his life, modelled his new compositions after his own compositional pedagogy."[32] Neither of these views is completely accurate, but Briner's is much nearer the mark.

Craft II is the first stage in the system of compositional pedagogy; it does not reveal Hindemith's own compositional method to his peers, but offers the beginnings of compositional training to student composers. In *Craft III,* Hindemith discarded or modified numerous rules maintained strictly in *Craft II* because he believed the student would be ready to handle the greater freedom (the same relaxation of the rules is apparent in the latter part of *Craft II*). In this he followed the pedagogical principle of many ancient compositional texts: a strict but simple basis is gradually embellished and some original rules are either discarded as inappropriate to new conditions or modified by license until an exercise is reached which is

28. *Craft I,* 157, 202.

29. There can no longer be any excuse for facile criticism of the *Craft I* analysis "method" of the sort found in P. J. Booth, "Hindemith's Analytical Method and an Alternative," *Soundings* 7 (1978), 117–36.

30. *Craft II,* viii.

31. Eberhart Zwink, *Hindemiths "Unterweisung im Tonsatz" als der Konsequenz der Entwicklung seiner Kompositionstechnik,* 15.

32. Andres Briner, *Hindemith,* 305.

"compositional" in character.[33] The *Craft* series never reached the stage we could call compositional; the closest Hindemith came was in the composition skeletons of *Traditional Harmony II*. In this sense, Briner is correct in denying a direct connection between the *Craft* and Hindemith's compositions. On the other hand, it is obvious from the textbook summary in chap-

33. Arnold Schering's *Dekolorieren* or Fux's five species of strict counterpoint could be used as examples. In an earlier draft of this study, I even suggested they might have been Hindemith's models for the exercises in *Craft II*. Fux seemed an obvious choice, since Hindemith quotes from his *Gradus ad Parnassum* at the beginning of *Craft I*. And the exercises on elaborated melody in *Craft II* more closely approximate Schering's *Dekolorieren* (in reverse, of course) than any of the Fuxian species.

The difficulties that will attend any attempt to pin down sources for the *Craft* theory can be gauged by Howard Boatwright's response to my mention of Schering and Fux: "The precedent for teaching by embellishing simple structures is much older than Fux. Hindemith's reference to Fux in the preface to *Craft I* has to do only with what he perceived to be a similar situation in history, not in methodology. The precedent in methodology is much older than Fux. Hindemith used to mention one medieval treatise in particular, Petrus dictus palmus ociosa, *Compendium de discantu mensurabili* (1336) which gives twelve modes of elaborating note-against-note structures that Hindemith said were similar to the training exercises of *Craft II*. Still older examples are found in *Discantus positio vulgaris, Quaedem de arte discantandi, Quiconque veut deschanter*, and *Anonymous III* (a Latin version of *Quiconque*). Hindemith knew all of these treatises, so I doubt if there is a specific relation to Fux, and certainly no reason to assume that Schering was an influence." Add to this the fact that in the first draft of *Craft I* Hindemith repeated Ernst Kurth's sharp criticism of Fux (see Schubert, "Vorgeschichte und Entstehung," 44). Hindemith's modern sources are by no means certain, either. I have already mentioned disagreement over the influence of Hans Kayser (n. 9, above). Hindemith's step-progression is often cited as derived from Schenker, but its character is actually much closer to Kurth's *Zug* (line) than to Schenker's. Hermann Roth, Hindemith's colleague and "theoretical confidant" during the writing of *Craft I*, was a student of both Schenker and August Halm, the latter being Kurth's principal source. The situation is further muddled by evidence which suggests that Schenker derived some of his essential ideas from Kurth—and not the reverse, as some have claimed. Kurth's Zug and his criticism of Fux appear in *Die Grundlagen des linearen Kontrapunkts: Bachs melodische Polyphonie* (Bern: Paul Haupt, 1917). Schenker first uses the terms Zug and Urlinie (primordial line) in 1920, in the essay accompanying his edition of Beethoven's Piano Sonata in A Major, Op. 101 (Vienna: Universal, 1920). In the following year, Schenker began a periodical series called *Der Tonwille*, whose reference in the title to Schopenhauer's term *Wille* can be traced to Halm through Kurth. (Hindemith owned a complete set of the *Tonwille* numbers.) Schenker's Urlinie at this stage of its development can be described as a critical response to Kurth: an attempt to vindicate Fux by containing Kurth's Züge in structures dictated by strict counterpoint. Hinter 1 that Hindemith himself was convinced that a connection *could* eventually be made (in *Craft IV* or *V*). In order to interpret Hindemith's compositional theory in a way that is suitable for analytic interpretation of his music, then, we must first abandon the twin assumptions that the *Craft I* analyses *are* analyses in the common sense of that term and that his compositional practice is nothing more than the *Craft* pedagogy put into action.[34]

---

demith almost certainly drew from both Schenker and Kurth, but probably more extensively from the latter. Although I have examined all the materials in Hindemith's estate which could bear on the question of sources, I do not find a clear direction in them. For example, his personal copy of Kurth's *Romantische Harmonik* (1920) is mostly uncut, and his copy of Schenker's *Kontrapunkt* (2 vols., 1911, 1920) contains marginalia with sharply negative opinions (from the handwriting and the nature of the comments, the marginalia come from 1937 or 1938, as Hindemith was working on *Craft II*).

34. Other problematic assumptions are that *Craft I* is primarily speculative theory or even a textbook in musical acoustics. It is no secret that Hindemith's appeal to the overtone series, combination tones, the triad as the chord of nature, and so on, has inspired a considerable critical literature. If the *Craft* is seen as attempting the presentation of a coherent system (which is fair), then most of the criticism is justified. The earlier drafts of the volume suggest, however, that much of Hindemith's work was an attempt at a de facto rationalization of the Series 1 ordering found in so many theoretical treatises.

No attempt will be made here to justify, correct, or extend the foundations of his system. I claim only that Hindemith's compositional theory is right for his own music, an examination of which shows beyond reasonable doubt that the fundamental principles, including the Series 1 and 2 constructs, do indeed form the basis of his practice.

THREE
AN ANALYTIC METHOD

The analytic method I propose here has a relatively modest goal. It is intended as a tool for description, not for prescription; that is, as an aid to interpreting technical, constructive features of Hindemith's music, and not as a network of logical rules showing how the music "must" be understood. It is, then, not a reductive theory as that term is usually employed nowadays, despite its five hierarchic stages. The stages are used to separate the different processes or components of the music and not to demonstrate a closed system of structural levels.[1] Only Stage III can properly be called integrative, and it is the one most open to individual interpretation.

1. The method differs from strictly applied Schenkerian analysis (following his *Free Composition*) in several respects: (1) though it is hierarchic, the method has no limited set of a priori constructs like Schenker's *Ursätze* to which a composition must be reduced (or conversely from which it is understood to evolve); (2) the largest member of the hierarchy, Stage I, admits the elements of form (rhythm) and harmony (tonality) but not melody, except in certain circumstances; (3) there is no fixed relationship or progression from Stage I through Stage V equivalent to Schenker's "composing-out"—the stages can interact in various ways depending on the length of the piece, its texture, and special emphases; (4) similarly, there is no fixed relationship of the primary elements (as in the Ursatz) but any number of possibilities for their "balanced cooperation"; (5) there is no single correct solution for the analysis of a piece, as must necessarily be the case with Schenker. The method differs in the same ways from Salzer's interpretation of Schenker, especially his readings of music after Brahms, plus the rejection of Salzer's attempt to create additional (though anomalous) background constructs with his "contrapuntal structures." My analyses of Stages IV and V often come close to Salzer's foregrounds when the composition in question is strongly harmonic (two cases are considered in this chapter), but depart radically when he imposes background structures which attempt to produce a closed system of harmony and counterpoint. In many cases, his background structures are not even functional; that is, the quasi-Schenkerian apparatus does not so much produce the insights of the analysis as merely accompany them awkwardly (or act as vague justification, a clumsy nod to tradition). I recognize that the orthodox Schenkerian will regret the loss of precision which comes with abandoning that method's limited system

Alternative readings of a composition are certainly possible (as Hindemith himself said), not only for Stage III but also for those stages which have greater richness of detail (IV and V), though less so for stages I and II. It is the essence of Hindemith's pedagogy and compositional practice that he permits different levels of definition for all the musical elements. In effect, any one of the elements has its own continuum of definition from greatest clarity at one end to obscurity or even randomness at the other, and the resulting network of definition levels is the most important factor in determining the technical character of a piece. To assign objective values to points on these continua and represent them in a graph might at first seem desirable, especially because of Hindemith's contention that the technical side of composition should hold no secrets, a point of view closely related to Stravinsky's zealous insistence on objectivity in composition. But as Hindemith also noted, "Even with the closest familiarity with the objective content of a work of art, the judgments of all observers will never completely coincide."[2] Even if a method of graphing the continua were possible, it would probably be undesirable, and without that precision of measurement the way is open for alternative interpretations. I accept the fact that some will find this a weakness, but prefer a system which makes such allowances to one with a false sense of closure (see the criticisms of analyses by Felix Salzer in the sections on stages III and IV, below).

STAGES I AND II: STRUCTURAL LEVELS

Stage I shows only the controlling structure: degrees representing tonal areas and a diagram of formal design. This tonal-formal interaction is not latent structure—the hidden secret of a composition—but is instead a description of what should be obvious, for the most part, to an intelligent, attentive listener. Following Kurth, Hindemith calls this the "total impression" or "total effect" of a piece (Gesamteindruck; Gesamtwirkung).[3]

Stage II shows the pillar chords (the *harmonische Hauptstützpünkte* of *Craft III* and the Zurich lecture) with voicings and any necessary cadence chords. In a short composition, the unit of reference is the phrase; in a longer piece, it may be the period or even section.

---

of harmony, counterpoint, and composing-out, and that the Salzerian will be uncomfortable with the rejection of the "contrapuntal structure." But I find that, even if it could account for twentieth-century tonal practices, the orthodox approach is too limited for a music based on the "balanced cooperation of the primary elements"; and that Salzer merely extends the boundaries of the Schenkerian system without justifying his method for doing so.

2. *Craft I*, 202.

3. *Craft III*, 146.

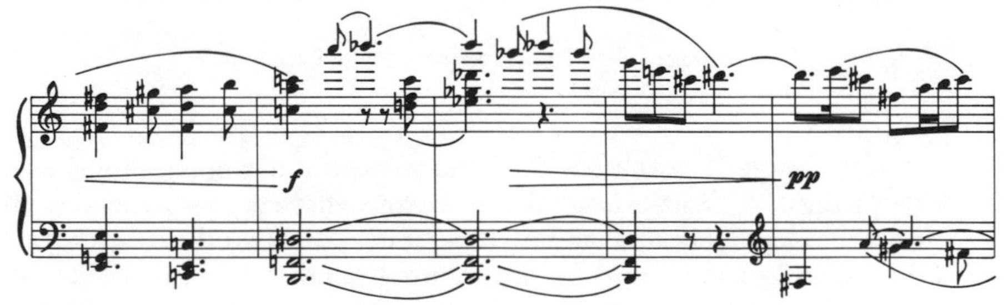

Example 3.1: *Ludus Tonalis*, Interlude in G

The "Pastorale" interlude from the *Ludus Tonalis* (ex.3.1) will serve as a demonstration piece for the different stages of the method. Even though its function is to connect the tonalities of the fugues in G and F, this interlude—a neobaroque siciliano—closes in G, and G is the tonic throughout. Each half of its binary form contains two phrases, the second and fourth phrases being identical except that the latter is transposed up a fourth.

A Stage I graph of the interlude appears in example 3.2. The third phrase is divided into two subphrases (c1 and c2) to separate the sequence in mm. 11–14 from the approach to the climactic dissonant chord of m. 16. Degrees are shown with symbols and noteheads (in the manner of a fundamental bass), but the symbols alone would be sufficient. (It is not necessary to know the meanings of the degree symbols at this point. An explanation is given in the section on Stage IV.) Slashes repeat the phrase divisions of the form plan. The open notes are reserved for degrees of pillar chords. The parentheses around IᵻI in the third phrase indicate an area of vague tonality as well as weak definition of the chord.

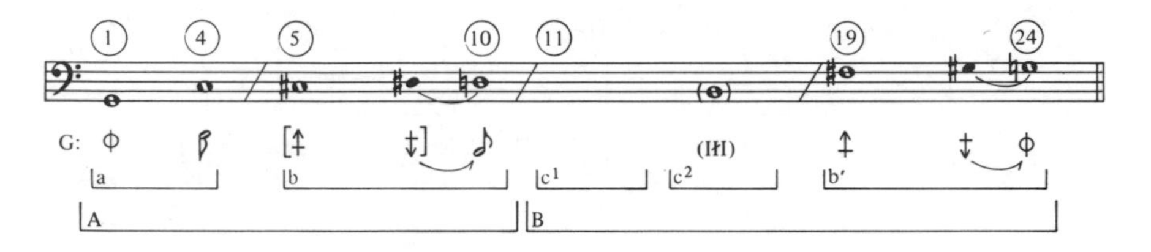

Example 3.2: Interlude in G, Stage I analysis

In the Stage II graph (ex. 3.3), the structural harmonies are shown with voicings. In the first chord, the inner voices have been separated from the outer-voice Gs because, although the inner voices produce the characteristic sound of the chord (minor-minor seventh), the tonal definition seems to be made clearly by the octaves alone on the first beat. Similarly, B♭5 in m. 4 is a minor seventh added to a chord first identified as a minor triad. The third phrase poses some problems. As frequently happens, the first chord of the phrase cannot unequivocally be taken as a pillar chord, a point of tonal orientation, and it has therefore been omitted. The climax chord, on the other hand, is obviously a point of harmonic orientation, but the exact content of its upper voices is not easy to determine. I have indicated all three voicings of the right-hand part, but prefer the last as the least dissonant (a single pitch doubling a note of the left hand's whole-note trichord) and as the apparent goal of the right-hand movements in this phrase.

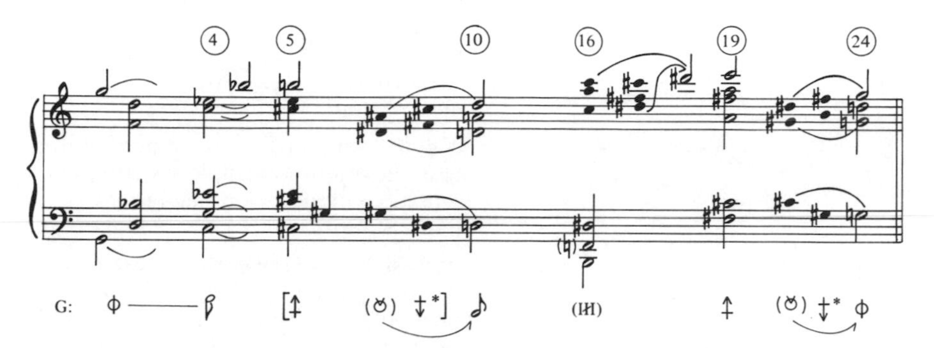

Example 3.3: Interlude in G, Stage II analysis

STAGE III

To construct a Stage III interpretation of the interaction of melodic, harmonic, and formal-rhythmic elements, it will be necessary first to introduce Stages IV and V. The description of Stage III appears at the end of this chapter.

STAGE IV: HARMONIC ACTIVITY

Glossary of Analytic Symbols

Hindemith's method of harmonic analysis is an updated fundamental bass theory. All twelve chromatic pitches can function as degrees within a key, giving us twelve chord symbols. A few of these symbols appear in *Craft II*, but the first complete presentation is in *Craft III*.[4] There are two groups: (1) the five principal tonal functions plus the tritone, which have special symbols; (2) the remaining six degrees, which are given Roman numerals derived from the interval labels of Series 2 (for example, II/III).[5] I find the labels in the second group are cumbersome and too easily confused with a commonly used symbol for secondary dominants. Simplified labels for these intermediate degrees are shown in the first item in the glossary below.

4. Ibid., 99.

5. Howard Boatwright says that "Hindemith no sooner introduced the Roman number combinations like II/III in the place of 2/3 than he declared them a 'nuisance.' "

1. (See ex. 3.4)	Degree symbols.
2. ? or ( )	A chord whose root or function is weak or doubtful.
3. *	A chord with a root other than that of best interval (for example, certain presentations of the major-major or minor-minor seventh chords).
4. φ (ℓ φ VƗ) ℓ	At least two levels of harmonic force can be distinguished within Stage IV: (a) (symbols in parentheses) chords of weak or doubtful function, either linear (contrapuntal chords) or weakly defined (root unclear, placed high in the chord, or chord value very low); (b) harmonic chords, those belonging to the degree progression.
5. φ ——————	Extension of a degree; at the surface level of the synopsis this means that successive chords have the same root; below that, it usually means extension of tonal control. Sometimes used for harmonic prolongation, though the symbol in item 6 is more appropriate.
6. φ ℓ φ or φ VƗ ♪ IƗI φ (slurred)	May mean (a) a neighbor-chord progression; (b) several linear or weakly functioning chords between statements of a clearly functioning chord or degree; (c) circular progression over a phrase.
7. ℓ VII φ (arrow)	The group of cadence chords in a phrase, period, or section; the final chord is the goal.
8. ~~~~~~~~	An area of ambiguous or indeterminable tonal basis.
9. Additional symbols: 4t = quartal (displayed in fourths) 5t = quintal (displayed in fifths) WT = whole tone (or a segment of the whole-tone scale) d = diminished (or octatonic-scale fragment) Pnt = pentatonic (or a segment)	
10. ♪/IƗI or IƗI/φ	The indefinite third relation: the degree could be either depending on how non-chord notes are interpreted. Any degree—including φ—may participate in this function. The lower note of the third is always below.

11. [VI♮ VII♪] ↕ — Secondary progressions (within brackets), referring to the chord or degree following the closing bracket.

C: Φ ‡ II I♯II I♮II ♪ ♉ ♪ VI♯ VI♮ VII ‡
or IIÌ or IIÍ or VÌ or VÍ

Example 3.4: Harmonic function symbols

Secondary progressions. The secondary chord or progression serves the same role in Hindemith's music as it does in traditional tonal music: tonicization of a degree in the key. The immediate question is what chords are to be regarded as secondary in a system that already includes all twelve degrees as part of the key and does not discriminate between the qualities of the chord built on any degree. In *Craft III,* Hindemith restricted the secondary function to the dominant and the lower leading tone of the tonicized degree and disallowed the use of the minor triad. He considered, but rejected secondary subdominants and upper leading tones: "they have nothing of the sharply decisive impulse of the [♪] and are barely distinguishable from the usual, non-secondary chord progressions."[6] Hindemith's procedure works for a harmonic vocabulary of triads and seventh chords, but is not very useful for his own music. In my analyses, the secondary progression symbol will be used in the following cases: (1) when a cadence falls on a nontonic degree, the cadence chords are shown as tonicization, as in [I♮I VII] ♪; (2) when a circular progression leading from and returning to a nontonic degree plainly includes the intervening chords or degrees under its sphere of influence, as in I♮I [VI♮ ♉ VI♮ I♮I ↕] I♮I. Simple neighbor-chord embellishments fall into this category—even, for example, I♮I [♪] I♮I (the traditional $\frac{5}{3}$–$\frac{6}{4}$–$\frac{5}{3}$ pattern).

Indefinite third relation. The indefinite third relation as a distinct function has no precedent in traditional harmonic theory, although the ambiguity it represents is well recognized in the theoretical literature (it is the essence of the problem of the *chord de la sixte ajoutée*). This function refers to a chord which—because of dissonance in the chord structure, difficulties in interpreting non-chord notes, or the presence of more than one fifth—could have either of two notes a third apart as its root. The indefinite third is common in areas where the intermediate functions are used (as in the mid-

6. *Craft III*, 129.

dle of the phrase) and in transitional or developmental areas. The relation can also be prolonged like other functions; that is, expanded to include several chords in a series, all referring to the same pair of roots. It may even be the tonal focus of a whole passage: in the diagram of tonal areas for the first movement of the Suite for Orchestra assignment in *Traditional Harmony II,* Hindemith indicated that mm. 6–14 (a transitional passage) should be heard as "moving between E and G♯" and they "should leave unsettled the question which tonic, E or G♯, is felt to predominate."[7]

The indefinite third is the most common example of a broader indefinite relation which can pair degrees at any interval. Even the tritone is susceptible: in another set of instructions for a class piece, Hindemith directed that the passage leading to the climax should move between D and A♭.[8]

Chord Roots

A system of harmonic analysis depending on degrees must have a method for determining chord roots. Hindemith gives rules in *Craft I,* and adds corollaries in *Craft III* and *IV* (chapter 21).

In *Craft I:* (1) the chord root is determined by locating the best interval nearest the bass (the root of this interval is the root of the chord); (2) doubled notes count only once; (3) if two intervals of the same type appear, the one whose lower note is nearer the bass has the chord root; (4) chords in which the bass and root are the same are stronger than those of the same type in which the bass and root do not coincide.[9] The sequence of intervals, derived from Series 2, is as follows: P5 (b), P4 (a), M3 (b), m6 (a), m3 (b), M6 (a), m7 (b), M2 (a), M7 (b), m2 (a), tritone (?).[10] (In this list, b = root below, a = root above.)

From *Craft III:* (1) doubling can have an influence on chord-root calculations insofar as it enhances the potency of any note: if this note is the root of the chord, the chord may be stronger—more clearly defined—than its chord class might suggest; (2) if two or more intervals in the chord share a note as root, emphasis on that note is greatly increased and may overrule the best root; (3) in those cases where the chord root found by the best interval or the previous corollaries is also a member of a tritone interval in the

7. *Traditional Harmony II*, 40.

8. Richter, "A Glimpse into the Workshop of Paul Hindemith," 134. The chords of Groups V and VI in the table of chord values in *Craft I* also represent indefinite relations: the quartal chord an indefinite fourth, the diminished seventh multiple indefinite thirds (and tritone?).

9. *Craft I*, 94, 97, 99.

10. *Craft I*, 96. The justification of Series 2 begins with the discussion of inversions of intervals on p. 64.

chord, the possible functions of the tritone determine the true root.[11] Therefore, in example 3.5a, below, the root is C. The best interval is C–E, the root of C–B♭ is also C, and C is not part of the tritone. In example 3.5b, the root is F♯. The best interval is C–E, to be sure, but the root of F♯–E is F♯, and the tritone C–F♯ is understood either as ↧𝅗𝅥 in B or 𝅗𝅥↥ in G, both of which suggest F♯ as the more significant note. As this indicates, Hindemith had considerable difficulty with chords containing tritones. This corollary is meant to account for the traditional root of the two types of diminished seventh chords.

Example 3.5: "Incomplete chords" (after *Craft III*, 222)

From *Craft IV:* For certain chords, the appearance of a familiar sonority in the lower voices can change the chord root. Hindemith uses this rule in connection with the minor-minor seventh and major-major seventh chords (see ex. 3.6a), but it can be extended to other, more complex sonorities as well (ex. 3.6b).

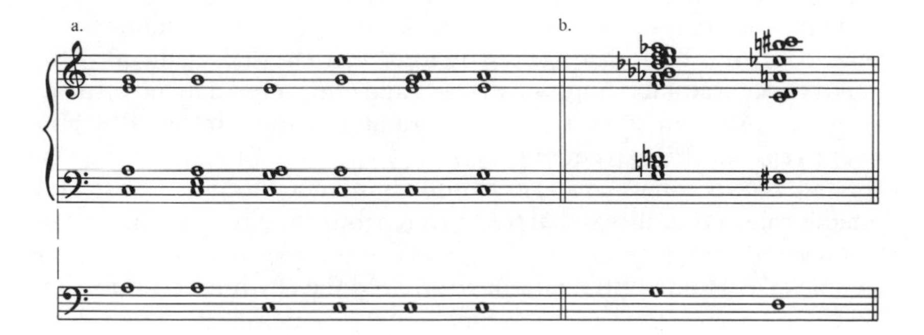

Example 3.6a: Chord-root analyses influenced by interval distribution (*Craft IV*)
Example 3.6b: Chord-root analyses of complex chords

In these four corollaries, Hindemith shows that he recognized chords are susceptible to varying interpretations, and that the best interval by itself does not account for the influence of a chord's context. The chord root method of *Craft I,* combined with these four corollaries, is quite sufficient

11. *Craft III*, 13, 224, 223.

for our needs, so long as it is used in connection with a flexible view of harmonic function.

Chords which can be understood without difficulty as related to the sets of the whole-tone or diminished scales (based on the augmented or diminished triads) normally have tritones and are treated using the third corollary above. In the Stage IV graph, roots are indicated in parentheses or with a question mark. Quartal chords and more complex chords based on pentatonic groupings—all common in Hindemith's music—are generally treated like the minor-minor and major-major seventh chords. Much depends on whether notes are doubled, fifths or familiar triadic formations occur in the lower register, or the context defines the vertical as harmonic in character. Even then, these chords are often without a clear root.

Criticism of chord-root reckoning. Like Hindemith's claims for the physical bases of the *Craft* theory, his method of determining chord roots has received extensive criticism. Charles Schackford, for example, comments at length on the perceptual difficulties connected with Hindemith's concept of chord root, even questioning his failure to consider implied roots.[12] William Thomson, on the other hand, offers the grudging compliment that Hindemith's method seems to have had considerable influence on later theorists, and that "whatever the methodological and empirical errors in its background formulation, Hindemith's method of root analysis is an advancement beyond the traditional framework of stacked thirds."[13]

Non-chord tones pose the most serious problem, since if nonchordal elements cannot be isolated, then neither can chordal elements. Hindemith's system admits chords of all types and one cannot depend on a limited group of chord stereotypes as in traditional tonal music. But Hindemith rejected the extreme position of Capellen and Schoenberg that everything has become chordal, that non-chord tones no longer exist. Hindemith's rule of thumb was that the "foreign tone should be less important rhythmically" or at least equal and unstressed (see exx. 3.7a and b). But in example 3.7c, Hindemith might have ignored the rhythmic criterion and decided in favor of A as the chord tone, not B♭: "generally it is a tone really

Example 3.7: Nonharmonic notes and chord-root determination (after *Craft I*, 165)

12. Charles Schackford, review of *Craft III* , 256ff.

13. Thomson, "Hindemith's Contribution to Music Theory," *Journal of Music Theory* 9 (1965): 59–60.

foreign to the chord—that is, the combination that occurs during the moment of its sounding belongs to a group of lower rank than the main chord." Suspensions and other traditionally accented dissonances, as well as only slight differences in chord values, are real obstacles. At one point Hindemith admitted that "it is often difficult to decide whether to consider a given tone as part of a chord or as a non-chord tone. If the rhythm then adds to the confusion, in that the added tones are not short enough to be unmistakably subordinate, a definite line cannot be drawn."[14] If this is the case with harmonic music, it is an even more serious problem with an unaccompanied melodic line.[15] But then what happens to the value and strength of the degree progression? Thomson's characterization of this problem as "a basic flaw in Hindemith's harmonic theory"[16] at first glance appears to be correct.

That chord roots or members cannot always be determined precisely should not, however, be construed as a defect in Hindemith's harmonic system. He often creates the contrary impression in *Craft I,* but even there he did not lay all the emphasis on harmonic function alone. Instead, he required the same kind of balanced cooperation among the components of harmony—harmonic function, chordal definition, non-chord figuration, and timbral progression (that is, harmonic fluctuation)—that he later required of the three primary elements of music, melody, harmony, and rhythm. This point may be difficult to grasp for the reader familiar only with *Craft I* and *II,* for it depends on the mature theory as expressed in *Craft III.* The presentation in *Craft I* is too much in the form of a modern analogue to a fussy traditional harmonic theory, demanding an identifiable chord, part of a progression, on every metric unit. The mature theory of the forties brings out the possibilities inherent in Hindemith's dependence on the Viennese fundamental bass tradition, especially the expanded scale-step of Schenker, and so offers a larger view of harmonic-melodic interaction and harmonic hierarchies.

There are a few inklings in *Craft I* of this broader conception of harmony. For some unusual harmonic constructions, "it would be better to take melodic influences . . . into account, rather than rely exclusively upon

14. *Craft I,* 165, 174.

15. Thomson, "Hindemith's Contribution," 64–65. Howard Boatwright offers the following on this point: "The chord root theory, as you have correctly shown, was modified greatly over the years, and was never as important in Hindemith's compositional process as *Craft I* led many people to believe. He was, at the time, trying to enlarge and advance harmonic *theory,* but in fact the basis of his compositional practice, even before *Craft I,* was not "chords," but melody supported by bass lines directed to certain stable points and cadences, made tonal by displaying sufficiently and at crucial points the main functions."

16. Thomson, "Hindemith's Contribution," 61.

harmonic analysis. These chords would then become subordinate to others more easily analyzed." In the analysis of the F-minor Sinfonia of J. S. Bach: "It is quite possible in listening to sum up the harmonic content as consisting of fewer chords of longer duration"[17]—almost a definition of the expanded scale-step.

In *Craft III,* a harmonic framework defined by formal articulation is good enough to establish tonal order. Any number of chords between may be of contrapuntal origin. Not every chord is a harmony. A hierarchy of function is linked to position in a phrase on the one hand, to chord value and definition on the other. Even ambiguity has a function: when chord roots need to be defined, they are. Seen from this perspective, the contradictions in chord-root and chord-tone determination disappear.

Harmonic Fluctuation

In his own compositions, Hindemith worked with timbral progression (harmonic fluctuation) in a more general manner than his instructions to students in the textbooks suggest. The broadest aspect of timbral progression is connected with the extremes of the chord-value groups: diatonic chords (triads, pentatonic groupings) versus whole-tone and diminished materials. In local contexts, fluctuation is so thoroughly mixed with non-chord figuration that no simple set of stereotypes can be established.

The accented dissonances—suspension, appoggiatura, accented passing tone, and so on—demonstrate the analytical problems that arise. For the progression given in example 3.8a, the addition of a suspension (ex. 3.8b) greatly alters the timbral effect but does nothing to the chord roots. A subtler but still noticeable change occurs if the suspension is lengthened (ex. 3.8c). Hindemith for the most part ignored non-chord tones as factors in the timbral progression and built harmonic fluctuation sequences on the underlying chords, although he did consider the effect on chord roots.[18] Because of these difficulties and the apparent discrepancy between Hindemith's compositional theory and his practice on this point, charts of harmonic fluctuation are not included in the analysis graphs; but the influence

Example 3.8: Suspensions and chord-root determination

17. *Craft I,* 98, 208–09.
18. Ibid., 165–74 passim.

of fluctuation values on chordal definition and function within the phrase has been kept in mind as harmonic synopses were developed.

Intratonal Relations

The basis of harmonic function at all levels is the continuum of intratonal relations expressed in Series 1. Just as Hindemith used this yardstick in *Craft III*[19] to judge the strength of various possible cadence progressions, we can use it to determine the strength or directional force of any sequence of chords. From the dominants through the mediants to II and VII, harmonic force gradually decreases, and the movements are milder, softer. The sharply directed melodic force of the tritone and the two leading tones means that chords built on them acquire disproportionate harmonic-tonal strength—greater than II, VII, and the mediants. Placement (accent, position in phrase), duration (including repetition), and the tonal context of the phrase all affect function. Some useful information may lie in the sequence of degrees in example 3.9, for instance, but nothing at all like that readily found in the traditional harmonic phrase: I–vi–IV–ii–V–I. Since Hindemith allowed any degree to function in the cadence with varying chord qualities no stereotypes like the traditional I–IV–V–I, I–ii–V–I, T–S–D–T, exist. The cadence as a rhythmic-formal event is the stereotype, and not a specific succession of chords.

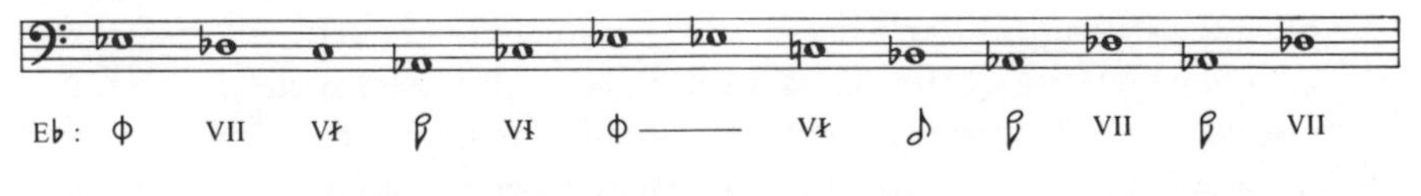

Example 3.9: An "arbitrary" succession of chord roots

If the degrees of example 3.9 are divided into two groups, as into two phrases, the picture of harmonic function changes considerably (ex. 3.10). The first phrase has a broad circular progression ϕ–ϕ with a relatively mild Vł ϕ cadence. The second phrase moves to and tonicizes VII: in the cadence, β has to be reinterpreted as [♪]. If the degrees are also given durations (ex. 3.11), the evaluation of certain chords may be altered once more: the opening tonic is not held long but is placed in a strong metric position (as is β in m. 2); Vł in m. 1 is enhanced slightly because it is held, [♪] considerably by the same means; the ♪ in m. 3 is obviously much weakened by its placement (it now simply passes from Vł to β).

19. *Craft III*, 137–45.

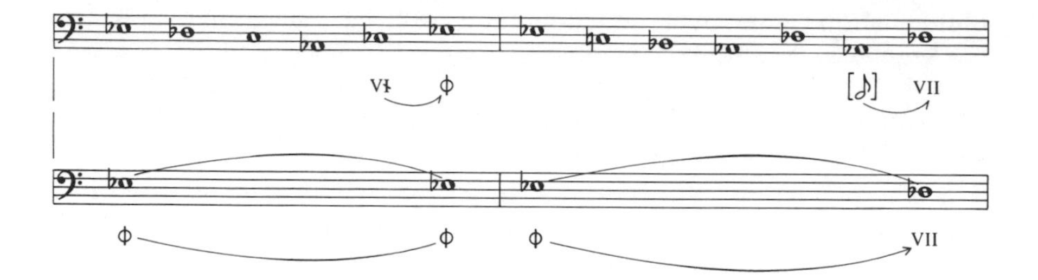

Example 3.10: The same, grouped in two phrases

Example 3.11: The same, placed in a metric framework

When voicings are added, chord values enter into consideration and affect the appraisal of the chords (ex. 3.12). The circular progression of the first phrase is compromised (though only slightly) by the fact that the quality of the second ϕ is weaker than that of the first; but the progression in the phrase is strengthened because the roots lie in the bass throughout, and the cadence because of the fifths added above the bass. Note that VI♮, despite its duration, becomes the weakest link in the harmony because its correct root lies high and contradicts the stereotype of the minor-minor seventh chord. In the second phrase, note especially the major triads in the cadence, and the relatively weak representation of VII in m. 3.

The final stage, for the purpose of my argument, is to add figuration to

Example 3.12: The same, with voiced chords

the chords: the result is the opening of the "March" interlude from the *Ludus Tonalis* (ex. 3.13). As one would expect of a march, harmonic definition is strong, though some residual doubts might remain about chord members (or even roots) on the second and fourth beats of mm. 1–3. In this short passage, the pillar chords are built on the degrees shown in the lower staff of example 3.10, the chords beginning and ending each of the two phrases (ex. 3.14). Chords with filled-in noteheads are other cadence sonorities. In a broader context such as the entire interlude these chords might become intermediate structural harmonies yielding to those that control period and section.[20]

Example 3.13: The same, elaborated (*Ludus Tonalis*, Interlude, E♭→A♭, mm. 1–4)

Harmonic function is always connected to the movement of the phrase, to formal design. The clarity of harmonic function is sharply

20. One important change would be the subordination of the degree VII in the harmonic-tonal hierarchy. This degree is quite strong in these four measures, in part because of the clear two-plus-two phrase structure, but the first beat of m. 5 shifts the tonal emphasis to B♭, the dominant. The tonal design of the entire March is as follows:

	March				Trio	March	
	1	2 ‖	3	4 ‖		‖ 1	2 ‖
m.	1	5	9	16	21–30	31	35
E♭:	ɸ—VII	𝅘𝅥𝅮-II	VII—ɸ—	𝅗𝅥 ɸ	𝅗𝅥—𝅗𝅥	ɸ—𝅗𝅥	ɸ—𝅗𝅥 𝅗𝅥 ɸ

affected by the delineation of the phrase, just as it is by the degree of melodic activity in a polyphonic texture. Harmonic prolongation or functional extension is necessarily linked to harmonic function. Extension of ϕ across the first phrase in example 3.13 is achieved by voiceleading with no contradictory melodic movements. The progression, whose voiceleading is summarized in example 3.14, is like an altered version of a traditional circular progression (ex. 3.15). In the second phrase, the pairings of intervals in the outer voices suggest linear origin and functional subordination to ϕ until the tonicizing cadence on VII. The step-progression A♭5–G5–F5 follows the pillar and cadence chords precisely, but the ascending step-progression in the same phrase moves indiscriminately through chords of various functional values: C5 (m. 3), D♭5, E♭5 (m. 4), F5.

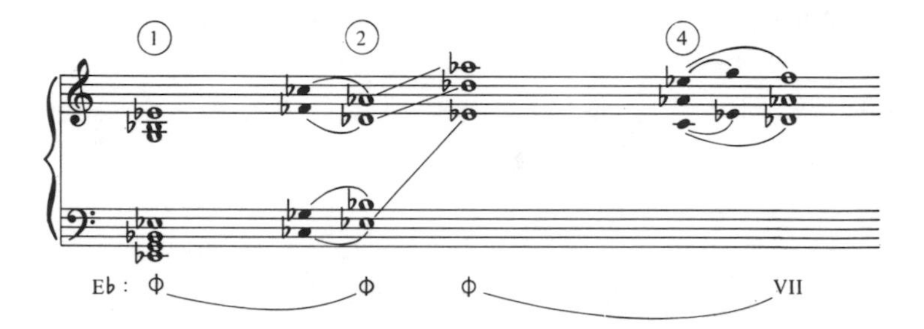

Example 3.14: Stage II analysis of the Interlude, E♭→A♭, mm. 1–4

Example 3.15: An analogy to a traditional progression

The more intimate the connection between harmony and melody—the more voiceleading is tied to harmonic progression—the more likely are patterns of prolongation, though underlying structures may or may not be traditional. Hindemith's *Craft* theory was meant to include traditional tonal music as a special case of its general principles, and it should be understood as possible for certain techniques associated with that music to arise when the writing is strongly harmonic. In a homophonic texture, as in the opening of the "March" interlude, the harmonic pillars are the organizing elements in a rich harmonic environment. The surface of the music is tightly controlled by harmonic progression, definite chord-to-chord movements, and the pillars represent a deeper level in the harmonic structural hierarchy. In a polyphonic texture, on the other hand, it is difficult to speak of harmonic progression in the traditional sense: the active melodic life reduces many of the progressions to mere successions of more-or-less well-defined harmonies. Only the cadence brings the harmonic material back into order; the pillars are often the only true bearers of harmony.

An excellent example of a prolonged passage in polyphonic texture is the opening of the Fugue in G from the *Ludus Tonalis* (ex. 3.16). It is almost impossible—and by and large pointless—to determine the harmonies with the same precision as in the march. Even the internal cadences are not very well defined (mm. 6, 8, 12, 15); the only clear points are the tonic opening and final cadence (m. 18). The voiceleading is spun out between these two points like the cables of a suspension bridge, an image of which Hindemith was especially fond.[21] There are, of course, elements of harmonic or tonal

Example 3.16: *Ludus Tonalis*, Fugue in G, mm. 1–18

21. Boatwright says that Hindemith would mention the George Washington Bridge specifically in this connection.

control observable within the section, but the essential harmonic constructive principle operates at the level of the whole section. A beat-by-beat harmonic analysis would be very artificial, as would a demand for equal status (level of definition) for all internal cadences. The degree of precision in the harmonic analysis must vary depending on the texture in a passage. To insist on the same level of analysis throughout may satisfy a desire for consistency, but can contradict the musical sense.

Motivic material, subject entry levels, and tonal-harmonic orientation are carefully coordinated in this fugue. The four degrees of the subject incipit (ϕ, 𝅗𝅥, ♪, VII) are also the positions of the internal cadences in the first section and (excepting VII) the entry levels. The formal design of the whole is distinctly tripartite with the principal degrees deliberately avoided in the second section (a series of alternating *stretti* and episodes) and emphasized again in the third section:[22]

	A		B						A'					
mm.	1 ———		18 ———					——— 46	47 ———					——— 75
				24	29	36	40			54	59	61	63	66
	ϕ	(VII 𝅗𝅥)	ϕ → VI♮	ʊ	III	VI♮ —		VII	𝅗𝅥	ϕ	(𝅗𝅥	♪)	ϕ —	

STAGE V: MELODIC ACTIVITY

General Characteristics

The two principal techniques of melodic development are the step-progression (connection by second) and arpeggiation (connection by other intervals). Arpeggiation is a reinterpretation of Hindemith's "harmonic

22. This is another of the pieces whose formal rhythms are based on a proportional scheme depending on the golden section. The design is as follows:

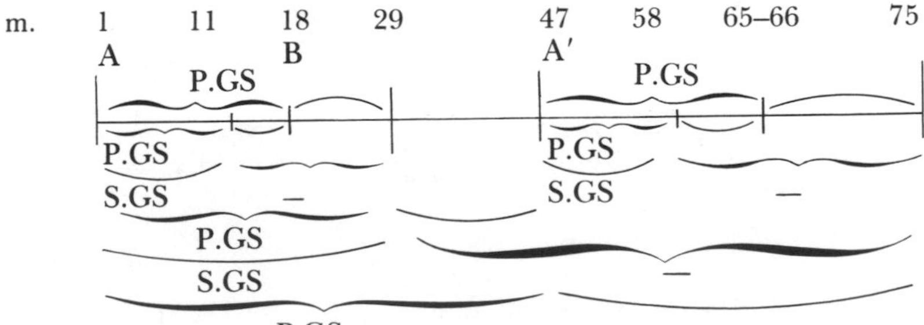

cells" (essentially, the harmonic content of a melodic line).[23] Single intervals in the bass are referred to as "harmonic steps."

Pitches in step-progressions do not require harmonic support: some members of a step-progression may be chord members, and some may be non-chord tones. The step-progression is not to be equated with Schenker's *Zug* (line) but is more nearly like Kurth's. In arpeggiations, the root of the interval or chord outlines need not be in the harmony. Arpeggiation cannot be equated with chordal figuration, but the latter is a special case of arpeggiation, as Schenker's line is a special case of the step-progression.

Step-progressions do not outline a particular interval, contain a particular number of notes, or move just along diatonic paths; they do, however, move in one direction only, barring embellishment and repetition. Arpeggiations are generally restricted to a limited number of interval and chord types (triads, common seventh chords, pentatonic figures, triads with split thirds or fifths). Any one pitch may belong to several patterns of step-progression or arpeggiation simultaneously.

Stage V shows most or all of the identifiable melodic activity in a passage; Stage Va is an interpretation of the significant, usually longer-range, connections. Preference is given to melodic patterns in the principal upper voice and the bass and to patterns interacting with the harmonic and formal-rhythmic articulants in phrase, period, or section. Much of the content of Stage Va will also be included in Stage III. Registral differentiation normally defines longer-range connections in the principal upper voice. This can occur occasionally in the bass as well.

1. Step-progression:

2. Doubtful extension of a step-progression:

3. Break in a continuing step-progression pattern:

Figure 3.1: Symbols for melodic analysis

23. *Craft I*, 183–87; *Craft II*, 63–70, 73–78.

4. Repetition:
(*Trauermusik,* III, 13–19)

5. Octave:
(*Trauermusik,* III, 7–10)

6. Embellishment:
(Mass, Agnus Dei, 3–4)

7. Implied note: refer to example for item 6.

8. Unfolding: (Schenker's symbol
[*Trauermusik,* III, 1–2])

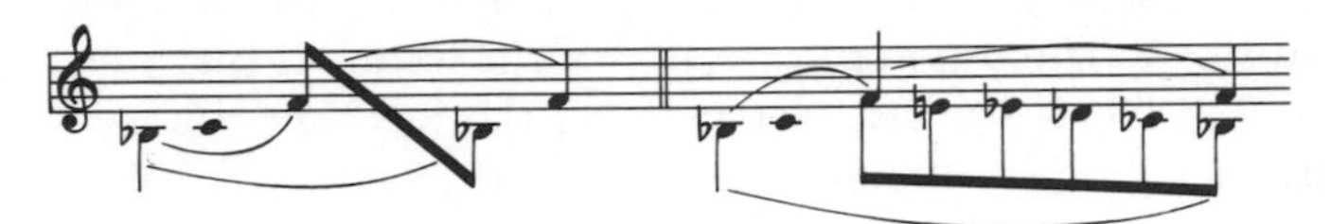

N.B.: No necessary connection to harmony; used for restricted purpose: if step-progression, arpeggiation, or combination retraces an already opened interval.

9. Recurrent pitch:

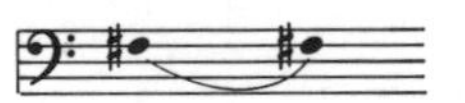

10. Doubtful connection:

11. Register transfer, octave:

Figure 3.1: *Continued*

12. Register transfer, other interval:

13. Neighbor:

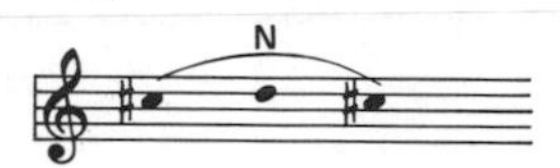

14. Turn:

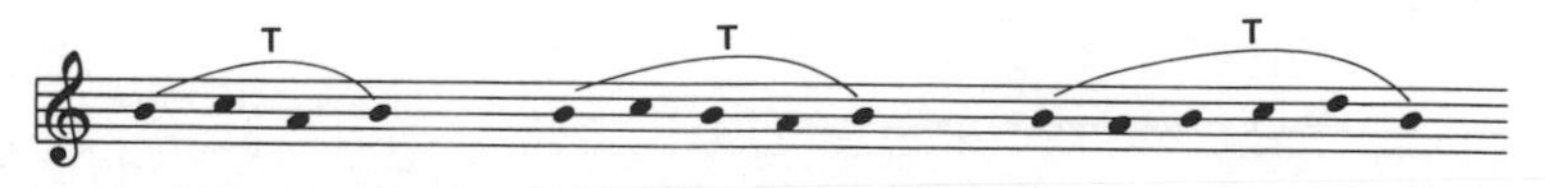

15. Arpeggiation (harmonic cell):

N.B. If desired, a label can be attached identifying the root of the arpeggiated chord as a degree in the controlling key (as in the second example above).

16. Embellished arpeggiation:
(*Trauermusik*, IV, 4)

17. Leading-tone functions:

Figure 3.1: *Continued*

An Example

The first period in the "Meditation" which opens the *Nobilissima Visione Suite* (1938) is analyzed in example 3.17. The obvious hierarchic arrangement of melodic events and the tendency to concentrate on a single step-progression across each phrase (sometimes two, one rising and one falling) are very characteristic of Hindemith in the late thirties, as is the three-

Example 3.17: *Nobilissima Visione Suite,* I (Introduction or Meditation), mm. 1–13 (melody only) with Stage V analysis

phrase period or two-phrase period with extended second phrase. Melodic construction, register, and dynamic and dramatic design are neatly interwoven. Rising step-progressions dominate the first two phrases, with the cadence arpeggiation of the first and the descending step-progressions of the second very near the end. In the third phrase, the step-progression connects with the highest pitch (B4) of the previous phrase and continues upward to the climax point, F5, in m. 11. A fairly rapid descent brings the phrase to cadence.

Of course, many more step-progressions are possible than those shown, but if the reader has opportunity to play through or listen to the example, little doubt can remain about the controlling features. Hardly any series of second connections could fail to provide *some* kind of information about the passage. The question is how significant such connections are to the listener's general impression, and therefore how much we should attempt to show in an analytic graph. A hypothetical step-progression from G4 in m. 3 through G♯ in m. 7 and A4 in m. 8 to B4 in m. 9 can be readily discarded, but one from C4 in m. 6 through D4 in m. 8 to E4 in m. 9 may be included, since the pitches are the low extremes in the line after m. 5. A connection from B4 in m. 9 through its recurrence in m. 10 to B♭4 in m. 12 imparts some information of interest and could also be included. Still, it is the obvious long-range step-progressions that provide the framework for the melody and the basis for analytical decisions about it. The consistency of Hindemith's practice, especially in the forties, greatly facilitates analysis of melodic activity.

Example with All Parts

Arpeggiations equal step-progressions as significant elements at different levels of melodic activity in the opening of the Third Piano Sonata (1936). A Stage V graph is given in example 3.18. The opening melodic gestures in the right hand present a series of interlocked arpeggiations which are interpreted mostly as triads. The pentatonic set is the agent of an octave transfer (downward) of all three notes of the B♭ major triad. The interlocking of arpeggiation, step-progression, and turn patterns at the cadence is characteristic. In the bass of mm. 3–4, an arpeggiated triad (D♭ major) has a root which is not the root of any chord set above it; it is a melodic phenomenon. In this context the triad is best regarded as an accidental result of two

Example 3.18: Piano Sonata No. 3 in B♭, I, mm. 1–10, Stage V analysis

harmonic steps. Extensive bass arpeggiation is less typical than development of step-progression patterns with an occasional harmonic step of a third, fourth, or fifth. In line with his notion of the two-voice framework, Hindemith generally took great care that the bass should have melodic character.

Arpeggiations are especially important from m. 4 on, where they function at different hierarchical levels. The arpeggiation of a D♭ major triad in m. 5, for example, is part of the arpeggiation of the D♭ triad with split third which controls right-hand melodic activity in mm. 4–6, but the split-third

Example 3.19: Felix Salzer's analysis

24. Felix Salzer, *Structural Hearing*, 2 vols. (New York: Boni, 1952; reprint, New York: Dover, 1962), 2: fig. X.

figure is part of the much broader arpeggiation of a half-diminished seventh chord (D♭5–E5–G5–B5) which runs from m. 4 to m. 9.

Felix Salzer identified the melodic shape of the upper part in this excerpt as shown in example 3.19.[24] If viewed as an interpretation of essential melodic activity, Salzer's graph is deficient in a number of ways. He was obliged by the constraints of his method to pick a single fundamental pitch at the beginning, from which all melodic activity of significance was presumed to proceed. He chose B♭4. (He could not choose F5, because the resulting melodic pattern in the middle ground is the unacceptable F5–B5–B♭5.) A better choice for such a source would be the entire arpeggia-

Example 3.19: *Continued*

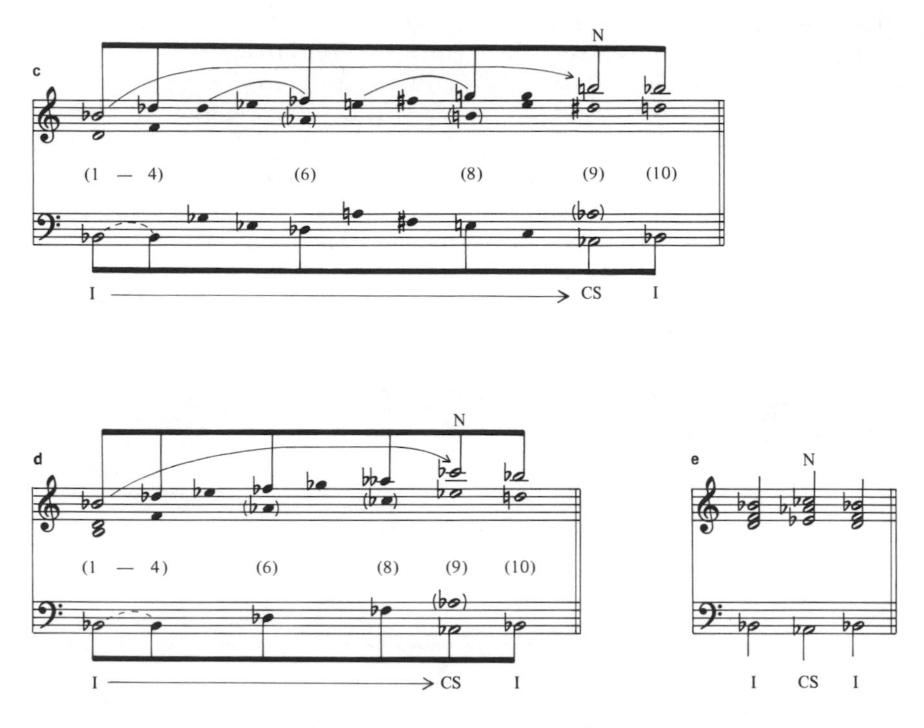

Example 3.19: *Continued*

tion of the B♭ major triad in m. 1. D5 in m. 1 makes the melodic connection to D♭5 in m. 4, the next pitch to occur in the same register. F5 makes a longer-range connection to E5 in m. 6 and even G5 in m. 8 (indicated by slurs in ex. 3.18). B♭4 initiates the step-progression of mm. 1–2. The connection of D5 to D♭5 is made by the two means Hindemith employed to achieve effective longer-range melodic connections: half-step motion and registral isolation.

In mm. 9–10, the upward motion of the arpeggiation is reversed in the half-step B5–B♭5, the technique used to change harmonic or diatonic cells. The final B♭5 is thereby separated from the half-diminished seventh arpeggiation. Salzer was correct in suggesting that B5 and the harmony that supports it are significant elements of the period encompassed by these ten measures, but he misidentified the note as a neighbor note. The importance of B5 lies in its position in the cadence, its function as the upper leading note, and the fact that it takes a register not used before. The immediate source of the pitch is the arpeggiation and octave transfer of m. 9; the result is the octave transfer of the opening triad (not just the pitch B♭): the main theme phrase is repeated in the fifth and sixth octaves, beginning in m. 10.

Arpeggiation as controlling longer-range feature is not very common. The more typical construction uses some arpeggiations at or near the surface of the melodic activity and more step-progressions operating at several levels, including that of phrase and period. This more characteristic usage appears in the opening phrase (mm. 1–4) of the "Pastorale" interlude in the *Ludus Tonalis* (ex. 3.20).

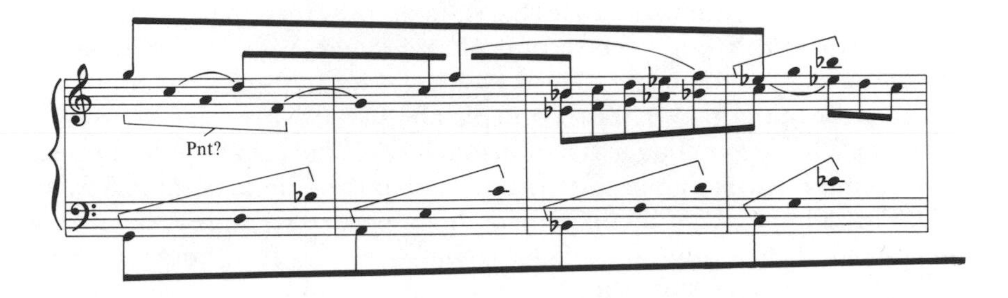

Example 3.20: *Ludus Tonalis*, Interlude in G, mm. 1–4, Stage V analysis

The principal exception is a phrase or period of developmental or transitional character, where tonality is not strongly defined. There, controlling arpeggiations occur commonly. For example, in the Third Piano Sonata excerpt (ex. 3.18) mm. 4–9 (the internal portion of the period) are harmonically the least stable and dramatically the most tense, as they lead to the high point of the period and its highest pitch, B5. The dramatic and dynamic high point of the "Pastorale" interlude is reached by the arpeggiation of a triad with an altered note (ex. 3.21). Here even the bass uses triad arpeggiations, though with intervening half-steps.

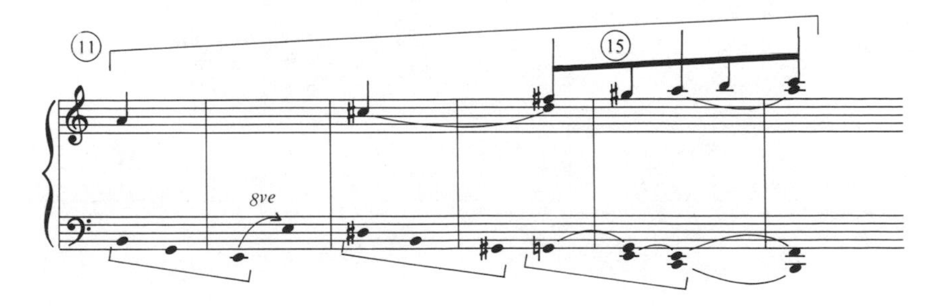

Example 3.21: Interlude in G, mm. 11–16, Stage V analysis (outer parts only)

STAGE III: INTERPRETATION

The function of the Stage III graph is to show as concisely as possible those aspects of melodic and harmonic process which lead from pillar harmony to pillar harmony (plus any longer-range melodic connections that may overstep the pillar harmonies). This is best described by example, for which the "Pastorale" interlude from the *Ludus Tonalis* will once again serve. The necessary preliminaries—Stages IV and V—are given in example 3.22. In the first phrase, the outer voices generate a step-progression pair in contrary motion, but note that the step-progression in the bass continues into and through the second phrase (Stage V). B♭5, freely introduced in m. 4, is the beginning of an ascending step-progression which controls the upper part in the second phrase: B♭5–B5 (transferred to B4)–C♯5–D5. The octave change from B5 to B4 leaves the upper register open; Hindemith returns to it in the third phrase at the climax point (C6 in m. 16). This connection of B5 to C6 (with the associated step-progression) is a good example of a long-range melodic connection made without reference to harmonic progression: the step-progression leaps past not just one, but two of the pillar chords. (Another step-progression operates in the right

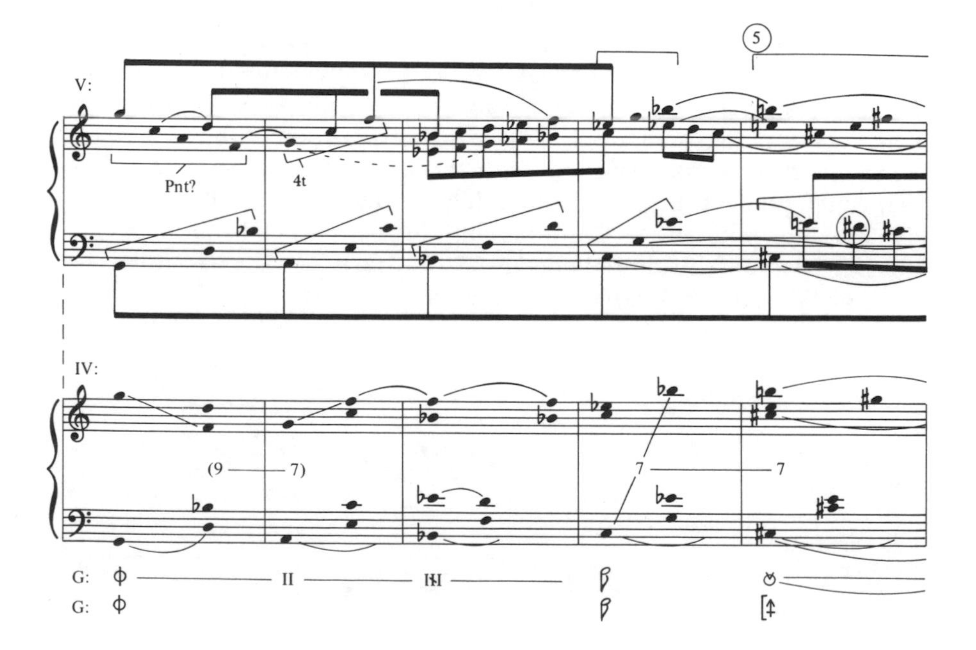

Example 3.22: Interlude in G, complete Stage IV and V analyses

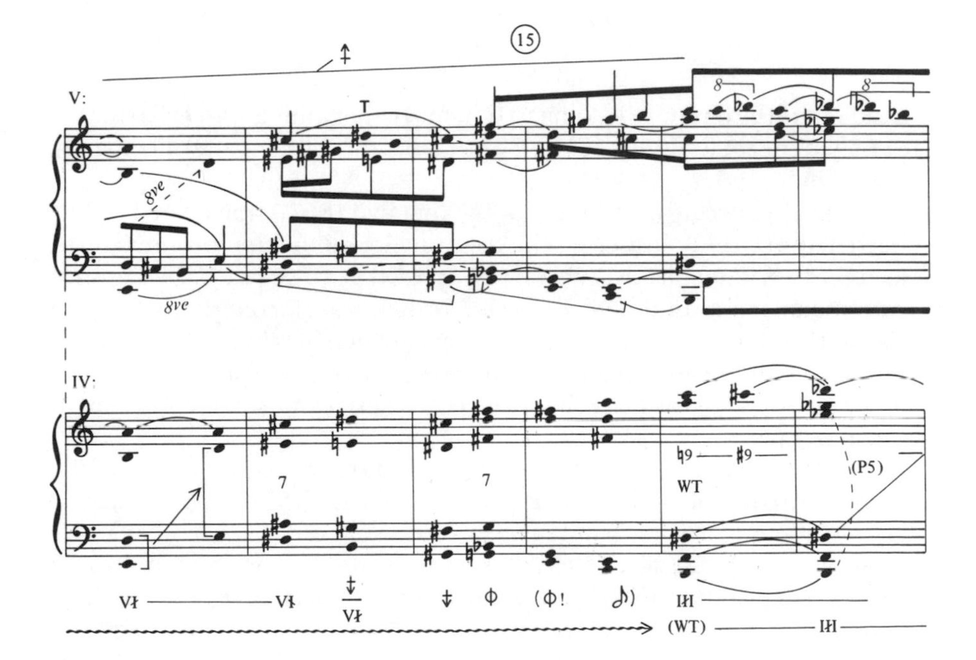

Example 3.22: *Continued*

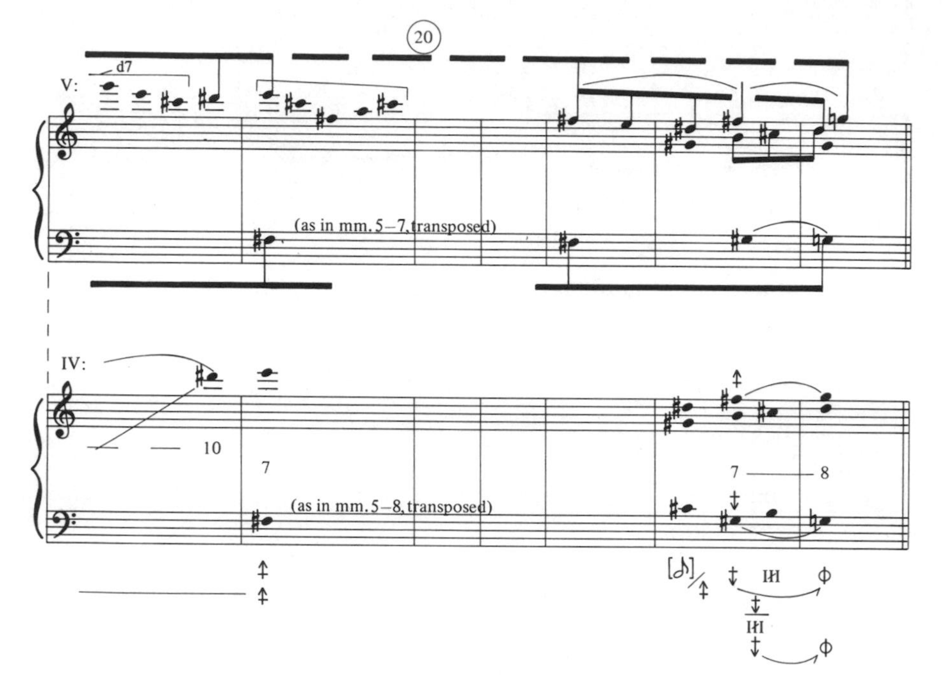

Example 3.22: *Continued*

hand in the third phrase leading to C in m. 16: beginning with D5 in m. 10, to C♯5 in m. 13, to C5 in m. 16, the opening part of the pattern being repeated in m. 15.)

The upper registral extreme of the first half (B5) is transferred downward in the second phrase, but the continuation of the step-progression in m. 16, C6, is immediately transferred upward to C7 to reach the registral extreme of the second half, D♭7. D♭7 is then transferred down again to C♯6 by the diminished seventh chord arpeggiation in mm. 17–18. Since E5 in the fourth phrase—parallel to B5 in the second—is also transferred down at the end of the piece, it is plain that register transfer is important in the upper parts.

Degrees in the first two phrases (Stage IV) are very clear because of the tenor's fifths doubling slow moving bass notes and, in the first phrase, triad arpeggiations in the left hand. The exact content of the harmonies above these degrees is not always clear because of pentatonic formations and some arpeggiations. My choices are given in the harmonic synopsis. The harmonic progression of the opening mm. 1–5 should not be interpreted as ϕ to ʊ, but as ϕ to ƥ, with a subsequent half-step shift to the ʊ: thus, ϕ ƥ, ʊ. The sonority—again a minor seventh chord—acquires a certain sense of stability because of its simple extension in mm. 5–8, but it is reinterpreted by the force of the cadence in mm. 9–10 as [↕].

In the third phrase, though the chords are generally easy to define because of strong metric placement and pattern repetition, the functions are not so easy to determine. Those presented in the synopsis are in G, but it is by no means clear that G is in control at any point in the phrase (D or B are equally plausible). The harmonic-tonal nature of the phrase is better indicated by the degree reduction shown below the synopsis: an area of indefinite tonality and function leading to an extended whole-tone sonority. Another abrupt shift in the fourth phrase returns tonal orientation to G, though even there the extension of the leading-tone chord to some extent compromises the function of the two leading tones in the degree progression.

Fluctuation values are carefully graduated in the third phrase: the minor seventh-major seventh-minor seventh dissonance sequences in the first two three-chord successions, then concentration on the major seventh dissonance beginning with the second chord of m. 14 accompanied by a separation of registers and the use of growling thirds in the bass, the inverted dominant ninth of m. 15—a sonority closely related to the whole-tone scale set—and the whole-tone sonority with minor ninth in the outer voices in m. 16. Hindemith uses the 7–9 voice exchange as minor seventh-major ninth in the first phrase, converting it to a major seventh-minor ninth exchange between mm. 15 and 16. The climax point (mm. 16–18) is an excellent example of the characteristic interweaving of dissonance (low fluctuation values), register, poor root definition, low tonal value (whole-tone derived sonority), long-range melodic connection, and dramatic progression or argument.

Example 3.23 gives my Stage III interpretation of the interlude. In this graph, the expropriation of Schenker's unfolding symbol (the two diagonal beams) deserves comment. This symbol shows motion within a single prolonged chord—subordinate harmonies may intervene, but the harmonic prolongation must be clear—and motion between already existing parts, notes already sounded, not merely implied.

The foreground of Salzer's analysis of this interlude in general agrees with my analysis of melodic activity and harmonic synopsis, even though the point of orientation and the manner of graphic presentation differ.[25] There are some errors of detail in Salzer's graph, however. Although he showed the minor-minor seventh chord of m. 1 in his foreground graph

25. Ibid., fig. 489. Discussion of the figure is in 1:239. For another analysis which agrees in many respects with mine, see William Christ *et al.*, *Materials and Structure of Music*, 2 vols., 2d ed. (Englewood Cliffs, N.J.: Prentice-Hall, 1973), 2: 450–54.

Example 3.23: Interlude in G, Stage III analysis

(a), he changed this to a G minor triad in the first middleground graph (b) for no apparent reason other than a desire to begin with a consonant chord. This misrepresents the harmonic character of the opening measure and there is in any case no reason to assume that the seventh chord is inappropriate to deeper structural levels in Hindemith's music. In mm. 5–9 greater importance is assigned to C♯5 than to B5 (C♯ is understood as a prolonged leading tone to D5 in m. 10). Here Salzer misread the harmony, ignoring the significant chord changes in the approach to the cadence and assuming prolongation of the C♯ minor-minor seventh chord through m. 9. C♯3 is certainly the bass for several measures, but it is displaced in the penultimate measure of the phrase by D♯3 in a characteristic cadence progression. C♯5 is retained as a leading tone by the soprano, a minor seventh is formed again (D♯3–C♯5), and both leading tones to D are present.[26] The entire passage may be read as a voiceleading pattern: 7–7–8 (ex. 3.24, in which the harmonies filling out both sevenths are minor-minor seventh chords).

Salzer also misinterpreted mm. 16–18. He placed emphasis on C6 and

26. I assume that the beam in the left hand from C♯3 in m. 8 through A, G♯, E, D♯, to D3 in m. 10 is an engraving error, for it makes no sense.

Example 3.24: Interlude in G, mm. 4–10, parallel seventh chords

D♯6 as the harmonic elements of the right hand figuration (graphs b and c), apparently because they continue and complete a progression of ascending thirds (C–D♯ = C–E♭) outlining a diminished seventh chord. But Hindemith offers only the diminished triad arpeggiation in mm. 15–16: the harmonic elements in mm. 16–17 are D♭7 (= C♯) and D♯6. C6 is a highly dissonant note, emphasized by placement, which gives way to D♭7 (less dissonant and part of the whole-tone basis posited by the left hand's trichord). D♭7 extends over two measures by arpeggiation and register transfer (C♯6) until its resolution to D♯6 (doubling of a member of the whole-tone trichord).

The relatively close agreement between Salzer's foreground graph and the content of Stages IV and V demonstrates that Hindemith's techniques can have a good deal in common with harmonic techniques of major-minor common practice. But the three errors cited above show that there are also significant points of divergence. When Salzer overlaid his foreground graph with stereotypes of large-scale tonal structure borrowed from (or created by analogy to) those of Schenker's theory, the unfortunate result was distorted middlegrounds and backgrounds which rule out any possibility of adopting his method for use in analysis of Hindemith's music.

PART II
MATHIS DER MALER (1933–35)

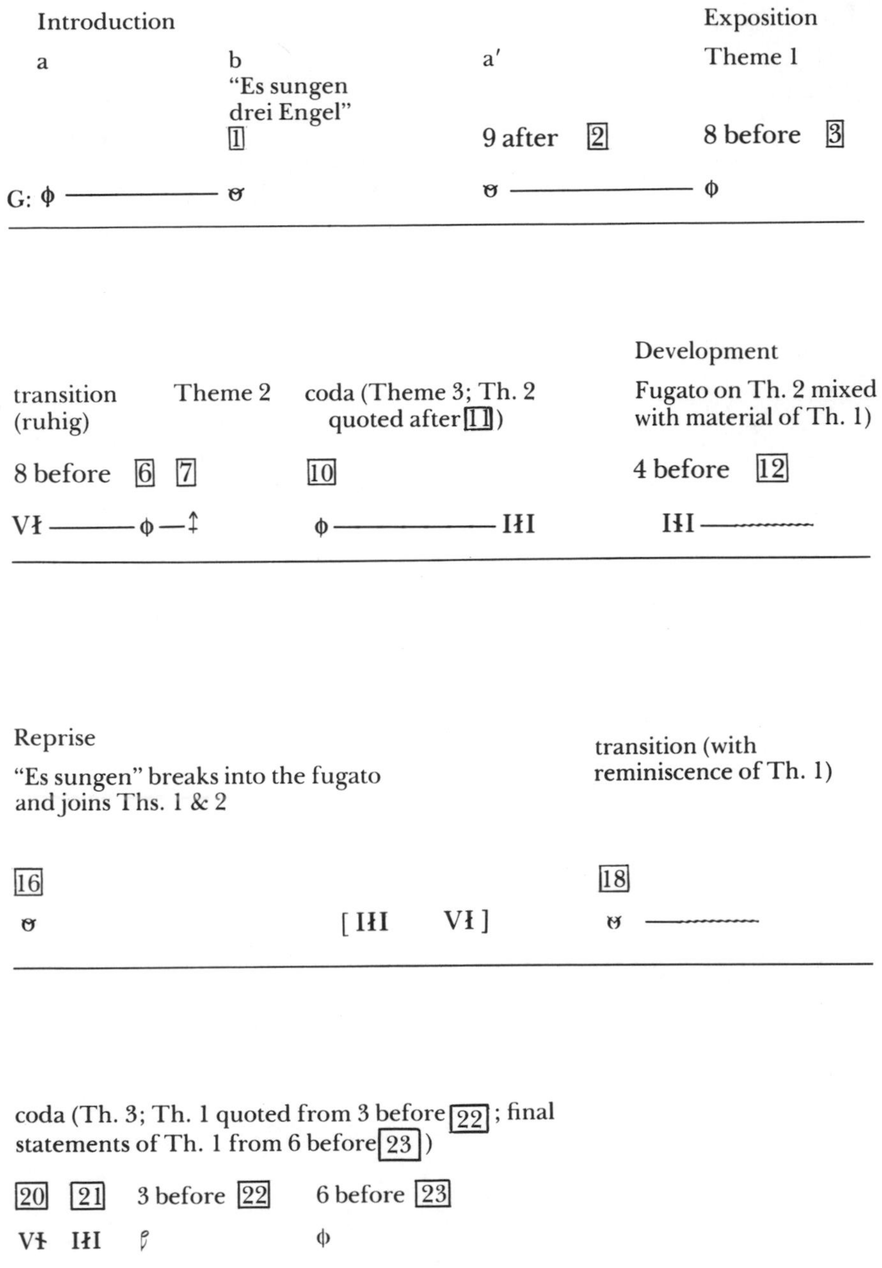

Introduction			Exposition
a	b "Es sungen drei Engel"	a′	Theme 1
	[1]	9 after [2]	8 before [3]
G: ϕ ————	♉	♉ ————	ϕ

			Development
transition (ruhig)	Theme 2	coda (Theme 3; Th. 2 quoted after [11])	Fugato on Th. 2 mixed with material of Th. 1)
8 before [6]	[7]	[10]	4 before [12]
VƗ ———— ϕ —↕		ϕ ———— IƗI	IƗI ————

Reprise		transition (with reminiscence of Th. 1)
"Es sungen" breaks into the fugato and joins Ths. 1 & 2		
[16]		[18]
♉	[IƗI VƗ]	♉ ————

coda (Th. 3; Th. 1 quoted from 3 before [22]; final statements of Th. 1 from 6 before [23])			
[20]	[21]	3 before [22]	6 before [23]
VƗ	IƗI	ℓ	ϕ

Figure 4.1: "Angelic Concert," tonal-formal design

FOUR

MODEL ANALYSIS: *MATHIS DER MALER*, "ANGELIC CONCERT"

The first movement of the symphony *Mathis der Maler* (1934) is identical with the Prelude to the opera.[1] Its title, "Engelkonzert" (Angelic Concert), refers to a panel of the Isenheim altarpiece by the German Renaissance painter Mathias Grünewald, the Mathis of the opera. The opening passages (the slow introduction, mm. 1–38, and the first period of the first principal theme, mm. 39–52) offer excellent examples of the compositional procedures typical of Hindemith's work at about the time he wrote *Craft I*. They also provide an opportunity to comment on Hindemith's only published analytic interpretation of his own music.

The tonal and formal plan of the whole movement appears in figure 4.1. The introduction is laid out in the form of a frame (mm. 1–8 and their transposed repetition in mm. 32–38) surrounding three statements of the medieval melody "Es sungen drei Engel" (fig. 4.2). This melody reappears in tableau 6 of the opera at the center of a lullaby scène in which Mathis recalls ancient mystic images in his attempts to reassure and calm the frightened Regina and again in tableau 7 shortly before Regina dies. The appropriateness of the melody in the context of the "Angelic Concert" needs no stressing, but it should be noted that the theme is given three times, as is the luminous G major chord of the introductory measures. Whether these repetitions refer simply to the three angels of the melody (there are more in the altarpiece panel) or extend to Christian number symbolism is impossible to say—but very characteristic medieval/Renaissance figure and number symbolism is certainly present in the Isenheim altarpiece, which may very possibly have influenced Hindemith's musical conceptions. (He went to see the altarpiece while working on the

1. The music of the symphony was composed first, while Hindemith was working on the libretto for the opera. See the histories in Geoffrey Skelton, *Hindemith,* 111ff.; Briner, *Hindemith,* 122–38. In several published sources, the assumption that the symphony was derived from the opera has led to erroneous conclusions; for example, Grout, *History of Western Music*, 705; Franz Wöhlke, "*Mathis der Maler*" *von Paul Hindemith* (Berlin-Lichterfelde: Robert Lienau, 1965), 52ff.

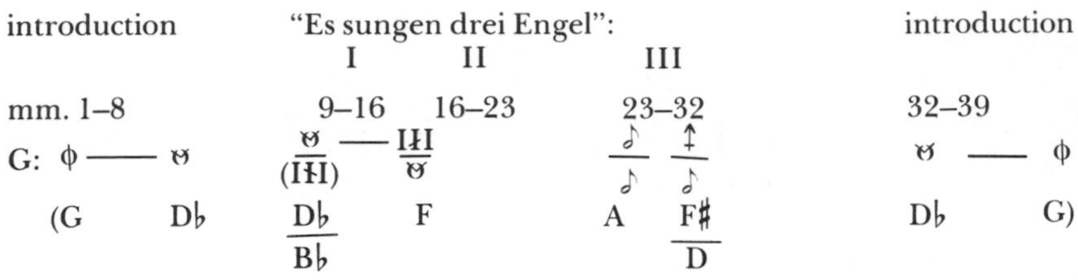

introduction	"Es sungen drei Engel": I	II	III	introduction
mm. 1–8	9–16	16–23	23–32	32–39
G: ϕ —— ʊ	ʊ / (IHI) ——	IHI / ʊ	♪ ↕ / ♪ ♪	ʊ —— ϕ
(G D♭	D♭ / B♭	F	A F♯ / D	D♭ G)

Figure 4.2: Introduction, tonal-formal design

opera, though after composing the "Angelic Concert."[2]) There is certainly some tonal symbolism: the passage from G to D♭ (ϕ to ʊ) gives in microcosm the tonal argument of both the symphony (I: G; II: C → C♯) and opera. The tritone relation might be said to have a trace of irony (if one recalls its Latin epithet, *diabolus in musica*); but its principal connotation is an opposition—heaven-earth, angelic-human, or serene-dramatic—which corresponds closely to the altarpiece, where the angels' concert is paired with the Incarnation. The tonality of the "Angelic Concert" (G) is also set off against the opening of the opera's first tableau (Mathis' "sonniges Land," an earthy image), in which the tonic is F♯, but emphasis is on its dominant, C♯ (ex. 4.1). In the introduction the tonal opposition is plain, though the symbolism of that opposition is not (the opening measures appear in both G and D♭; the angels sing in D♭). Apparently the intent is only to foreshadow the tonal symbolism of G and D♭ in the symphony and the opera.

Example 4.2 translates figure 4.2 into a Stage I graph (with the addition of critical tones in the upper voice). The brackets in mm. 7–9 show the outer voices in the three chords of the cadence leading from ϕ to ʊ. (In *Craft I,* Hindemith says three chords are necessary for a convincing cadence when no tritone interval is in the voiceleading.[3]) The smooth diatonic motion of the upper voice is matched with the unstable diminished triad in the bass. This diminished triad establishes tension in intratonal relations and fluctuation values which the final cadence chord resolves. The cadence by this means is made more distinctly functional than it might otherwise be. Some ambiguity or uncertainty remains throughout the passage quoting "Es sungen drei Engel," not in the harmonic-tonal successions, which are strong enough, but in the major-third transpositions of

2. Skelton, *Hindemith,* 118. Wöhlke, "*Mathis der Maler,*" draws attention to the fact that there are three themes in the exposition and that three of the five angels in the panel play musical instruments (42).

3. *Craft I,* 139.

Example 4.1: *Mathis der Maler,* Tableau I, mm. 5–8

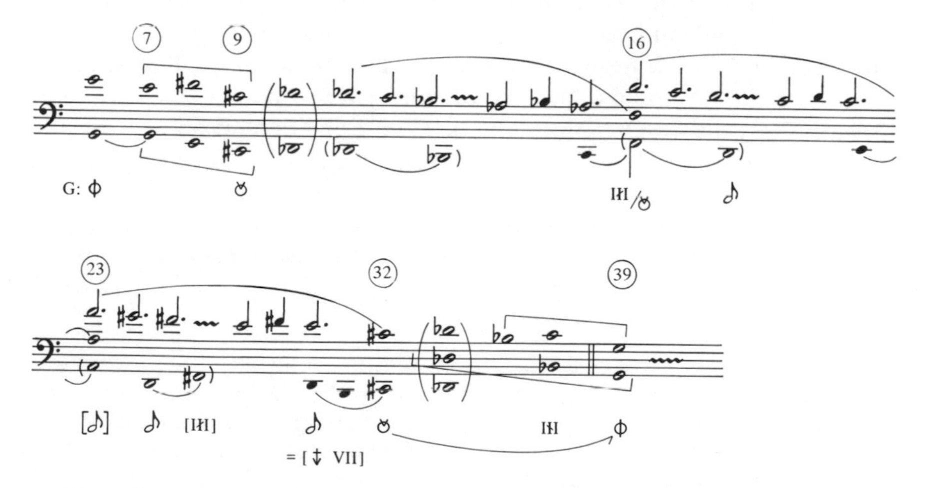

Example 4.2: *Mathis der Maler,* "Angelic Concert," mm. 1–39, Stage V analysis

the melody. These transposition levels form an augmented triad outline and lead through the octave to D♭, at which point the introductory measures are repeated, the cadence this time leading to G. The top of the dynamic and dramatic curve in the introduction is reached at the point of the primary golden section (the first dotted half beat of m. 24), and the secondary golden section lies at the pickup to m. 16, so that the second statement of "Es sungen" lies between these two points. The introduction, then, is not merely symmetrical; it is, in terms of Kayser's *Harmonik,* a balanced, organically proportioned structure.[4]

A Stage IV harmonic analysis of mm. 1–8 is given in example 4.3a. The essential harmonic rhythm is almost the prolongational stereotype of traditional harmony: I . . . . . II V I becomes ɸ . . . . . [(ʊ) IłI] ʊ. The gradual increase in dissonance level (fluctuation values) above the pedal point G is readily audible, as is the distinct difference in fluctuation values between the cadence dissonances of mm. 7–8 and the chord of resolution (the D♭ octaves in m. 9). The path upward out of the G (or G major triad) even has something of the flavor of a journey through the overtone series.

Example 4.3b shows a Stage V melodic analysis of the same passage. Arpeggiation dominates at first, but then an extended step-progression moves out of A5 to reach F♯ in m. 8 (a coincidence of the highest points of melodic and harmonic tension in the phrase). Because all the melodic activity of the passage rises, as if to regain the register of the highest note of the G major chord (G6), that note has been shown as implied—as has G♯6 and other notes below it that would correctly be placed with the D♭/C♯ bass of the cadence.

The first statement of "Es sungen drei Engel" is made by three trombones in unison with an accompanimental line in the strings (tripled by octave duplication). In example 4.4, only the lowest strain of the accompaniment (in the cellos) is shown against the trombone melody. The two broad arches of this secondary line are formed from a combination of step-progressions and arpeggiations, the latter entering necessarily into calculation of the harmonic basis of the passage (Stage IV). The melody does not have a single clear stepwise frame either, but is a combination of step-progressions (first half) and arpeggiations (second half). The ambiguity between major and relative minor so common in modal melodies is apparent here as well and is reflected in the harmony, which gives emphasis to D♭

4. In this connection it is important that the return of "Es sungen drei Engel" to form the reprise (m. 230ff.) lies very near the primary golden section of the main body of the movement (that is, not including the 38 measures of the introduction), and that the three statement levels are reproduced (mm. 230–67). (Mm. 39–342 = 304 mm.; add 10 for 20 mm. in $\frac{3}{2}$ meter = 314 mm.; 314 x .618 = 194; 194 + 38 = 232.)

(ϕ) only at phrase beginnings, the cadence positions being VƗ (m. 12) and IƗI (m. 16). A wholly unambiguous determination of the harmony is prevented by the arpeggiated figuration. In the first half of the passage, the figures are pentatonic but are succeeded by a strong linear descent toward B♭. Chord symbols in parentheses are sonorities formed on second or third beats and may or may not be regarded as belonging to harmonic progression. In the second half, the major-triad arpeggiation of the melody and generally clear harmonic basis contrast with diminished triad or seventh outlines in the figuration—an instance of noncoincidence between harmony and the implied harmonic content of the melody (melodic degree progression).

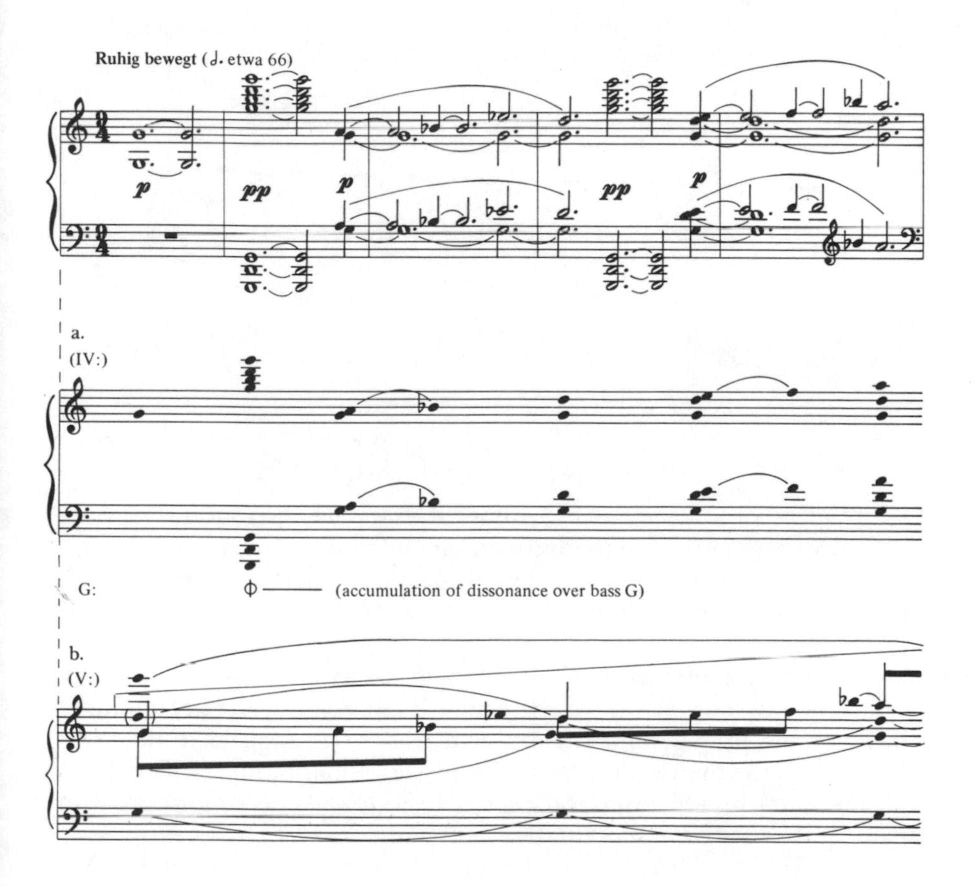

Example 4.3: "Angelic Concert," mm. 1–9, score and Stage IV and V analyses

Example 4.3: *Continued*

To avoid overbearing detail, I have shown only a partial summary of the melodic movements of the accompaniment (again tripled in the strings) in mm. 16–24, the second statement of the angels' melody. This is equivalent to a Stage Va melodic reduction of that part (ex. 4.5). Most of the extended arpeggiations of diatonic or pentatonic character, especially in mm. 20–23, have been omitted to show the single overriding feature: the step-progression of mm. 16–18 which regains the register of the beginning of the piece and prepares for the climactic use of that register in the third statement of the theme, mm. 24ff. The arpeggiations of mm. 20ff. dramatize the point by repeating the registral recovery. The counterpoint of theme and bass is 1:1, almost in the manner of exercises in *Craft II* (ex. 4.6).

The distinction between the two halves of the theme emphasized by design changes in the accompaniment is also apparent in the harmony: where the chords of the first half are all in root position, most of those in

Example 4.4: "Angelic Concert," mm. 9–16, Stage IV and V analyses

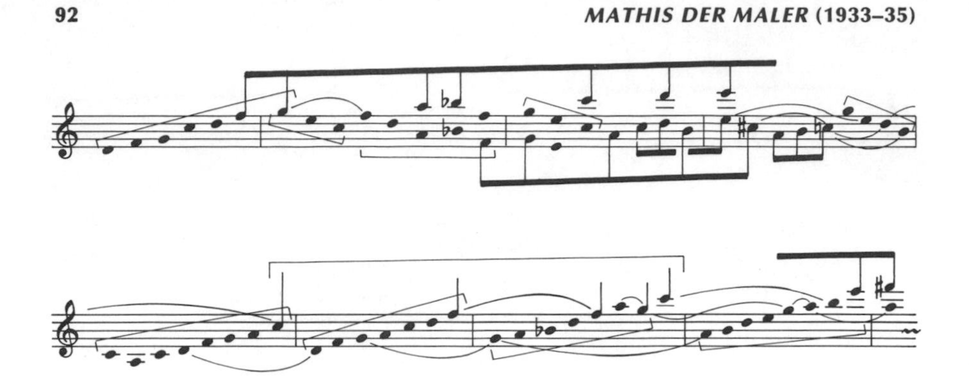

Example 4.5: "Angelic Concert," mm. 16–23, violin part, Stage V analysis

Example 4.6: "Angelic Concert," mm. 16–23, counterpoint of melody and bass

the second have their roots in an upper part (ex. 4.7). The whole passage is given as in D, since the nominal tonic at the beginning, F, gives way to its traditional relative minor very quickly (though cadences are in fact to the dominant, A). The asterisk above the system indicates a chord whose upper-voice content is not clear because of the arpeggiation figures. The harmonic progressions in the cadences may be characterized as modal. Otherwise they are freely chosen but concentrate on degrees and possible sonorities available in the minor key. Parallel fifths in all three cadences are used for harmonic or root reinforcement.[5]

The counterpoint of theme and bass in the third setting (mm. 24–32) is essentially a varied (and of course transposed) version of the counterpoint of mm. 16–24. Around this is set a profusion of extended step-progressions and arpeggiation figures. The passage is not really polyphonic, however; it is actually very strongly harmonic, so much so that I have constructed a 1:1 setting to which the remainder of the figuration can be related in the traditional sense of diminutions (ex. 4.8). For instance, the derivation of the violin figuration in mm. 24–26 from the upper voices of example 4.8 is shown in example 4.9.

5. *Craft III*, 35–36.

Example 4.7: "Angelic Concert," mm. 16–23, Stage IV analysis

Example 4.8: "Angelic Concert," mm. 24–32, Stage IV analysis in the form of a harmonic reduction with voiceleading

Example 4.9: "Angelic Concert," mm. 24–26, violin part, analysis of figuration

The harmony of this setting is similar to that of the second statement in its quick movement away from the major key suggested at the outset to the minor (but now IƗI, not the relative VƗ) and in the two broad, clear movements toward the dominant. In this setting, however, chord roots lie in the bass almost throughout (again, note fifth doublings as harmonic reinforcement). The distinction between the two halves of the theme is made by the harmonic articulation of the dominants and by obvious timbral and registral means: in the first half, the full orchestra is used across the widest registral distribution so far, but instruments drop out in groups in the second half. The first flute's A6 is the highest note in the introduction, the basses' and tuba's F♯1 the lowest. Thus they finally reach the registral extremes of the initial chord, G1 and G6, and we can recognize the opening measures (1–8) as a microcosm of the shape of the whole introduction: the opening chord with wide distribution, the *Wellenspiel* that gradually regains the register of the chord (as F♯6 in m. 7, but beyond G to A6 in mm. 24ff.).

The final measures of the introduction are the same as mm. 1–8, transposed at the tritone. The range is narrower, however (upward in the bass to D♭2, downward at the top to D♭6) and timbral disposition is reversed: winds have the static chord and strings carry the line. In Hindemith's recording of the symphony (1934),[6] a subtle but important difference obtains between these measures and those of the opening. In both he pushes the tempo forward slightly toward the cadence chords, but in mm. 33–39 he does this much earlier, with the result that the D♭ major chords in the winds are somewhat blurred by entries and motion in the strings—a characteristic blending of dramatic quality (tension), tonal hierarchy, and timbre.

Hindemith's analysis of mm. 39–54, the opening period of the faster main section of the "Angelic Concert," is reproduced in example 4.10.[7] His comments on this graph were restricted almost entirely to a few remarks on harmony and tonal plan. The English translation of the first part of this passage unfortunately obscures its meaning, and I have therefore newly translated it:

> The strongly chordal plan of the harmonic degree progression [Stufengang, labeled 5 in Hindemith's figure] is attributable to the endeavor

6. Re-released on Telefunken in 1973 in the set *Paul Hindemith zum 10. Todestag* (KT 11036/1–2).

7. *Craft I*, 220–22.

*) The organ-point is disregarded in the analysis.

Example 4.10: "Angelic Concert," mm. 39–54, Hindemith's analysis from *Craft I*, 220–22

Example 4.10: *Continued*

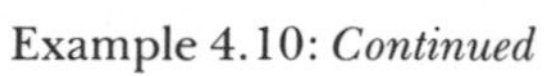

Example 4.10: *Continued*

> to give as narrow as possible tonal definition to larger chord groups—as contrasted with the free motion of the individual voices. Because the tones of the harmonic degree progression in mm. 9–13 [that is, mm. 47–51] produce an arpeggiated chord of Group VI, a gentle but very poignant cadencing is aimed toward the B of mm. 13–16 [51–54]. In the tonal summary [6 in Hindemith's figure] the same procedure is discernible: here too, groups of central tones ["tonicized notes," upper staff of Hindemith's 6] are chordally related in order to achieve a thoroughly quiet, softly extended tonal foundation [Untergrund], despite all the activity of individual segments.[8]

He appeals to this notion of contrast of functions elsewhere: "The degree-progression give us a means of combating the effect of harmonic fluctuation. . . . If the chords have very varied harmonic weight . . . the degree-progression may be very smooth, consisting largely of third-relationships and leading tones." The idea is to achieve variety and richness, to aid "the free unfolding of the harmony," but at the same time to remain intelligible.[9] So here the stability of the harmonic-tonal plan through its several levels is the foil to the profusion of melodic life and rapid shifts in harmonic definition (fluctuation values).

Actually, Hindemith's explanation of this passage involves some question begging. The general effect is quite clear and can be described pictorially as something like "angels at joyous play." The active music making of fundamentally quite untroubled beings corresponds neatly to active melodic life above a "thoroughly quiet, softly extended tonal foundation." But it was unnecessary to appeal to several layers of harmonic-tonal organization: the effect of stable basis is achieved very well by the three pedal points (on G, C, and B) which Hindemith excludes from his harmonic reckoning. This problem is a reflection of a general difficulty with the early *Craft* theory: although it advances well beyond most harmony texts current in its day, it does so unevenly and in many instances not far enough. The exclusion of the pedal point is a reactionary vestige, a product of overconcern with harmonic detail.

One peculiarity in the harmonic analysis is the fact that G is ignored in the tonal reckoning of the first half of the passage (C is chosen instead), despite the clear cadential preparation of the end of the introduction and the strong and obvious pedal point. At another point (mm. 45–47), degrees are grouped in such a way that an obvious cadence chord is left out, even though Hindemith placed strong emphasis on the role of the cadence chord in his theory.[10] In fact, I think the three pedal points by themselves

8. Ibid., 222–23.
9. Ibid., 144, 145.
10. Ibid., 138.

(with their cadences) explain the harmonic content of the whole passage adequately:

mm. 39–42 46 47 51 54
G: ϕ— VII ♭— ( ) IłI—

The tonicizing chords in the cadences produce a clear tension-relaxation effect in conjunction with their cadence chords by contrast of quality (diminished versus major, or $\frac{8}{5}$), dissonance level, and root definition.

Hindemith's analysis of melodic activity, especially step-progressions, ignores the possibility of expanded arpeggiations (analogous to expanded step-progressions) and, partly because of that shortcoming, underrates the significance of upper-voice registral placement and isolation. On the other hand, it concentrates on the most readily audible step-progression connections and ignores some short-range successions. In the first draft of *Craft I*[11] he analyzed these step-progressions somewhat differently (ex. 4.11). In mm. 39–42, he traces three step-progressions, but I would also include the arpeggiation that reaches D6 in m. 43 (ex. 4.12). The register thus opened is left alone, to be regained in m. 50 (in step-progressions Hindemith shows) and then followed upward to F♯6 (reached as IłI is gained). The whole plan is not unlike that of registral use in the introduction.

Example 4.11: "Angelic Concert," variant reading of the melodic degree-progression, mm. 39–47 (from the first draft of *Craft I*)

Example 4.12: "Angelic Concert," mm. 39–47, upper part, Stage V analysis

Hindemith warns us that we might come to different conclusions than he does about any of the several analyses offered at the end of *Craft I*. Here, an interpretation of the later *Craft* theory forces changes in the reading, changes that avoid the limited harmonic perspective that hampers the theory in *Craft I*.

11. *Craft I* (1935–36 draft), 153.

FIVE

A COMMENT ON TABLEAUX 6 AND 7

When the work of Grünewald was rediscovered in the early 1920s (thanks to the reassembly and exhibition of the Isenheim altarpiece), it was hailed primarily for its expressionistic qualities. What Hindemith saw is recorded in his notes for the premiere performance of *Mathis der Maler* in Zürich in 1938:

> If I have attempted to present in a form appropriate for the stage what I read into the few dates in the life of Mathis Gothart Nithart and what the connections to his works have allowed me to imagine, I have done it because I can think of no more lively, problematic, humanly and artistically moving (therefore, in the best sense, dramatic) figure than the creator of the Isenheim Altarpiece, the Karlsruhe Crucifixion, and the Stuppach Madonna. . . . Although he knew well the complex artistic fashions of the on-going Renaissance, he chose in his own work to develop to its fullest unfolding the materials and manner of the past, rather like J. S. Bach two hundred years later, who appears as a conservative [Bewahrer] in the stream of musical progress. [Mathis] fit into the still powerful machinery of state and church . . . but in his paintings he could report with sufficient clarity how the wild tumults of the era, with its suffering, its sickness, and its wars, had deeply affected him.[1]

The autobiographical character of the opera—for which Hindemith wrote his own libretto, his first major literary effort—has been stressed by several writers. Much of the artistic personality Hindemith read into Grünewald's "few dates" is in fact Hindemith's own. The central question posed—how can one justify continuing to create art that is not politically engaged in a time of dangerous political uncertainty—was one very immediate to Hindemith in Berlin in 1934. In the story, Hans Schwalb, the leader of the peasant revolt, taunts Mathis with the pointlessness of art in wartime and with the irresponsibility of his simply standing aside ("Every time one of us is struck, so are you!"[2]). The solution to which Mathis eventually comes

1. Cited in Andres Briner, *Paul Hindemith*, 136–37.
2. I.1.81–82.

(once transfigured as St. Anthony and with the help of St. Paul the Eremite) is surprisingly personal, a combination of the craftsman doing what he can do best, religion-based morality, and a romantic conception of the power of art:

> Go back to both [people and your task]. Let all
> you create be an offering to God, and He will
> be alive in
> every work. If you turn humbly to your brother,
> unselfishly giving what is most sacred to you
> with your
> greatest skill, you will be at once bound and free:
> a strong tree in the soil of your land.[3]

For Hindemith, this meant "do what you must in all conscience, despite competing demands on you." Indeed, he described his later self-imposed exile in Switzerland as a time of "good music and a clean conscience."[4]

The libretto draws together the strands of Hindemith's life and career in the late twenties and early thirties, and the music for the opera does the same: it achieves a perfect synthesis of stylistic and technical elements of his music from the period of the New Objectivity and his rediscovery of historical musics. Of the latter Hindemith said, "Old folksongs, polemical songs from the Reformation period, and Gregorian chant make the nourishing ground for the *Mathis* music."[5] This was the historical reflection of Op. 11, no. 5, on a grand scale, which, as it happened, produced a compositional style rich and comprehensive enough that he could spend most of the rest of his career working out its implications.

In chapter 4 I discussed at some length the beginning of the "Angelic Concert," the first movement of the symphony and the "Prelude" to the opera. Here I will comment on the constructive principle of the sixth and seventh tableaux and on some technical details of the music.[6]

3. VI.3.35–40. The translation is mine.
4. Geoffrey Skelton, *Paul Hindemith: The Man behind the Music*, 161.
5. Briner, *Hindemith*, 138.
6. A general analytic survey of the opera has been published by Franz Wöhlke: *Mathis der Maler*. Andres Briner has discussed the opera's compositional genesis, in *Hindemith*, 122–38. Geoffrey Skelton has interwoven that history with an account of Hindemith's uncertain relations with the Nazi government during the same period, in *Hindemith*, 106–24. Walter Salmen has written on Hindemith's use of old folk songs and historical musics: " 'Alte Töne' und Volksmusik in Kompositionen Paul Hindemith," *Yearbook of the ISCM* (1969): 89–122. Dieter Rexroth has traced stylistic and plot themes through all the major operas, including *Mathis*, in "Das Künstlerproblem bei Hindemith," *HJB* 3 (1973): 63–79. Another summary of major themes in the operas appears in James D'Angelo, "Hindemith's Opera *Die Harmonie der Welt*."

The symphony was the first of the *Mathis* music to be completed, partway through the writing of the libretto. The "Angelic Concert" is used in its entirety in the opera, but the second and third movements became the basis for the opera's sixth and seventh tableaux. The sixth tableau is essentially an expansion of the third movement of the symphony, with some interpolated and reworked material. The seventh tableau contains all of the symphony's second movement, "Grablegung," as an interlude between the first and second scenes. The remaining material is new except for the short third scene, which is a condensed, partly transposed version of the Grablegung, and a final quotation from the "Angelic Concert."

Franz Wöhlke distinguishes eleven sections in the third movement, "The Temptation of Saint Anthony," with an axis of symmetry at the point of the demons' plague (m. 237). Not all of this material is used in the opera, nor is it consecutive. The distribution is given in figure 5.1, which compares opera and symphony material.[7] Figure 5.2 shows the design of the opera's tableau 6. Three sections of the instrumental music were omitted, others were expanded, and additional material was inserted—most notably the striking paraphrase of the "Angelic Concert" in scene 1, part 2. The result is a most convincing dramatic and psychological flow: from the instrumental recitative at the beginning (model for the many that Hindemith wrote in later years) through the magical lullaby scene (in which "Es sungen drei Engel" is recalled) and the several temptations to Mathis' collapse and the final apotheosis. Although the constructive method may seem uncharacteristic of Hindemith, it is not: the *Nobilissima Visione Suite, Marienleben II, Ludus Tonalis,* the *Weber Metamorphosis,* the Whitman Requiem, and *Harmonie der Welt* were all built in a similar way. Nor is such a method difficult to reconcile with the five-stage method of *Craft III*. Since specific thematic or harmonic materials come relatively late in the planning, "building a large structure on the basis of" is equally "incorporating preexistent materials into an already planned structure."

The angels' melody makes its third appearance in the final tableau (a summary of the design appears in fig. 5.3). The symbolic significance of this ancient melody, which Böhme labels "Alter Ruf zu Christo" (An old call to Christ), changes through the opera. In the "Angelic Concert," the connection between a "call to Christ" and the Incarnation panel of the altarpiece is simple and obvious. In the sixth tableau, as Mathis and Regina escape into the forest, the song becomes a call for help: the last of the fifteen couplets of text given by Böhme is "God keep us from the pains of Hell / that we poor sinners not there fall."[8] Of the three text couplets which Regina sings to this melody, two are entirely Hindemith's own, with

7. Wöhlke, "*Mathis der Maler*," 54–58. Figure 5.1 is based in part on Wöhlke.

8. Franz Böhme, *Altdeutsches Liederbuch* (Leipzig: Breitkopf & Härtel, 1877), 647.

Symphony:	1–18			193–236	19–78
Opera:	beginning to 9 after (1)	Sc.1: A and B	Sc.2: C	D (in part)	E 9 before (59) to (63)

Symphony:	87–142	143–92	(193–236)	237–307	308–77
Opera:	(not used)	(63) to 5 after (67)	(see above)	(not used)	6 after (67) to (72)

Symphony:	378–408	409–68	469–520		521–37
Opera:	11 after (72) to (73) (paraphrased)	(not used)	(73) to (80)	Sc. 3: F	G to end

Figure 5.1: *Mathis der Maler*, tableau VI (opera) and movement III (symphony)

no relation to the original text. In the final tableau, the song becomes Regina's call to Christ to take her in death (confused in the delirium of fever with a call to her dead father, Hans Schwalb). The interlude which follows refers both to the Entombment panel and to the death of Regina. The

Introduction	Scene I	
	A (Mathis/Regina)	B (at (19) : “Es sungen . . .”) 1 2 3
E♭?———C♯ D♭?	D	G F♯—A—D

Scene 2: Temptation of St. Anthony

(27)	C (Bounty:Countess)	(33)–5 (Merchant:Pommersfelden) E♭	(39) (Trio) B♭
F♯	D		

D	(44)	(49) + 4	(52)	(56)
(Beggar/	Seductress/	Martyr:Ursula)	(Learned Man: Capito)	(Warlord:Schwalb)
D	B?	D	E♭	E♭

Scene 3: St. Anthony in the hermitage of St. Paul

E (Chorus)	F	G	(97)
C♯	D	E	(D♭)——— D

Figure 5.2: *Mathis der Maler,* tableau VI, tonal-formal design

three presentations of the song represent three stages of life: birth, middle life, and death. In each instance, the situation of the characters is bound up with a reference to Christ.

In case the point of such symbolism should be lost, Hindemith gives

Scene I: A				B	
Sehr breit—	Sehr langsam—	Lebhaft—	Sehr langsam	recitative	Lebhaft
	Ursula			Regina/Ursula	
4 mm.	19 mm.	43	8	7	174
	G♯	E	G♯ ⟶	B♭	

(B)	C	Scene II:	
Langsam ("Ruf zu Christo")	Zwischenspiel	Ruhig bewegt	
Regina	(*Grablegung*)	Albrecht—	Mathis—
41	43 (+1)	12	4
ends B♭	C ⟶	C♯	

M—	A+M—	M—	A		Scene III:
					Mathis
15	15	15	11 (+1)		28
D♯–D	G–?	D♯–	D	F♯	A ⟶ C♯

Figure 5.3: *Mathis der Maler*, tableau VII, tonal-formal design

one of the most familiar baroque musical emblems at the opening of the seventh tableau: a cross motive for the text—"this is the crossroad, where death and life separate" (ex. 5.1). The harmony is rooted on D (though the chord, a minor-major seventh, is a sharp dissonance); the B♭-minor triad

Example 5.1: *Mathis der Maler*, Tableau VII, beginning

Example 5.2: Tableau VII, mm. 6–9

arpeggiation of the cross motive is expanded in the voice part (shown with asterisks in ex. 5.1); and the effect of the passage is a contradiction of melodic and harmonic orientation that suggests bitonal constructs and the indefinite third relation (perhaps D: $\frac{\phi}{V♮}$). As it happens, D is not the tonic: the tonal center of Ursula's three-part aria is G♯ (which we cannot know at this point). Hindemith takes the third B♭3–D♭4 from the cross motive and uses it to open the slow first section of the aria, the harmonic course of the first phrase being from II toward the tonic (ex. 5.2). The fast central section of the aria, on E (G♯: V♮), uses the battle motive that is prominent in the third tableau.[9] The eight-measure reprise moves toward the B♭ tonic that clearly controls scene IB (see fig. 5.3). The first phrase (ex. 5.2) is re-

Example 5.3: Tableau VII, end of scene I, A

9. Wöhlke, "*Mathis der Maler*," 36.

peated entire, but immediately afterward the harmony becomes very uncertain again, reaching B♭ by means of a chromatic step-progression in the voice, then a rather sharp leading-tone cadence in the orchestra (ex. 5.3).

A similarly interesting passage which extends the dominant-function cadence dissonances is the close of scene IB (ex. 5.4a). The modulation to

Example 5.4a: Tableau VII, end of scene I, B

the key of the interlude is accomplished by a simple descending arpeggio (ex. 5.4b).

Example 5.4b: Tableau VII, transition to scene I, C (Zwischenspiel)

In both scenes where Hindemith quoted materials from the symphony, he wrote new arioso counterpoints for the voice parts with occasional linkages to the principal melodic material of the original (Regina in VII.1B; Mathis in VII.3). In each case, the effect is a delicate blend of reminiscence and contemplation.

PART III
THE MUSIC BEFORE *MATHIS*

SIX

THE EARLY MUSIC (TO 1925)

During my time as a soldier in the First World War I was a member of a string quartet which served our commanding officer as a means of escape. . . . His dearest wish was to hear Debussy's String Quartet. We rehearsed the work and played it to him with much feeling at a private concert. Just after we had finished the slow movement the signals officer burst in and reported . . . that the news of Debussy's death had just come through on the radio. We did not continue our performance. It was as if the spirit had been removed from our playing. But now we felt for the first time how much more music is than just style, technique, and an expression of personal feeling. Here music transcended all political barriers, national hatred and the horrors of war. Never before or since have I felt so clearly in which direction music must be made to go.[1]

Hindemith's account of this experience is obviously colored by hindsight, since such an early appearance of his notion of a supranational ethical community of music makers is difficult to reconcile with some of his own activities in the following years. The "other" Hindemith emerges quite clearly from another reminiscence—this time, Max Rieple on a performance of Hindemith's *Kammermusik* No. 1, Op. 24, no. 1, in Munich in 1923:

A few weeks earlier I had been involved in a concert by the American George Antheil . . . and witnessed a bombardment of tomatoes, eggs, and even stinkbombs. I prepared myself for something similar on Hindemith's first appearance in Bavaria's conservative capitol. And I was right. Scarcely had the last measures of the fox-trot imbedded in the piece subsided than the hall turned into chaos. Whistles blew, boos resounded, chairs flew through the air—a hellish noise filled the large room. Hindemith, in the meantime, had disappeared backstage with the other musicians. As the spectacle reached its height, he reappeared—thoroughly calm—seated himself at the percussion . . . beat with all his might on the drums, and let the slide whistle howl. The honest *Münchener* were so taken aback by this unexpected behaviour that Hindemith was the victor in an unequal battle.[2]

1. Skelton, *Hindemith*, 49.
2. Max Rieple, "Begegnungen mit Paul Hindemith," *HJB* 1 (1971): 150.

Epater le bourgeois or moral reflection? Nose-thumbing or positive interaction with the traditions of German culture—or, even more broadly, European Christian culture? This dilemma was posed early in Hindemith's career, and for many years before *Mathis* he tried to heed both calls at once and wavered between them.[3] The brash young radical received more attention, especially through the operas or instrumental works for larger ensembles, while the reflective historicist worked underground, as it were, in the solo sonatas, quartets, and songs. The sonatas of Op. 11 feature the interplay of French and German elements, of Debussy and Reger; the sonatas of Op. 25 show their New Objective transformation. In Op. 25, no. 3 (for solo cello), a "constructed" exterior conceals a debt to the subtlest compositional techniques of the expressionists. But only in the *Kammermusiken* of Op. 36, the Concerto for Orchestra, Op. 38, and *Cardillac*—the stylistic summa of the early period—does Hindemith clearly bring all the elements of style and technique together, laying the foundation for the synthesis of the early 1930s.

SONATAS, OP. 11, NOS. 4 AND 5; OP. 25, NO. 1

Hindemith began as a performer and matured quickly. He played the Beethoven Violin Concerto in concert at the age of eighteen and was appointed concertmaster of the Frankfurt State Opera orchestra at the age of nineteen (in 1915). By that time he had also been composing actively for two or three years, with several opus numbers under his belt (in later years he thought of everything he wrote before 1918 as juvenilia). After war service, during which he continued to compose while playing the piano for officers' clubs and the violin in his music-loving colonel's quartet, he turned abruptly and permanently from the violin to the viola. He played the viola in the Rebner Quartet (the first violinist was his teacher Adolf Rebner) until 1921 when the Amar Quartet was formed to premiere his String Quartet, Op. 16. In the next year, this new group began touring and, until it was disbanded in 1929, was among the most active and successful proponents of contemporary chamber music in Europe. Hindemith composed two quartets especially for this group (Opp. 22 and 32), as well as solo sonatas for the individual players. In the series of pieces under two opus numbers (Opp. 25 and 31) which contain these solo sonatas, he included two for himself.

The sonatas of Opp. 25 and 31 were written between 1922 and 1924.

3. See Andres Briner, "Ich und Wir: Zur Entwicklung des jungen Paul Hindemiths," in Rexroth, *Erprobungen und Erfahrungen*, 27–34; Dieter Rexroth, " 'Nun beginne ich mich zu bedeuten'—zur Biographie des jungen Hindemiths," in *Hindemith-Zyklus Nordrhein-Westfalen 1980–81*, 28–42.

An earlier opus, 11, contains works from 1918–19, some with roots extending as far back as 1914. Of the five sonatas in this opus, four are accompanied: nos. 1 and 2 for violin, no. 3 for cello, and no. 4 for viola. No. 5 is the first of the unaccompanied sonatas for viola. All these sonatas readily reveal Hindemith's familiarity with eighteen- and nineteenth-century sonata literature and his debt to Brahms, Strauss, and Reger, but also to Debussy and the German composer most influenced by him, Franz Schreker. In the two violin sonatas, Brahms is most in evidence, but Hindemith tries to open up Brahms's tightly closed motivic-harmonic structures with gestures drawn from Debussy and the more radical middle-period Reger. Op. 11, no. 4, which is certainly the most frequently performed of Hindemith's works for viola and probably the most frequently performed of all his early works, turns round the relationship, the influence of the Quartet and late sonatas of Debussy being paramount. In the opening measures of the Fantasy (first movement), in fact, Hindemith's own personality threatens to be subsumed (see ex. 6.1). But we can forgive him easily—these measures are so strikingly beautiful and so perfectly suited to the viola, which is placed in its most sonorous register, with the piano chords below giving a blend of modal yet chromatic flavors strongly reminiscent of passages in Debussy's sonatas for violin and cello. In addition, Hindemith now firmly controlled formal processes, developing the emotional and constructive arch of this improvisatory prelude in the most skillful and satisfying manner.

The second and third movements are linked to one another in the nineteenth-century cyclical manner. The second movement is a theme with four variations. The third movement, though it is labeled *mit Variationen,* is actually a sonata movement in which further variations on the theme of the second movement have been inserted. The theme, which may have been written in 1914 or 1915, is marked "Quiet and simple, like a folk song." The first variation continues the mood with a soft pastorale in triple eighths, but the second is a whimsical Debussyian Pierrotesque in whole-tone scale figures. The third and fourth variations are really a single unit,

Example 6.1: Sonata for Viola and Piano, Op. 11, no. 4, I, opening

the viola declaiming figures from the theme, while the piano's arpeggios of the third variation turn into cascading octaves in the fourth. The octaves quickly collapse into the main theme of the third movement, an excellent concatenation of the thematic and the improvisatory. After a lyrical second theme, the theme of the second movement comes back in the guise of variations five and six, which substitute for a development section. There are a reprise and a coda (variation seven) which thoroughly mix and unite the themes in a final dramatic flourish.

By Op. 11, no. 4, Hindemith had learned to control musical-emotional architecture with sure skill and intuition. In Op. 11, no. 5, however, he came closer to finding a consistent, individual compositional voice, despite the fact that this sonata also does not hide its stylistic sources. In fact, the sonata shows hardly an inkling of non-German influences. The greatest debt is to Reger, whose sonatas and suites for solo violin, viola, and cello form the major part of the late romantics' contribution to this corner of the string literature. The sonata is cast in the traditional four-movement form. The first is a compact sonata design, but is more a developmental than sectional form, built entirely on the two double-stopped chords that begin it and the angular sixteenth-note figure that follows. The second movement is slow, a freely developed two-part form which is one of the most openly romantic pages in Hindemith's music, with an expressive theme, rich triadic harmonic progressions, cadenzas, and a drawn-out coda. Its opening measures are shown in example 6.2. The third movement is a scherzo and trio, the former full of exaggerated Regerian irony, the latter legato and expressive. The finale is a passacaglia whose theme is an expansion of the main theme phrase of the first movement. Throughout this sonata, the harmonically bound texture but chromatic chord progressions and prolonged half-diminished or dominant chord types, chromatic half-steps, dynamic and tempo changes (including dramatic crescendi and even a coda

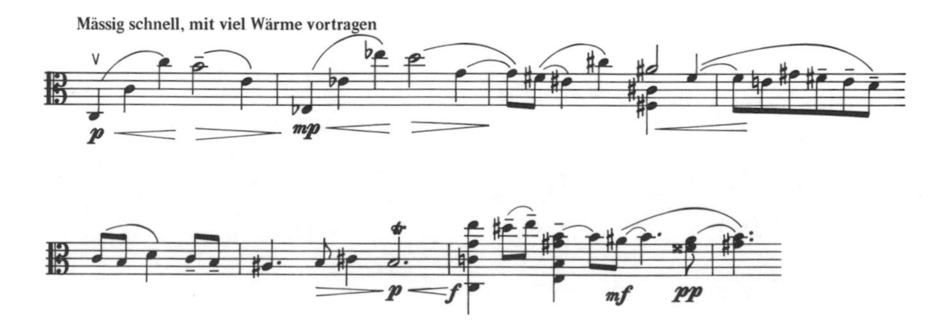

Example 6.2: Sonata for Viola Unaccompanied, Op. 11, no. 5, II, mm. 1–7

acceleration in the first movement) all show Hindemith's roots in the late nineteenth century.

In one sense, however, the passacaglia is a special case. The movement is labeled "In form and tempo of a passacaglia"[4]—perhaps a twinge of conscience, since it is difficult to trace the theme. Hindemith's point of view is really that of a musical gloss: not interaction with the work of his contemporaries, but a powerful historical reflection—Hindemith in the musical language of 1919 contemplating in form and tempo the great D-minor Chaconne of J. S. Bach. The motivation for using the traditional passacaglia design here was quite different than in the later New Objective works. Instead of "emptying out" the traditional forms, turning them into neutral types which could be exploited for the composition of new music, here Hindemith still thought in terms of the nineteenth-century dialectic of demand for originality and reverence for the masters. The former required constant progress, constant evolution from the masters, the eventual result being the extremes of expressionist atonality on the one hand and the counter-romanticism of the New Objectivity on the other. But a different combination of the ingredients also gave the substantial literature of historical reflection: a music designed both to be new and also to offer a new way of hearing, of interpreting, its traditional model, a kind of music criticism carried out in the medium of music itself. Brahms was the first real master of this kind of composition. In the passacaglia of Op. 11, no. 5, Hindemith stands closer to Brahms, Reger (who sometimes wrote musical glosses on Brahms), Busoni, and Berg, than he does to his work of the late twenties. Admittedly the point is complicated by the fact that historical reflection did not disappear during the twenties, but was assimilated into (or at least remained a significant undercurrent in) the counter-romantic music of the New Objectivity, just as the techniques of German expressionism were assimilated into its quasi-geometric linear counterpoint. Hindemith became a master of both kinds of assimilation.

We must also distinguish between Hindemith's historical reflection in this passacaglia and deliberate archaism. He did not abandon contemporary stylistic concerns to take refuge in an outmoded manner as Reger did in some of his last works. The simplistic arguments of Adorno notwithstanding, historical reflection is not automatically unhealthy archaism, although the point on a continuum where the one threatens to become the other is not easy to locate. I am convinced that Hindemith never lost contact with his present, in 1919 or later. To illustrate the point with images of which Hindemith later was very fond, I quote Dorothy Sayers's description of a fictional Oxford college: "a stone quadrangle, built by a modern architect in a style neither old nor new, but stretching out reconciling hands to

4. Hindemith also uses the phrase "Im Form und Zeitmass . . ." in the finales of Op. 11, nos. 1 and 2.

past and present."[5] How a person in the twenties or thirties would react to such a building would depend on his aesthetic ideology: to insist on the "constant progress" view would mean seeing it as mediocre archaism; to insist on a strict traditionalism would mean finding it decadent dilution. But Sayers gives the emphasis to reconciliation, as does Hindemith in his 1925 letter to Schenker ("work with and not against one another"). Neither of the extreme views could accept the idea of a pluralism of musical style, but it is clear that, even at an early stage in his career, Hindemith had done so. From this to his concept of musical community was a small step.

In Op. 11, no. 5, since the large-scale traditional harmonic framework is for the most part intact, we can use Schenker's method as our primary analytic tool. But it will still be difficult to explain all the features of the surface of the music purely in traditional harmonic terms, though most can be referred to chromatic alterations or functional substitutions of the kind found in some textbooks of that period (including the *Harmonielehre* of Louis and Thuille from which Hindemith studied as a conservatory student) (exx. 6.3 and 6.4).

I have not supplied graphs based on the analytic method presented in

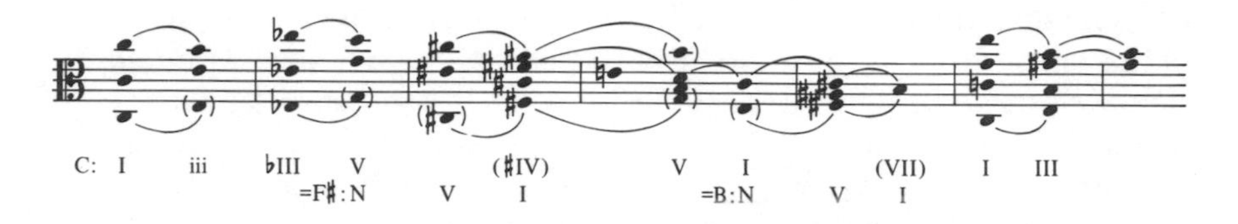

Example 6.3: Op. 11, no. 5, II, mm. 1–7, harmonic-voiceleading analysis

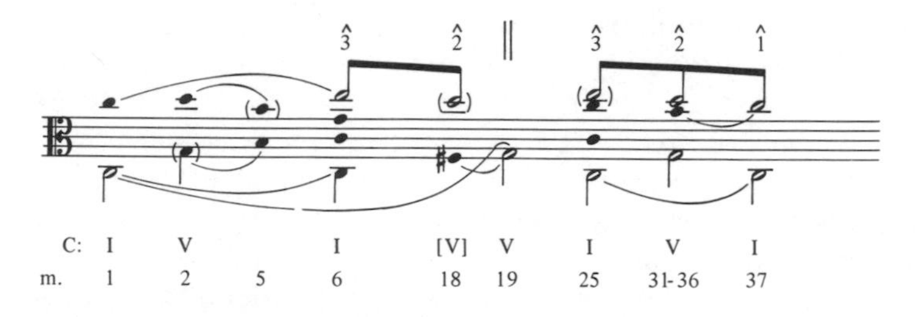

Example 6.4: Op. 11, no. 5, II, analysis of tonal structure (after Schenker)

5. Dorothy Sayers, *Gaudy Night* (New York: Avon, 1968), 7. I cite this after the paperback reprint edition. My argument in this paragraph depends heavily on Leonard Meyer's discussion of style change in *Music, the Arts, and Ideas* (Chicago: University of Chicago Press, 1967), 104–33.

chapter 3, because the results would largely duplicate those of a Schenkerian analysis. Chordal definition is still bound closely to the traditional cadence and its dissonances; for example, the triads of the opening versus the half-diminished, diminished, and major-minor seventh chords of the pre-dominant and dominant prolongations (mm. 13ff., 31ff.). (The same applies to the first movement, but attention to the dominant dissonances is greater.) The special features of Hindemith's later practice that require a different analytic approach are not much in evidence: modal melodic cells and cadential progressions, melodic activity in polyphonic texture freed of clear harmonic support (lines spun between the harmonic pillars, or large-scale step-progressions), intratonal relations to replace the older functions, and surface control of chordal definition (harmonic fluctuation).

The scherzo exhibits greater freedom of harmonic detail. In example 6.5 I have juxtaposed the score for mm. 1–12, the first section of the scherzo proper, with a simple harmonic reduction (roughly Stage IV) and Schenkerian readings of foreground and middleground. Two significant

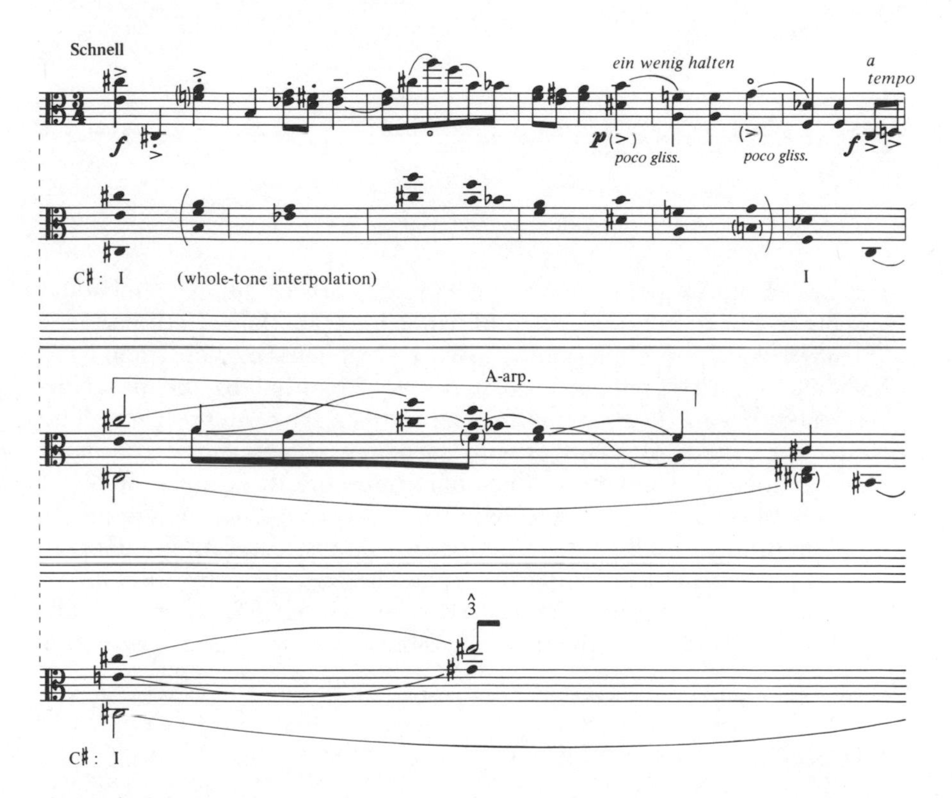

Example 6.5: Op. 11, no. 5, III, mm. 1–12, analysis of harmony and voiceleading (after Schenker)

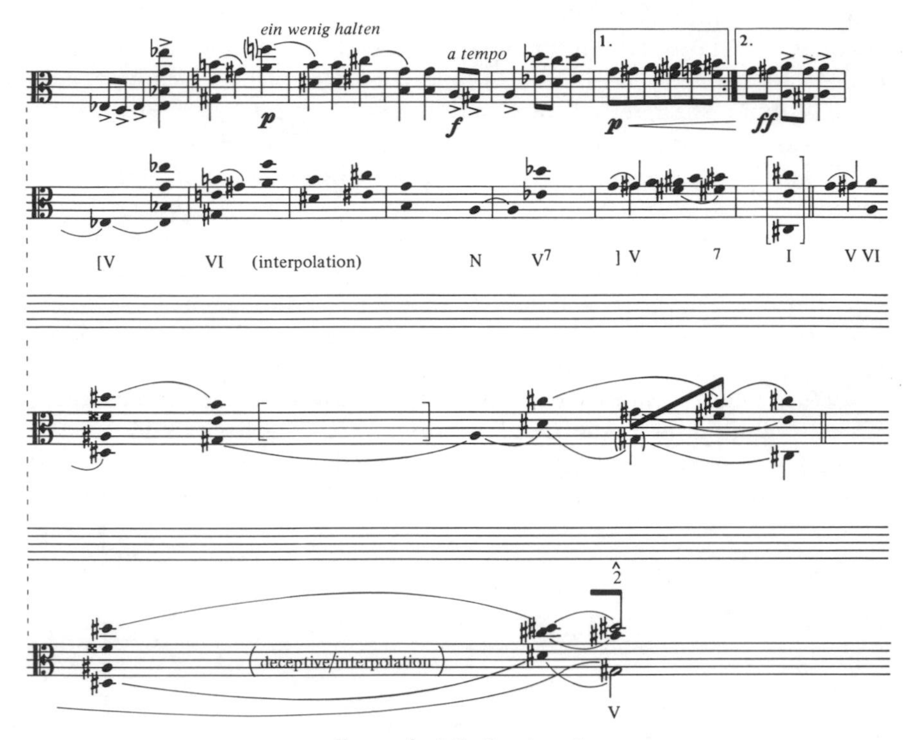

Example 6.5: *Continued*

stretches of the music cannot be interpreted with traditional functional symbols and have to be regarded as ironic interpolations. Both passages depend primarily on whole-tone constructs. In the first of these (mm. 1–5), the tonic sonority can be understood as expanded by means of an augmented-triad arpeggiation. The second is a true interpolation. The greater the length of passages with such interpolations and the more poorly defined the elements of the tonal framework (here the tonic chord has a split third, $\hat{3}$ is displaced from its tonic bass, and $\hat{2}$ over V is implied), the greater the possibility the framework will be abstracted away and other kinds of pitch-structural complexes replace it. Precedents for this kind of development may be found in the works of Schoenberg, Scriabin, and others.[6] But for Hindemith, the many possible stages between major-minor

6. See Allen Forte, "Schoenberg's Creative Evolution: The Path to Atonality," *Musical Quarterly* 44 (1978): 133–76; James Baker, "Scriabin's Implicit Tonality," *Music Theory Spectrum* 2 (1980): 1–18; idem, "Schenkerian Analysis and Post-Tonal Music," in David Beach, ed., *Aspects of Schenkerian Theory* (New Haven: Yale University Press, 1983), 153–86; Jim Samson, *Music in Transition* (London: E. J. Dent, 1967).

harmonic music and a wholly atonal syntax were merely tools to be used as he needed. With the exception of the most extreme solutions, he explored all approaches. Indeed, the variety of techniques and stylistic idioms he employed without compromising his compositional identity is remarkable.

In common with many of his contemporaries, Hindemith used special devices to replace the tonal framework for harmonic orientation: mottoes (chord, figure, or short progression), ostinatos, or prolongations of dissonant sonorities. All play some role in Op. 11, no. 5, but they become the principal means of tonal definition in the five movements of Op. 25, no. 1 (1922): a three-chord motto in the first movement; a two-measure progression with careful definition of the bass in the second; a chord in the third (the most subtle of the five movements); an obvious ostinato in the fourth; and a recurrent progression with bass-register definition in the fifth. The first movement's motto is treated as a dissonant prolongation[7] (ex. 6.6). At the end, in a characteristic coda reduction, the second and third chords of the motto are filtered out (ex. 6.7). In this piece, the interpolations have become the whole fabric of the music.

The opposite extreme of suppression of the tonal framework occurs in

Example 6.6: Op. 11, no. 5, I, opening measures

Example 6.7: Op. 11, no. 5, I, closing measures

7. See Robert Morgan, "Dissonant Prolongations: Theoretical and Compositional Precedents," *Journal of Music Theory* 20 (1976): 49–92. For criticism of Morgan's methods, see Baker, "Schenkerian Analysis and Post-Tonal Music": 158–61.

the "Signal," the first movement of the Violin Concerto, Op. 36, no. 3 (*Kammermusik* No. 4) (1925). The bass sounds only eight notes (with many repetitions), the pattern being tonic–dominant alternation with one short whole-tone prolongation:

I:							II:
mm.	1–8	9–11	12	13--17	18–23	24–26	(attacca)
B♭:	I	V———	———	———	I	V	(I)
(bass)	B♭	F	E♭ C♯	BA	B♭	F	(B♭)

Set above this throughout is a tremendous complex of dissonant sonorities, trills, flourishes, and trumpet calls. In the second and third movements, most of the elements of the later style are present. It would take little taming of the harmonically disengaged and motivically indifferent passages shown in examples 6.8 and 6.9 to conform to the manner of the mid-forties. In fact, Hindemith uses a device very common later: the progression B♭–D in mm. 1–23 of the second movement is the same as the tonal course of the whole movement and of the whole concerto:

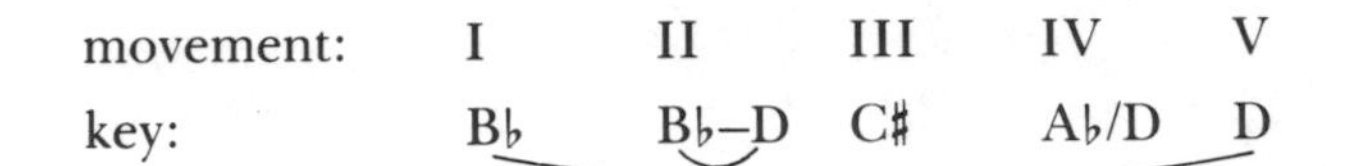

movement:	I	II	III	IV	V
key:	B♭	B♭–D	C♯	A♭/D	D

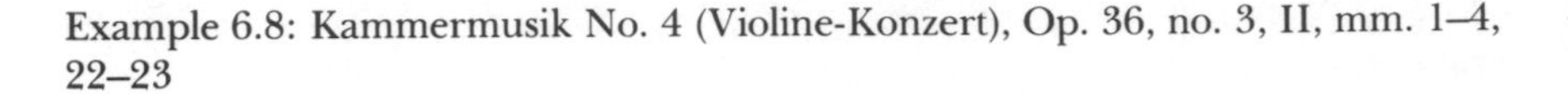

Example 6.8: Kammermusik No. 4 (Violine-Konzert), Op. 36, no. 3, II, mm. 1–4, 22–23

Example 6.9: Op. 36, no. 3, III, mm. 1–7

SONATA FOR SOLO CELLO, OP. 25, NO. 3

The third in the series of solo sonatas, Op. 25, no. 3 (1922), is a technically anomalous but musically quite successful composition that is one of the few transitional pieces Hindemith wrote before his determined plunge into the New Objective manner in early 1923. All but the last of the Sonata's five movements were written in one day in July 1922. Even though written very quickly, the sonata is a perfect synthesis of competing stylistic and technical claims. It blends features of traditional tonal or modal harmony with the careful, dense motivic development of the late romantics and Viennese expressionists, and with the anti-romantic irony, raucous unconcern for pretty colors, and objective formalism which characterizes Hindemith's New Objective music from 1923 on. The difference in stylistic and technical consistency between the sonata and its contemporaries—the *Kleine*

Kammermusik, Op. 24, no. 2, the "1922" Suite, Op. 26, and even *Marienleben*—is striking.

The fact that Hindemith included this piece in the list of his "approved" works in the first edition of *Craft I* shows that he regarded it as fit for scrutiny using the methods of the *Craft* theory; that is, as controlled by organized tonal principles. But it exploits such a dense mat of chromatic materials modeled in the manner now generally associated with nonserial atonal music that the principal point of my discussion will be an assessment of the interaction of the atonal chromatic surface and dense motivic development with demonstrable tonal processes. Two separate analytic methodologies will be necessary: the analytic method from chapter 3 above and—for characteristically atonal procedures—Allen Forte's set-complex analysis.[8]

Given Hindemith's endorsement of the sonata, the appropriateness of an analytic method based on the *Craft* principles is not in question. But the applicability of set-complex analysis is another matter, not because the Sonata fails to be atonal—indeed, it is exceptional for the relatively small number of complex interval structures (pitch-class or pc sets) it employs, their recurrence, and complementation—but because it plainly balances atonal and tonal procedures. Forte, however, deliberately avoids "such features of the music as tonality, large-scale linear connections, register, or orchestration" to explain with clarity and concision the multiple relations of "unordered pitch-class sets that underlie melodic configurations, combinations of horizontal lines, and segments of various shapes."[9] Schoenberg's atonal music, the paradigm for this repertory, "is characterized not only by the use of 'new harmonies' without reference to a tonal basis, but also by the complex deployment of those components, creating a new dimensionality appropriate to the new music."[10]

The hierarchic levels of a set-complex analysis are not in any sense equivalent in content to Stages I–V, but they are concerned with approximately the same dimensions of a composition. The set complex and its nexus set(s) and Stages I and II, for example, both deal with the whole composition, but are not analogous in any other way. The set complex is the hierarchic superior of the independent pitch structures in an atonal composition, but it is not the same as a tonal background: "It is tempting to compare Schoenberg's detailed way of segmenting the musical continuum with the traditional diminutions of tonal music. Both are hierarchic, but

8. Allen Forte, *The Structure of Atonal Music* (New Haven: Yale University Press, 1973).

9. Allen Forte, *The Harmonic Organization of "The Rite of Spring"* (New Haven: Yale University Press, 1978), 29, 23.

10. Allen Forte, "Sets and Nonsets in Schoenberg's Atonal Music," *Perspectives of New Music* 11 (1972): 63.

they are essentially different with respect to the concept of musical space."[11] For this reason, any simple analogy between the set complex and Schenker's middleground or background stereotypes must be rejected out of hand.

To make a meaningful comparison of analytic results, I will treat tonal process as a constructive principle superior to the multiple relations of pc sets, the set complex. The relation of melodic configurations (specifically, motivic design and development) to pc-set structures must be considered, even though Forte disassociates pc-set structures from any necessary connection to melodic or thematic process. Pc sets underlie melodic configurations, which include motives. They are not equivalent or identical, nor dependent. But since I have taken a step away from these latent structures in favoring tonal process, I must accept a closer connection between motive and "significant set" whenever possible. For example, set recurrence and complementation, which are major criteria in set segmentation, need to be reassessed from this point of view. We must take into account that musical presentations vary widely with respect to clarity or emphasis, internal repetition of elements, duration of elements or of the set, registral placement, and so on, and that most of these factors are usually considered significant in tonal process.[12] Therefore, set recurrence as a criterion for significance has to be demoted to a status no greater than that of any related motivic-thematic configuration in the tonal process.

The sonata consists of five movements arranged symmetrically around the central *Langsam* (slow) movement. The outer movements are relatively long, moderately fast, heavy, and marked, but the second and fourth movements are short, the second being a quiet intermezzo, the fourth a pianissimo scherzo in triplet eighths.

The first movement is built in a simple rondo-like form: A B A′ B′ A″. A (mm. 1–7) is characterized by three- and four-note chords and brusque triplet eighths. B (mm. 8–16) presents a theme in triplet eighths which first concentrates on reiterated fifths in the lowest register and then on arpeggiations. A′ (mm. 17–24), a development section, starts with a main-theme variant which follows rhythms exactly and contours generally and continues with development of a pair of triplet-eighth fragments. The reprise of B is transposed and the arpeggiations are altered. A″ begins with a false reprise (mm. 32–34), followed by a literal, though truncated, repetition of A and a coda. The analysis presented here concentrates on the first A section (mm. 1–7), with details of other sections considered where appropri-

11. Ibid.

12. See William Benjamin, review of Forte, *Atonal Music*, in *Perspectives of New Music* 13 (1974): 180; also, "Ideas of Order in Motivic Music," *Music Theory Spectrum* 1 (1979): 31–33.

ate to the argument.[13] The set-complex analysis is given below followed by the graphs of tonal process and discussion of the extent to which the two analyses inform one another.

The score for mm. 1–7 is shown in example 6.10 and a segmentation chart in example 6.11. The quadruple-stopped opening chord, which forms the set (0, 1, 5, 7), Forte's label 4–16, functions as a kind of source set (not in the serial sense) for tonal, thematic-motivic, and pc-set relations. The chord divides into two internal components, each with a motivic role: perfect fifth below and minor sixth above, linked by an enharmonic minor seventh. This structure is reminiscent of the much-maligned device of polytonality, which was nevertheless both significant and fashionable in the twenties. Whatever the other aspects of its structure, the first chord is also a bitonal construct. The likelihood that the cellist would strike the open notes first and then the upper pair in the chord reinforces the visual impression.

The roots of the two intervals form the extremes of the chord (C–C♯), and Hindemith treats this relationship (or more generally the half-step) as motivic and structural not only in this movement but in a cyclical manner throughout the sonata. The second and third movements close plainly on C, the first and fourth on G (approached by its ↕), and the final movement, which begins indistinctly, on a C♯ major triad. Thus, the entire tonal movement in the Sonata is contained in capsule in the first chord. As the cellist begins with the low C–G open strings and proceeds to the upper E♯–C♯

Example 6.10: Sonata for Violoncello Unaccompanied, Op. 25, no. 3, I, mm. 1–8

13. For a set-complex analysis of the entire movement, see Neumeyer, "Early Music of Hindemith," 137–42, 157–58. Analyses of the other movements of the Sonata may also be found there, 21–40, 142–57.

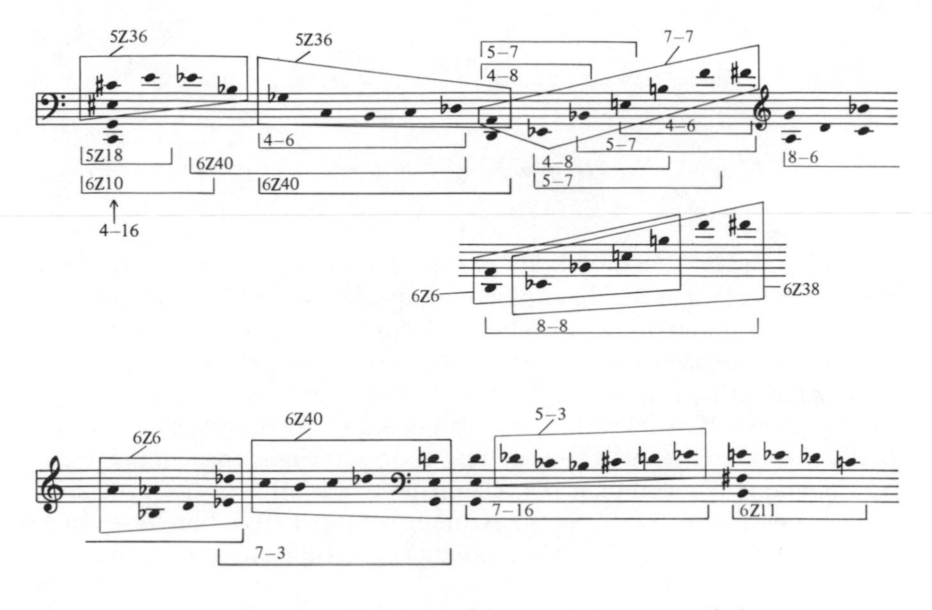

Example 6.11: Op. 25, no. 3, I, mm. 1–8, pc set analysis

stop, so the sonata begins with four movements which, if not always securely rooted in C, cadence in C or its dominant G before ending in C♯.

The pc set of the opening chord (4–16) recurs most obviously in the second reprise of A, but also in several other places in transposed, reordered forms. The eight-note complement, 8–16, appears as well (0, 1, 2, 4, 6, 7, 8, 9) at the beginning of section A′. This octad contains a transposed form of the tetrachord (ex. 6.12). The parallel with the opening measures may be made even plainer by constructing a transposition of mm. 17–18 to the level of the opening (ex. 6.13). Pc sets 4–16 in mm. 16–17 (with sets linked to it before and after) and 8–16 support a complex collection of pc sets from the opening measures of the composition, so that motivic-thematic and pc-set structures are dense and tight in this first reprise.

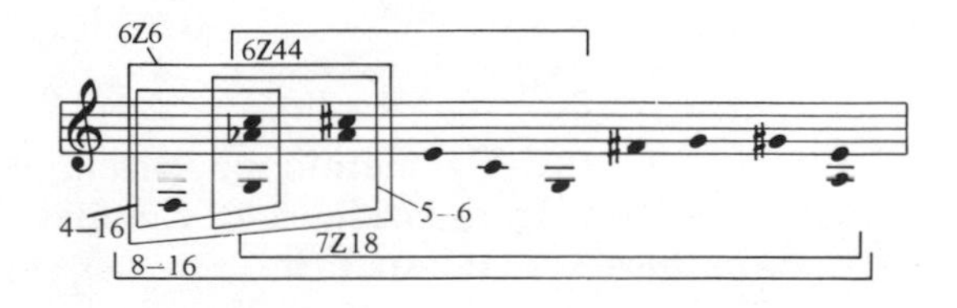

Example 6.12: Op. 25, no. 3, I, mm. 17–18, pc set analysis

Example 6.13: Op. 25, no. 3, I, mm. 17–18 transposed to the level of mm. 1–2

The pentads 5Z18 and 5Z36 which arise immediately from the first chord also recur and their complements appear. Pentad 5Z36 recurs immediately, transposed at t = 8. These two forms of the set share only pc 1, positioned at opposite ends of each set's display in association with interval class (hereafter ic) 4 (E♯3–C♯4; D♭3–A2). The complex nesting of sets and complements which follows in m. 2 is generated by development of the perfect fifth component of the opening chord through repeated half-step transpositions. The complement-related hexachords that result are of considerable significance in the pc-set structure of the composition (especially in the second reprise and coda). (Note that 6Z6 reappears already in m. 3, at t = 11.)

A number of complement relationships not yet mentioned are created in this opening section. In m. 1, set 4–6 (11, 0, 1, 6) is the complement of the octad in m. 3. In mm. 3–7, sets 5–3 and 7–3 appear and, with other sets in those measures, gain emphasis through repetition. Hexachord 6Z11 (m. 7) is the complement of 6Z40 (which appears three times); these hexachords, however, are not significant outside section A or A″.

In addition to set occurrence, recurrence, and complementation, there are interesting examples of shared subsets in section A. These are listed below.

Sets	*Measure(s)*	*Shared subset*
6Z40 (10, 11, 0, 1, 3, 6)	1–2	5Z36 (11, 0, 1, 3, 6)
6Z11 (11, 0, 1, 3, 4, 6)	7	
6Z40 (10, 11, 0, 1, 3, 6)	1–2	4–6 (11, 0, 1, 6)
6Z40 (6, 9, 11, 0, 1, 2)	1–2	
6Z6 (9, 10, 11, 2, 3, 4)	2	4–8 (10, 11, 3, 4)
6Z38 (3, 4, 5, 6, 10, 11)	2	
6Z6 (9, 10, 11, 2, 3, 4)	2	4–8 (9, 10, 2, 3)
6Z6 (8, 9, 10, 1, 2, 3)		

The juxtaposition of C and C♯ mentioned earlier is important throughout the first movement. In the cadence of the first short phrase (mm. 1–2), the tensions inherent in the first chord because of its C2–C♯4 outer-voice dissonance are rapidly broken. The neighbor-note figure of m. 2 carries C up an octave, C♯4 down an octave (C♯ = D♭), and both C3 and

D♭3 can be understood to move to an implied D3 over the open fifth D2–A2 (see ex. 6.14). This movement parallels a gradual decrease in chord tension from ϕ to II.

The first three sections are linked by means of several of the properties of the opening chord, including the half-step relation (ex. 6.15). In section B, the perfect fifth is raised a half-step (roots: C2–C♯2) and the two bitonal dyads are articulated separately (the minor sixth is inverted to a major third). The minor ninth in the outer voices is preserved (C♯2–D3), but the set type is not. At the opening of section A′, the set is transposed up a fifth, the minor sixth again inverted to a third, and that third restated a half-step higher to give C5–C♯5 in the upper voice (and form another version of the opening tetrachord).

It is puzzling that the prominent minor third, C♯4–E4, in the upper voice in m. 1 is not a significant motivic factor in the movement. Apart from its use in combination with the minor seventh of the opening chord in mm. 3–7, it has no important role. Instead, it is the ascending half-step that is most prominent in the transition to section A′, the second part of that section (which reaches the piece's upper registral extreme), and the lead-in to the false reprise of A″.

Graphs of the tonal process in mm. 1–7 appear in example 6.16. In general, melodic activity can be characterized as a mixture of arpeggiations, harmonic steps, and step-progressions. Because of this and the fre-

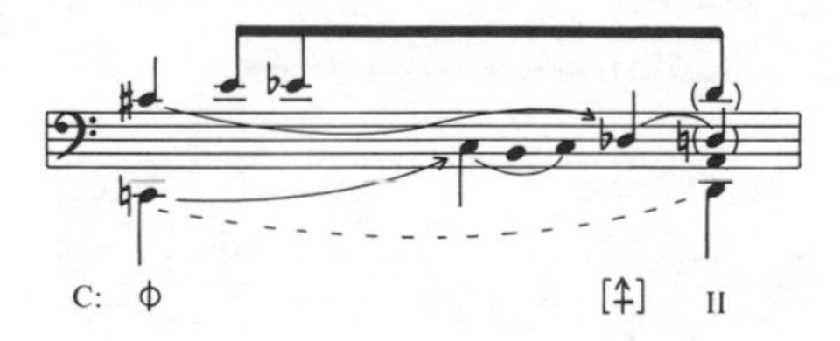

Example 6.14: Op. 25, no. 3, I, mm. 1–2, harmony and voiceleading

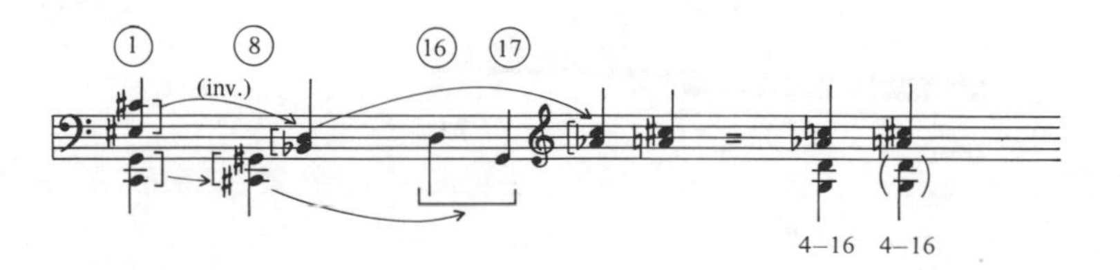

Example 6.15: Op. 25, no. 3, I, the first three sections linked by properties of the opening chord

quent octave transfers, there are some loose ends in the step-progression patterns. The broadest feature of the upper voice (see Stage III) is the arpeggiation of a diminished seventh chord in mm. 1–4 (with repetition of the last segment in mm. 5–6). The step-progression connections from E4 also deserve mention as organizing factors in mm. 1–3. In a very unusual procedure, the bass step-progression C2–D2–E♭2 (mm. 1–2) surges upward by means of register transfer to join the upper-voice step-progression at F4 in m. 2. The extreme bass register is isolated, carrying only C2–D2–G2, the bass of a simple opening harmonic progression in traditional tonal harmony.

The harmonies are not difficult to define for a composition of this period due to the articulating perfect-fifth simultaneities, multiple-stopped chords, and obvious arpeggiations. The opening chord (Stage IV in ex. 6.16), though complex, is functionally clear thanks to the fifth C2–G2. The arpeggiated chord that occupies the second half of m. 1 is shown as representing the indefinite third relation ϕ and IHI because of the inherent ambiguity of the half-diminished seventh chord (here the technically correct

Example 6.16: Op. 25, no. 3, I, mm. 1–8, Stage III, IVa, IVb, and V analyses

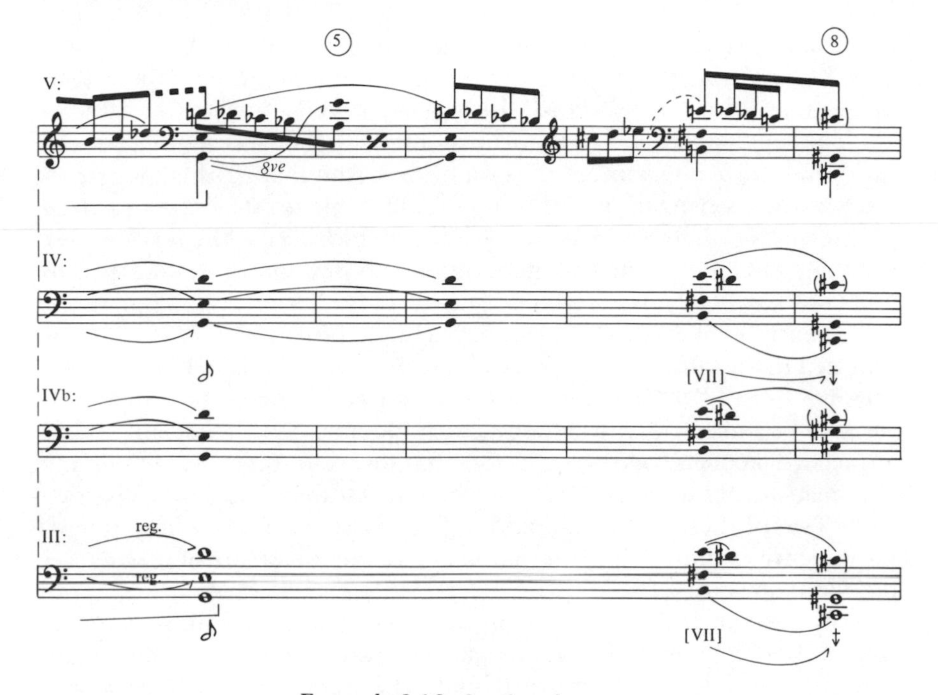

Example 6.16: *Continued*

root is E♭, but the chord is displayed as a seventh chord on C) and because the aural impression changes as the chord is presented in arpeggiation. The fifth D2–A2 forms the second clear point of harmonic definition, the chords that follow (again defined by fifths) acting like neighbor chords, as the bass D3 is struck and held in m. 3. In all of m. 3 D3 is the bass, but the exact harmonic content above it is not easy to determine. The notes given in Stages III and IV belong to the longer-range diminished-seventh chord arpeggiations shown in Stage V. In other words, I have used melodic criteria: harmonic claims of these sevenths are no better than those of the seventh left out, B♭3–A♭4. The chord of m. 4 is an arrival point. The traditional dominant is reached, the compound fifth G2–D4 rests in the outer voices, the rising tendency of the diminished-seventh chord arpeggiation is arrested as the original register of the upper part is regained, and one of Hindemith's half-step shifts—though with a register transfer, D♭5–D4—signals a pattern change (this time a cadence).

A Stage IVb showing a voiceleading reduction of Stage IV has been added to example 6.16. For the most part, this reduction simply acts to correct the octaves to which voices have been displaced by register transfer and the diminished-seventh chord arpeggiation. The arpeggiation disappears, but one or two interesting features emerge which the melodic analysis of Stage V ignores, in particular the three-note step-progression from B♭3 (upper voice, second chord) through A3 to G3.

The set-complex and tonal-process analyses, though essentially separate, can inform one another in certain ways, with motivic-thematic processes as the intermediary. A direct joining of pc-set structures to step-progressions or harmonies is not possible, but aspects of the set-complex analysis can be tied to motivic generation and development, and then to tonal process.

The ic potential of 4–16 (0, 1, 5, 7) should be considered first, as it is reflected in the table which Forte calls an "interval vector."[14] For 4–16 the vector is 1 1 0 1 2 1 (one entry each for ics 1 and 2, none for ic 3, and so forth). The two entries in ic 5 suggest possible emphasis on that ic, but nine tetrachordal pc sets have two ics 5 (one has three). Ic 1 is represented only once in 4–16, but three of the nine tetrachords with two ics 5 also have two ics 1. Two of these three, 4–6 and 4–8, are also used in the movement, prominently in mm. 1–7. The relationship of their structure or ic potential to 4–16 is obvious.

In other words, 4–16 is not an unusual set. Its interval emphases in this composition emerge only from its particular musical presentation as the quadruple-stopped opening chord. Once the ic potential of the set is realized in a particular form as a presented pc set, factors other than its inherent structure and potential relationships enter into interpretation.

The complementary hexachords 6Z6 and 6Z38, on the other hand, are the only six-note sets which have four entries in both ics 1 and 5 (along with set 6–7, which is not used in this piece). In this respect, these two sets contrast sharply with the other hexachords used in the first section, 6Z10 and 6Z40, which have no particular ic emphasis. In effect, the pair 6Z6 and 6Z38 realize in hexachordal form the interval structure emphases of the first chord: the outer-voice C–C♯ becomes a strong bias toward ic 1; the open fifth C–G becomes a bias toward ic 5.

In m. 1, 5Z18 is directly produced by the first chord and the melodic gesture C♯4–E4. This first melodic interval in the movement completes the tetrachord in the sense that ic 3 is the only ic not in 4–16. Since 5Z18 and 5Z36 are Z-relatives, having identical interval vectors, a direct sequence of pc-set generation from the source tetrachord can be observed through the first phrase: 4–16 ⟶ 5Z18 (harmonic completion) ⟶ 5Z36 (Z-relative) ⟶ 5Z36 (transposed, at t = 8) ⟶ 6Z40 (twice).

The first 5Z36 and 5Z18 share the trichord (1, 4, 5). The succession of

14. For a systematic discussion of the relation of the interval vector to ordered presentations of a set, see Allen Forte, "The Basic Interval Patterns," *Journal of Music Theory* 17 (1973): 234–73; also *Atonal Music,* 63–73.

intervals in the 5Z36 suggests a protomotivic relation to 4–16 except for the anomalous minor third (ex. 6.17a). Compare also the ics formed by the upper notes in relation to the initial F3 (ex. 6.17b). The presentation of these pitches gives each interval about equal weight with the exception of the half-step, which is easily heard as a shift from the cell of the minor third to that of the fourth E♭4–B♭3. The dotted quarter duration of E4 helps to isolate these interval cells.

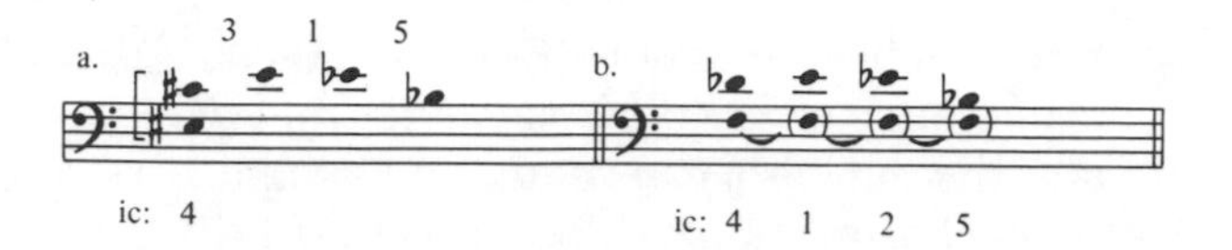

Example 6.17a: Interval succession in 5Z36 (m. 1)
Example 6.17b: Intervals formed with the initial F (E♯) in m. 1

The second 5Z36 sets forth its intervals so differently that it seems designed for minimum association with the first form of the same set. The tritone suggests the disjunction immediately, but there is in fact a motivic relationship: the second 5Z36 is nearly a retrograde of the first. If the second 5Z36 is transposed to the level of the first, the pc sequence of the first set ($^{1}_{5}$ 4 3 10) becomes 10 (4) 3 4 5 1 in the second. Although it is one of the group of sets generated from 4–16, the second 5Z36 is presented in a way that obscures the connection. This may be because Hindemith sought a distinctive cadence formula, as shown in example 6.18. The same formula is used in m. 4, where 6Z40 is again produced (ex. 6.19). A similar cadence figure in mm. 7–8 gives rise to the statement of 6Z11. If the hexachords 6Z40 and their complement 6Z11 are reserved for cadence, then, the role of the pentad contained in 6Z40 in mm. 1–2 is at once to make the hexachord motivically distinct even as it furthers the generation of material from the source set.

The discussion of the first phrase is summarized in example 6.20. The first chord presents the source tetrachord for pc-set structures and motivic materials, as well as the first element of harmony (ϕ with its fifth) and the

Example 6.18: Cadence formula in m. 2 Example 6.19: The same figure in m. 4

Example 6.20: Summary of pc set evolution in mm. 1–2

first outer-voice notes. The second note (E4) generates the first set from 4–16 (5Z18) and establishes patterns of movement in the upper voice: arpeggiation (eventually the diminished-seventh outline) and step-progression (two come from E4). The next two melodic notes (E♭4–B♭3) continue one of the step-progressions from E4, begin a descending arpeggiation, and produce the Z-relative of 5Z18, 5Z36. This figure is the first melodic presentation of the significant interval classes in 4–16. The continuation of the descending melodic figure generates a transposed recurrence of 5Z36 with a sharply altered motivic figure, nearly a retrograde of the figure of the first 5Z36. The propagation of sets from 4–16 is thus extended to the phrase cadence. The hexachordal superset 6Z40 provides the bass for the cadence, continues the bass step-progression, and, through an implied note, finishes the descending step-progression of the upper voice begun in the first 5Z36.

The interlocked hexachord pair following the cadential fifth in m. 2 continues the generation of sets from the source tetrachord. The design of this arpeggiated figure obviously mimics the first chord: half-step and perfect fifth are exploited, the fifth-plus-tritone outline of the first chord is reproduced (ex. 6.21a), and the two events are joined in bass and upper voice by step-progression connections. Note the bass fifths in example 6.21b.

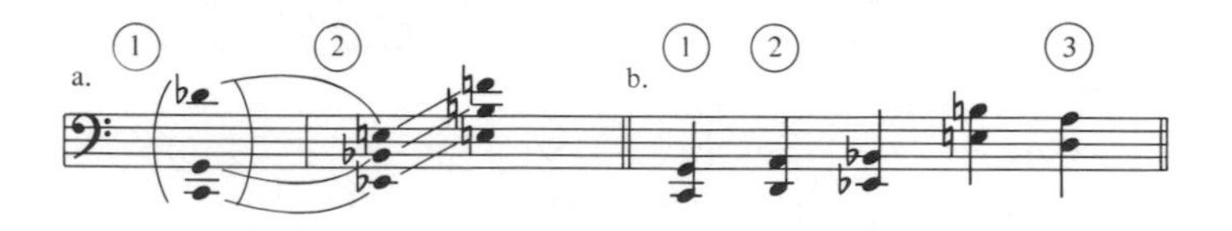

Example 6.21a: The source chord 4–16 in the arpeggiations of m. 2

Example 6.21b: The bass fifths in mm. 1–3

The melodic pentads of the opening are also related to the events of m. 2. The last three notes of the first 5Z36 reappear as the first triplet figure of the arpeggiation (ex. 6.22). The same trichordal set, in a permutation that

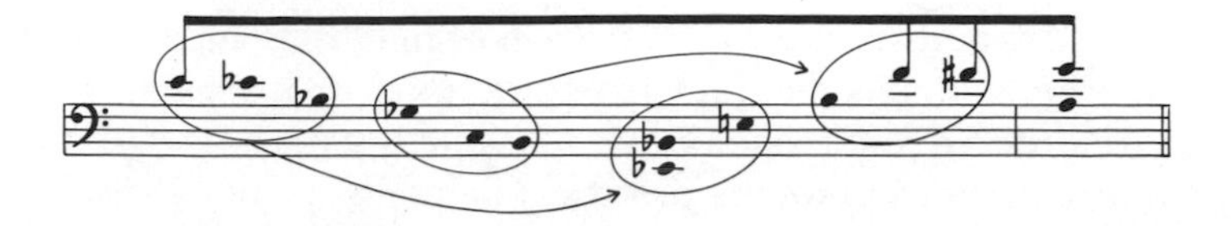

Example 6.22: Some trichordal connections in mm. 1–2

suggests a transposed retrograde, begins the second 5Z36, another aspect of the retrograde relationship, and this version inverted becomes the second triplet-eighth group of the arpeggiation in m. 2 (note that the fifth B–F♯ remains constant). The roles of the trichords are thus reversed in the two measures: the first begins a descending figure and an upper-voice step-progression, but in m. 2 the same pcs are used in the bass to begin an ascending arpeggiation. The second trichord, in its inversion in m. 2, carries the step-progression from m. 1 upward.

The change of design in m. 3 results in little change in the pc-set structures or their relationship to other features of the music, but it creates some further variants of motivic materials. Even in the first figure, Hindemith maintains the emphases of the beginning, harmonic and melodic (ex. 6.23). Furthermore, there are structural parallels in the multiple-stopped chords (ex. 6.24). The close of the A section (mm. 6–7) is a development of the cadence formula of m. 2: set 7–3 in mm. 3–4, repeated in mm. 5–6, contains the chromatic steps of that first cadence, which form the motivic basis of the set 5–3 in mm. 6–7 and the upper voice in 6Z11.

Though it is possible to demonstrate the interaction of pc-set structures and tonal process in other compositions of this period, none equals

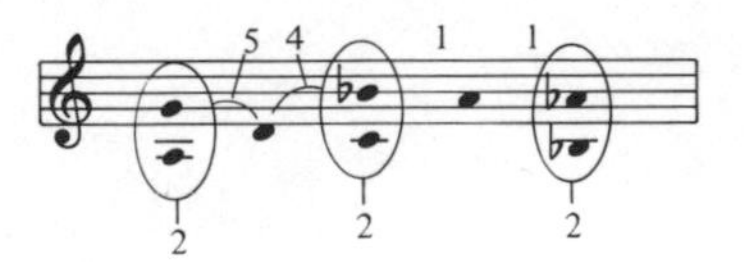

Example 6.23: Intervals, successive and vertical, in m. 3

Example 6.24: Interval relationships of the multiple-stopped chords, mm. 1–4

Op. 25, no. 3, in density and concentration of materials and musically successful synthesis of techniques. Chromatic pitch materials within tonal process are ordered and related by pc-set structures as little or as much as Hindemith pleases. As motives or other elements do not necessarily influence pc-set structures, the set structures have no immediate effect on the technique or procedures of tonal process. "From the beginning, the atonal syntax was only one among the available compositional means for Hindemith."[15] He never did make the leap into Schoenberg's "new dimensionality." Op. 25, no. 3, which we can describe as a great accomplishment of musical intuition, may be the closest he ever came.

15. Hans Heinz Stuckenschmidt, *Neue Musik* (Berlin: Suhrkamp, 1951), 176. Hindemith only rarely used such complex pc-set structures in his later music. See my discussion of the Fugue in D♭ from the *Ludus Tonalis* in my "Genesis and Structure of Hindemith's *Ludus Tonalis,*" *HJB* 7 (1978): 90–94.

SEVEN

DAS MARIENLEBEN, OP. 27 (1922–23; REVISED 1936–48)

"Das war nicht leicht zu machen" (That wasn't easy to do) was Hindemith's comment on his Rilke song cycle, *Das Marienleben,* completed in 1923.[1] In the autograph score he expressed a similar sentiment in a less restrained manner: below the final stave of the last song, he scrawled a line from the fifth poem, "und dann sang er Lob!" (and then he sang praise!).[2] Such confessions were unusual for Hindemith, who was proud of his ability to produce substantial quantities of music quickly, especially in these early years of his career.[3]

What is more remarkable is that Hindemith considered revision of the cycle shortly after its premiere performances and publication. In the "Introductory Remarks" to the second version (1948), Hindemith revealed that the very positive critical reaction "soon led to timid attempts at improvement."[4] There are no extant revision sketches from this period, but the remark is corroborated by one of the first reviews: "Hindemith will shortly undertake a revision of the entire cycle."[5] His intention to redo *Marienleben* is, thus, not the result of some post-*Craft* enthusiasm: it dates from one of the first performances of the original version and is yet another item of evidence that historical reflection and conscious craft were components of his early work, too. When he wrote the first volume of the *Craft* more than ten years later, he seized on the possibility of a "corrected" *Marienleben* as a demonstration piece for the book's theories: "He is considering rewriting the entire *Marienleben* and providing it with a foreword to be sent out as the vanguard of the book."[6] Neither revision nor foreword appeared be-

1. Briner, *Hindemith,* 43; also, Kurt von Fischer, ed., *Paul Hindemith: Sämtliche Werke* VI/1: *Klavierlieder I* (Mainz: Schott, 1983), xiii.

2. Fischer, *Klavierlieder I,* xiii. This page is reproduced in facsimile in *Hindemith-Zyklus Nordrhein-Westfelen 1980–81,* 97.

3. See comments recorded in Briner, *Hindemith,* 17, 25, 42, and reviews reproduced in Fischer, *Klavierlieder I,* xiv–xv.

4. Hindemith, *Introductory Remarks,* 3.

5. Karl Holl, "Musikleben: Frankfurt a. M.," *Die Musik* 16 (1924): 297.

6. Gertrude Hindemith to Willy Strecker, 14 July 1936.

fore *Craft I,* but the idea bore fruit in new sketches for several songs. When the second version was published in 1948, it was accompanied by an explanatory essay.

Obviously, the impetus for revision was different in 1936 than it had been in 1924. Hindemith changed compositional styles halfway through the first version and, had he rewritten the cycle in 1924, he would certainly have eliminated the stylistic disparity by rewriting the first group of songs to conform to the linear-contrapuntal, New Objective style he achieved in the later ones.[7] The second version, on the other hand, was to be a "practical elucidation"[8] of the *Craft* theory and compositional pedagogy. This was not meant to result in a sharp change of style, but only to perfect technique with the aid of tools provided by the theory, such as the step-progression and harmonic fluctuation principles.

Because Hindemith closely associated the revised *Marienleben* and the *Craft* theories, in the "Introductory Remarks" he stressed the shortcomings of the original version: its composer "like everyone else . . . relied on his musical instinct, since he knew nothing better," and, further on, the problems addressed in the revision "run parallel with the great issues in the general development of composition in our time."[9] These are obvious polemical signals: the earlier version is rejected because it is merely intuitive, lacking the disciplined organizational principles that the *Craft* provides. The *Craft* was the product of Hindemith's struggle to find something better, as he saw it—more orderly, more enduring—than the aesthetics of the twenties (of which he, admittedly, was one of the foremost representatives) allowed him. Symbolically at least, he withdrew his early music by revising not only *Marienleben,* but also the operas *Neues vom Tage* and *Cardillac.*

It is understandable that Hindemith should have criticized the 1922–23 *Marienleben.* He needed to justify his extensive revision, but apparently he also felt genuinely that certain of the songs were in need of improvement. Unfortunately the two versions of *Marienleben* became metonyms for Hindemith's early and mature styles.[10] His post–World War II critics read this in terms of the sharply polarized atonal-tonal debate and Hindemith's rejection of serial techniques (repeated in the "Introductory Remarks"). As a result, one finds extraordinary accusations against the revised version. For example, to Dika Newlin, *Marienleben II* was a "repudiation of development," the tonal and cyclic organization actually weaken it, and Hindemith made "inartistic concessions to the hearer." Rudolf Klein claimed that Hin-

7. Walter B. Hilse (in "Factors making for Coherence in the Works of Paul Hindemith, 1919–1926," Ph.D. diss., Columbia University [1971], 242–45) also draws attention to the stylistic disparities in the first version.

8. *Craft I* (1st German ed.), 252.

9. Hindemith, *Introductory Remarks,* 3, 5.

10. See also letters cited by Briner, *Hindemith,* 176.

demith had even lost control of the compositional process—a most uncharacteristic judgment on Hindemith's post-*Mathis* music.[11]

The longest negative critique is by Rudolf Stephan, who focuses entirely on the differences in the two versions and comes to the foreseen conclusion that the first version is superior to the second because the early style is fresher, freer, and more subjective; where the later style is weighed down by abstraction and the insistence on tonality.

> We have noticed how in the first version . . . several *strata* of style tend to overlap. Symptomatically enough Hindemith endeavors to smooth out all extremes [in the second version]. . . . Hindemith has retreated to the middle way of least resistance. His renunciation of any radical spirit speaks clearly through his more recent compositions and is pressed into a direct formula in the final section of the preface to the new version. . . . Not even the historic importance of the first version can be approached by the new one. The somewhat motley style of Op. 27 may have been more unified, but at the expense of spontaneity. In place of spontaneity one is faced with the concoctions of an unstable theory and with a handful of practical formulae which are used by Hindemith and his imitators within the confines of respectable academicism.[12]

Stephan's argument, in addition to its all too obvious Adorno-influenced polemic, also fails as analysis, particularly in the comments on the three Passion-Resurrection songs, where his position can easily be contradicted by his own method. He says of the original version of "Vor der Passion," for instance, that certain surface characteristics "remind one strongly of Schoenberg's songs."[13] Yet in its second version, "Vor der Passion" displays pitch materials and structure more consistently modeled in the manner that Allen Forte has demonstrated is characteristic of Schoenberg's atonal music.[14] One need only reflect that Hindemith arrived at this later version

11. Dika Newlin, "Music Chronicle: The Case of Hindemith," *Partisan Review* 16 (1949): 412; Rudolf Klein, "Von Hindemith zu Hindemith: Bemerkungen zu den beiden Fassungen des 'Marienlebens,' " *Österreichische Musikzeitschrift* 19 (1964): 67–72. Von Fischer also reproduces—with pointed juxtaposition—two completely different evaluations of *Marienleben I* by Adorno from 1923 and 1928 (*Klavierlieder I*, xv).

12. Rudolf Stephen, trans. Hans F. Redlich, "Hindemith's *Marienleben:* An Assessment of Its Two Versions," *Music Review* 15 (1954): 275–87. The quotation is from p. 286. A recent, but somewhat bizarre, rendering of much the same argument may be found in Glenn Gould's "A Tale of Two *Marienlebens*," liner notes to Columbia recording M2 34597 (1978).

13. Stephen, "Hindemith's *Marienleben*," 284.

14. See Forte, *Atonal Music*. For a detailed comparison of the two versions of "Vor der Passion" using Forte's method, see Neumeyer, "Early Music of Hindemith," 107–35. Briner also comments on the "false conclusions" to which comparisons of the two cycles can easily lead (*Hindemith*, 186).

by application of the tonal rules of the *Craft* to recognize that Stephan's critical comparison is much too facile and simplistic. The invoking of the atonal-tonal dichotomy is pointless, as it is inadequate to describe either cycle or their relationship. If Hindemith had wanted them, arguments for even the first *Marienleben* could have been found in the *Craft* theory (especially in its later forms): his notion of *Gesamttonalität* could embrace both his early eclectic and neo-objective styles.

We may well ask, then, how the two *Marienlebens* ought to be judged, how compared with one another, if the devices of this older polemic, represented by both Hindemith and his critics, are no longer acceptable. We should remind ourselves that Hindemith was not the first composer to revise earlier works nor the first to get into trouble with critics because of it. The fact that two mature versions of a piece exist invites comparisons, but the more we can separate the assessment of the two *Marienlebens* from the tonal-serial dichotomy, the better.

Some important clues to the interpretation of the two versions lie in the stages of the revision process itself. The issue in the first revisions (1936–37) was not stylistic change but technical improvement, following directly from *Craft I,* where Hindemith commented, "To the composer, as well as the teacher, the book offers new perspectives on his materials . . . the advantages which these methods offer the composer in his creative work . . . may be observed only in one's own work."[15] In the next group of revisions (from 1941–42 and 1945), a second issue emerges, and with it arises the I/II, early/late, atonal/tonal dichotomy: the relationship of style and its associated techniques to the composition's "message." The style of the earlier *Marienleben* was not merely different from Hindemith's post-*Mathis* manner; it lacked something that was essential to him by the early 1940s. By then, *Marienleben I* was an expression of an attitude which he rejected as "unsound," as lacking ethical force, so the style was changed to perfect its relation to the correct message. It was not the style of his early music, but the aesthetic governing that style that caused Hindemith the most trouble.[16]

His technical arguments in the "Introductory Remarks" tend to obscure his real intentions, and critics who stressed the tonality/atonality, expressionism/neoclassicism polarity have missed the point. Hindemith did not object to the expressionist or sharper neo-objective manners or techniques, but to what he saw as their implicit ethical indifference. Like others of his generation, he had a substantial concern for music's place in culture. He was frankly afraid that music was losing its moral bearings, its

15. *Craft I,* 9, 202.

16. Giselher Schubert, "Ein Komponist in seiner Welt: Zu Hindemiths später Entwicklung," in *Hindemith-Zyklus,* 46.

high cultural values. If the purely harmonic style of entertainment music was indulgence in the sensuous,[17] it was only the "most cultivated ear" (as he put it in the Zurich lecture) that could grasp apparent atonality as another level of tonal order. The attraction that writers on music theory held for Hindemith in the twenties and thirties was the possibility they offered for a technical reconciliation of tradition and modernity. The romantic image of the composer as rule breaker, as larger than system (and larger than life), may have been acceptable as late as the expressionist decade (to 1914) (though Stephan still tries to defend it in 1952). But in the chaos that ensued it seemed important to many to draw back, to cultivate one's own walled garden. This did not necessarily mean cultural atavism—the tempo of experiment was quick in the twenties, but it is symptomatic that experiment soon coalesced into system during those years: in Haba's microtones, Hauer's and Schoenberg's twelve-tone methods, and several chromatic harmonic systems. Hindemith at first was very optimistic. He plainly thought that tradition and modernity could be reunited, that Schenker could find an *Urlinie* even in Hindemith's own music, just as he thought the Weimar republic could survive. The same optimism characterized his involvement with the Jugendmusikbewegung in the late twenties. It was only when he had to leave Germany at the beginning of World War II that the real crisis struck, that he drew back to his notion of an ethical musical community as a personal psychological defense. The immediate results of this we can see in the *Craft*-related pieces of 1941–42: the second *Marienleben* revisions, *Ludus Tonalis,* the Sonata for Two Pianos (with its recitative on an old English poem, "This World's Joy"). In the end, Hindemith's vision turned out to be as personal and as romantic (in several senses) as Schenker's defense of the tonal masters or Adorno's serial socialism. Yet, as the music from the early 1940s shows, that vision was also musically fruitful.

A critical comparison of the two published versions of *Marienleben,* then, is a much more complex undertaking than a simplistic dichotomy would permit. The 1922–23 version was meant for performance and was very successful. It had the timbral and harmonic sensitivity of Hindemith's earliest music and the rhythmic vigor of his linear counterpoint. It is relatively short and nowhere obscure. On the other hand, it is stylistically inconsistent, juxtaposing songs with subtle harmonic coloration and text expression to rough neo-objective music. The revision began in 1936 as a straightforward cleanup of technically weak passages and whole songs with the aid of the *Craft* principles. In the 1941–42 revisions, however, *Marienleben* became a wholly different piece serving a wholly different purpose. The *Ludus Tonalis* and the series of sonatas Hindemith had begun with the

17. *Craft III,* 198.

Violin Sonata in E (1935) were in fact the practical demonstrations of the theory that the *Marienleben* was supposed to be. The sonatas in particular are generally compact, musically convincing structures that elucidate the theory in application and strike a perfect medium between music for amateurs (the Sing- und Spielmusiken of the late twenties) and virtuoso display pieces. Hindemith made the revised song cycle a more abstract but more personal demonstration of compositional (and tonal) principle.

The 1948 version thus achieves a great compositional synthesis with a fundamental inner unity expressed at every level. Hindemith's full forces were applied: key symbolism; cyclical connections created by the resurrection, annunciation, and passion motifs; the planning of broad dynamic and expressive high points throughout the cycle; and the binding of the whole by the consistent application of the technical procedures of the *Craft* theory. Admittedly, the second version is also long, its expression frequently abstract, and the key symbolism inscrutable. These problems arose in the 1941–42 sketches, when Hindemith imposed the key-symbolism scheme described in the "Introductory Remarks." This new factor upset the balance between what we might call the personal and general, or even subjective and objective, functions of the *Craft* theory. The theory as personal confession and the theory as compositional tool were so completely fused that they could no longer be separated. *Marienleben II* is in a certain respect like the *Art of Fugue:* although in a good performance it can be very moving, it is ironically a most difficult composition to present successfully. This is due at least in part to an aesthetic imbalance between Hindemith's grand cyclic structure and the unpretentiousness of Rilke's poems, which he called "a little book that was presented to me, quite above and beyond myself, by a peaceful generous spirit."[18]

Hindemith transcribed six songs from the revisions for soprano and orchestra:

1. Four songs which agree with the 1936–37 versions, not those of *Marienleben II*.

"Geburt Mariä"	30. V. 39	Blusch
"Argwohn Josephs"	31. V. 39	Blusch
"Geburt Christi"	(undated)	Blusch
"Rast auf der Flucht nach Aegypten"	5. VI. 39	Blusch

2. Two songs which agree with *Marienleben II* (1959).

"Vor der Passion"
"Vom Tode Mariä II"

18. Letter to Hugo Salus, 28 June 1913, quoted in M. D. Herter Norton, *Translations from the Poetry of Rainer Maria Rilke* (New York: Norton, 1938), 245.

This version removes two fundamental shortcomings of *Marienleben II:* (1) it is much shorter (twenty-three minutes instead of seventy), but provides a summary of the argument and narrative (songs 1, 5, 7, 8, 10, and 15); (2) it is richly colored—the timbral variety dissipates the air of abstraction that hangs about *Marienleben II*. The transcription is eminently performable and is, in my opinion, the most successful of the three versions. That it has been ignored in the critical literature and in the repertoire of performance is very regrettable.[19]

The focus of the following essay is the nature and extent of changes in the revision and the way in which these reflect Hindemith's application of his *Craft* principles. The subjects are two songs treated very differently: the first song of the cycle, "Geburt Mariä" (Birth of Mary), which changed very little; and the third song, "Mariä Verkündigung" (Annunciation to Mary), which changed substantially at every major stage.

STAGES OF REVISION: SKETCHES AND OTHER HOLOGRAPHS

The sketches for *Marienleben I* are contained in three different sketchbooks.[20] None is dated, but it is plain from the fair copy that the songs were composed in three series: in June and July 1922 (nos. 1, (2), 5, 8, 11); in November and December 1922 (nos. 4, 6, 10, 12); and from April to July 1923 (nos. 2, 3, 7, 9, 13, 14, 15). The second series of sketches has been lost, but all extant sketches are complete and consecutive, with remarkably little rejected or reworked material. The fair copy was done while the composition was in progress, not afterward. The songs are not in the published sequence but in the order of composition.

Two series of sketches from 1936 and 1937 contain revisions for nine songs (nos. 1–3, 6–8, 13–15). These sketches were the basis of the first three volumes of fair copies labeled *Neukomposition* (which also include nos. 4, 5, and 10). Hindemith used a fourth *Neukomposition* volume in 1941–42 (nos. 9 and revisions of 3 and 14). These four sets of fair copies were obviously meant to be printer's copy for the publication of the *Craft's* "vanguard." Instead they became sketchbooks themselves, as Hindemith pasted in changes, and crossed out and wrote over whole passages, even whole pages. Occasionally changes were so extensive that they were separately dated. With the fair copy of *Marienleben I,* these volumes are the most important holographs in the history of the cycle.

19. These settings have been published in Henry W. Kaufmann, ed., *Paul Hindemith: Sämtliche Werke* VI/5: *Sologesänge mit Orchester* (Mainz: Schott, 1983), 97ff.

20. On the sketches, see the introduction and critical notes in von Fischer, *Klavierlieder I*.

Sketches for the songs in *Neukomposition IV* (as well as for "Vom Tode Mariä II") are in a looseleaf notebook which also holds sketches for the Sonata for Two Pianos and the *Ludus Tonalis.* The only holographs for any of the *Marienleben* versions or revisions which are not now in the Paul-Hindemith-Institut belong to this group: three leaves representing very nearly the final version of "Mariä Verkündigung" were removed and given to M. D. Herter Norton in 1946, probably as an early appreciation for the intended, but unrealized, collaboration on an English translation suited to the songs.

The first evidence of the abstract key symbolism discussed at length in Hindemith's "Introductory Remarks," which plays such a dubious role (to some) in *Marienleben II,* appears with the *Neukomposition IV* sketches. The symbolism scheme is based on a Series 1 sequence with E as tonic; each degree takes on an association with a character and some mood or abstract idea. For instance, Christ is the ϕ (E), as Godhead the center of being; Mary, the ♪ (B), the symbol of the human, the personal, of earthliness; the angels, the ♩ (A), heavenliness or the abstract. A list of the songs, their lengths in the second version, and the Series 1 sequence are all given on the back of one leaf in this notebook. A closely related document is reproduced in figure 7.1: jottings on p. [6] of Hindemith's copy of the Rilke poems.[21] These no-

Maria	H	H	1	Geburt Mariä		17.7.36
		C	2	Darstellung Passacaglia		23.7.37
		H/E	3	Mariä Verkünd.		25.7.37 5.5.41
		H/C	4	Heimsuchung		11.7.36
Josef	F					
		F	5	Argwohn		11.7.36
		A	6	Verkünd. Hirten		28.7.37
		E	7	Geburt Christi		21.7.37
Jesus	E					
		C/As	8	Rast auf d. Flucht		19.7.36
		F	9	Hochzeit zu Kana	Fuge	16.III.41
Engel	A	E/As	10	Vor der Passion		11.7.36
		Es	11	Pieta		
		E	12	Stillung		
Tod	Es G					
		C/Es	13	Tod I	Basso ost.	26.7.36
		Es/G	14	II	Variationen	19.3.41
		A	15	III		29.7.37

Figure 7.1: Handwritten list in Hindemith's copy of Rilke's *Marienleben*

21. Kaufmann, *Sologesänge.*

tations could not have been made earlier than 1937 and could be as late as 1941. In the second column are the keys of the songs in the 1936–37 revisions. The keys conform to the principal keys of the published second version except that the keys for nos. 13 and 14 are reversed, and "Mariä Verkündigung" was newly written in 1941. From this evidence it seems likely that the Series 1 symbolism was not a factor in the 1936–37 revisions, but was invented after these prototypes of the *Marienleben II* versions were completed. If true, this could explain some of the awkwardness in the scheme as well as the motivation for the revisions done after 1941. In any event, the development of the key symbology is closely entwined with the three songs in the 1941–42 sketchbook, which are the three most often rewritten (nos. 3, 9, and 14).

The stages of composition and revision may be summarized as follows: *Marienleben I* was written in three separate series from June 1922 to July 1923. Hindemith contemplated revision as early as 1924, but apparently did not begin until 1936, in connection with the writing of *Craft I*. The second set of revisions was carried out in 1941–42, at another important juncture: the revision and refinement of the *Craft* theory in the earliest forms of the three-part exercises. These new sketches incorporate the abstract tonal symbolism of which Hindemith makes a great point in the "Introductory Remarks." A great number of internal changes was made in 1945, but the fair copy of the second published version was not finished until July 1947.

"GEBURT MARIÄ"

O was muss es die Engel gekostet haben,
nicht aufzusingen plötzlich, wie man aufweint,
da sie doch wussten: in dieser Nacht wird dem Knaben
die Mutter geboren, dem Einen, der bald erscheint.

Schwingend verschwiegen sie sich und zeigten die Richtung,
wo, allein, das Gehöft lag des Joachim,
ach sie fühlten in sich und im Raum die reine Verdichtung,
aber es durfte keiner nieder zu ihm.

Denn die beiden waren schon so ausser sich vor Getue.
Eine Nachbarin kam und klugte und wusste nicht wie,
und der Alte, vorsichtig, ging und verhielt das Gemuhe
einer dunkelen Kuh. Denn so war es noch nie.

The songs in which the greatest number of changes were made—including the two composed entirely anew—are those in the 1923 series of sketches. The songs altered least, including the one not changed at all, come from the 1922 sketches. This underscores the assertion made earlier in this study that from 1936 on Hindemith felt a greater affinity for his early music than he did for the formalistic, linear-contrapuntal work of his middle period.

The first song of the cycle, "Geburt Mariä," is a good representative of the 1922 group. Hindemith said of its second version: "Little has been changed. Measures 21–32 replace a version that was too independent in its harmonic harshness, and thus gave too much importance to a section serving as a bridge between two more significant structural members."[22] "Geburt Mariä" was one of the first songs composed for the original version, and the revision sketches suggest that it may have been the first song rewritten. Those changes Hindemith did make were carried out in 1936; the *Neukomposition I* version is the same as that in *Marienleben II*.[23] Several of the 1936–37 revisions did not survive the change in Hindemith's attitudes in the 1940s as his theories matured and his practical compositional experience with them increased, but "Geburt Mariä" did, which suggests that its style and technique were acceptable to him at every stage of his career.

Hindemith inserts musical quotations twice in *Marienleben I*. In "Mariä Verkündigung," the piano right hand plays the first line of the Christmas chorale "Von Himmel hoch," a subtle reference to the immaculate conception. In "Geburt Mariä," Hindemith quotes the opening of the medieval Eastern hymn "Surrexit Christus hodie" as the essential motive in the song's principal theme. In examples 7.1a–c, the first phrase in two of the several surviving versions of this hymn and the opening of "Geburt Mariä" are shown together for comparison.

The direct source for "Geburt Mariä" is probably the one shown in example 7.1d: the violin entrance in the second movement, mm. 9ff., of the sonata "Die Auferstehung" (The Resurrection), the eleventh in a cycle of fifteen violin sonatas "zur Verherrlichung von fünfzehn Mysterien aus dem Leben Mariäs und Christus" (to glorify fifteen mysteries from the lives of Mary and Christ) by the baroque composer Heinrich Biber. This second movement is a passacaglia in which the theme is the entire "Surrexit Christus" melody. In m. 9, the violin begins a canon with the passacaglia bass (which at this point has reached the third line of the hymn); the pause on G5 in m. 12 is necessary to make the canon work. The result is a motive very like Hindemith's in shape and rhythm, although it contains a leading tone. Hindemith knew Biber's sonatas and regarded them highly.[24] Whether

22. Hindemith, *Introductory Remarks*, 6–7.

23. Only two notes were changed in the transfer of sketch to fair copy: left hand, mm. 19–20, was A4, became G4; voice note, m. 79, was B4 (as in *Marienleben I*), became A4.

24. Heinrich Strobel, *Paul Hindemith*, 66; Briner, *Hindemith*, 151. Hindemith gave a lecture-recital on Biber at Yale in February, 1942, the notes for which survive. Nicholas Harnoncourt, in the preface to an edition of the Sonata Representativa in A (Vienna: Doblinger, 1977) reports that "Hindemith once referred to

Example 7.1: Four versions of "Surrexit Christus hodie"

consciously or not, he almost certainly borrowed from Biber's "Mariensonaten" the opening motive of his own cycle on the life of Mary.[25]

The "Surrexit Christus" motive permeates the 1922 setting of "Geburt Mariä." The song divides into four sections of approximately equal weight (A B C A), but the thematic material of each section is developed directly from the principal motive. This gradual thematic transformation, fre-

Biber as the most important Baroque composer before Bach" (p. 3). The fifteen sonatas were released in a performing edition by Robert Reitz (Vienna: Universal, 1923). An earlier, but faulty edition (in which some of the scordatura tunings were misread) is found in *Sechzehn Violinsonaten von H. F. Biber*, ed. Erwin Luntz, *Denkmäler der Tonkunst in Österreich*, vol. 25 (Leipzig: Breitkopf & Härtel, 1905). See also Eugen Schmitz, "Bibers Rosenkrantzsonaten," *Musica* 5 (1951): 235–36. Hindemith did his own figured-bass realizations of the fifteen sonatas as well: see Howard Boatwright, "Hindemith's Performances of Old Music," *HJB* 3(1973):39.

25. Biber's sonatas may have affected the formal structure and procedures of at least two songs in the cycle. His fourth sonata, "Die Darstellung Jesu im Tempel," is cast as a single movement, a large chaconne or passacaglia. Hindemith's "presentation" song, no. 2, "Die Darstellung Mariä im Tempel," is also a passacaglia. Biber's fifteenth sonata, "Mariäs Kronung," has as its middle movement an aria with variations, and the second of Hindemith's three songs on the death of Mary, no. 14, also concerned with Mary's accession to the throne of the Queen of Heaven, is cast as a theme with variations.

quent repetition, and static harmonic plan in each section are devices Hindemith used to minimize contrast and maintain the song's lullaby character.

The changing-note figure of the "Surrexit Christus" motive and its harmonization with neighbor chords—that is, the simplest circular progressions (ex. 7.2)—reappear in the later sections. In section B, the lower parts are preserved (though transposed), but the root of the embellishing chord is made clearer. The voice presents new material, but the right-hand figuration of the piano is based on the changing notes (ex. 7.3a). In section C, chord qualities and the neighbor chord's degree are changed, but the right hand carries a neighbor note and the voice the whole "Surrexit Christus" motive (though now situated a minor third above the tonic) (ex. 7.3b).

Example 7.2: *Das Marienleben*, "Geburt Mariä," mm. 1–4

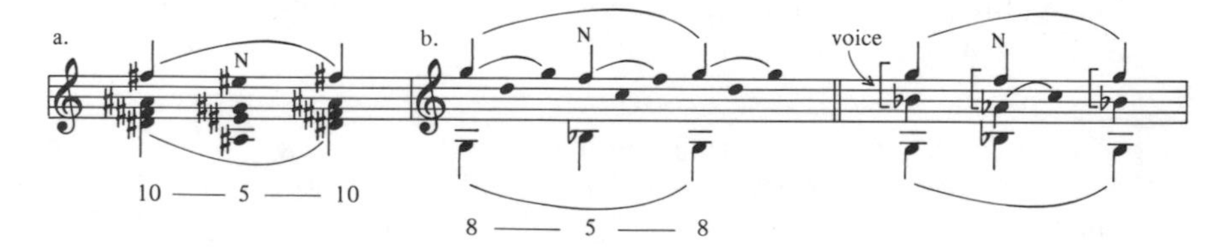

Example 7.3: Neighbor-note figures in sections B and C

Hindemith's setting follows the sentence sequence of the poem rather than its verse structure. There are three verses, each a quatrain with the rhyme scheme abab. No rhymes extend across verses. The first verse consists of a single sentence with two virtually independent clauses, which are set separately in sections A and B. B, despite its motivic and harmonic connection to A, is plainly set apart by the low dynamic level (ppp) at beginning and end and by the triplet-eighth figuration (elsewhere movement is in quarters), perhaps to give appropriately hushed utterance to the reference to the Christ ("in dieser Nacht wird dem Knaben die Mutter geboren, dem Einen, der bald erscheint"). Section C sets all of the second verse (again one sentence with two independent clauses) and the first two lines of the third. The third verse consists of three sentences, the first being one line set with the internal reprise in C (from m. 66). Hindemith placed the second clause of the second sentence in the reprise of A (from m. 80). The final sentence ("Denn so war es noch nie"), like the clause in section B, expresses a thought detached from the hushed activity of the rest of the poem. Hindemith emphasizes this separation in his setting, giving the voice a new figure, another arpeggiation of the characteristic chord on the ϕ (ex. 7.4).

Example 7.4: "Geburt Mariä," final vocal phrase

The tonal plan of the whole—B D♯ G B—outlines the augmented triad, a not uncommon symmetrical design in Hindemith's earlier music. Within sections B and C, tonal focus weakens or shifts, but the original orientation is regained. In every section except C, the tonic-chord quality and voice disposition are the same at beginning and end. This suggests very broad circular progressions, even harmonic prolongation, of each section's controlling tonic chord, not just the degree. The Stage II graph contains only four pillar chords (ex. 7.5). The identity of the first and last chords combined with the simple augmented triad outline could even suggest harmonic prolongation across the entire song. (Note also that the chord on IłI is simply a transposition of the first chord.)

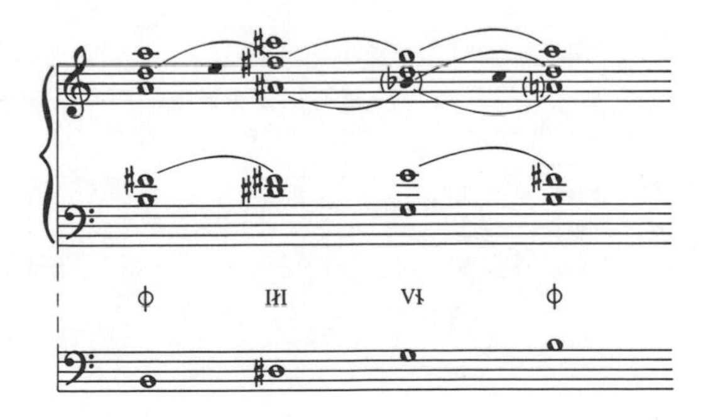

Example 7.5: "Geburt Mariä," Stage II analysis

A detailed analytic graph of the song is presented in example 7.6. Because of the clear identity of the chords (except in section C) and the limited number of changes, Stages IV and V are joined in a single graph. Despite the many harmonic prolongations, the reader is warned against reading this graph as if it were a foreground (that is, with melodic activity always tied to the harmonies by voiceleading).

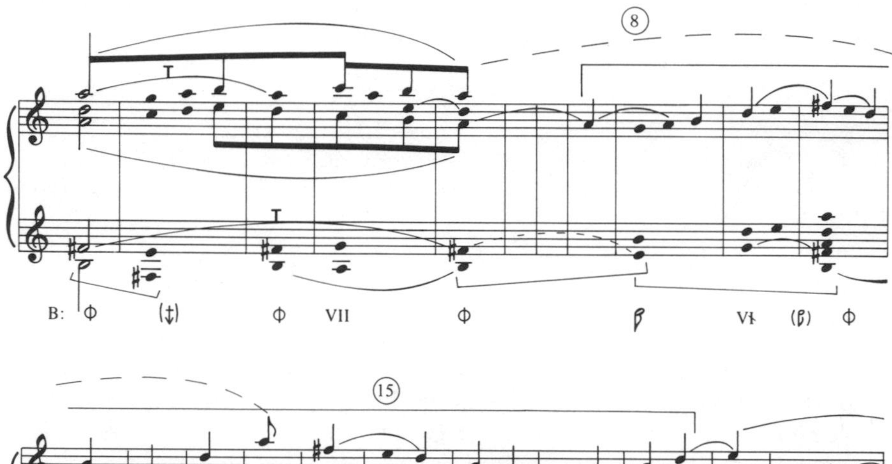

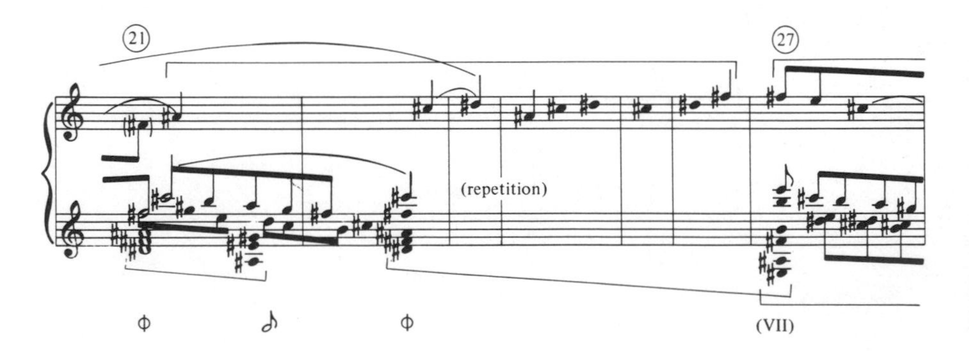

Example 7.6: "Geburt Mariä," complete Stage IV and V analyses (combined)

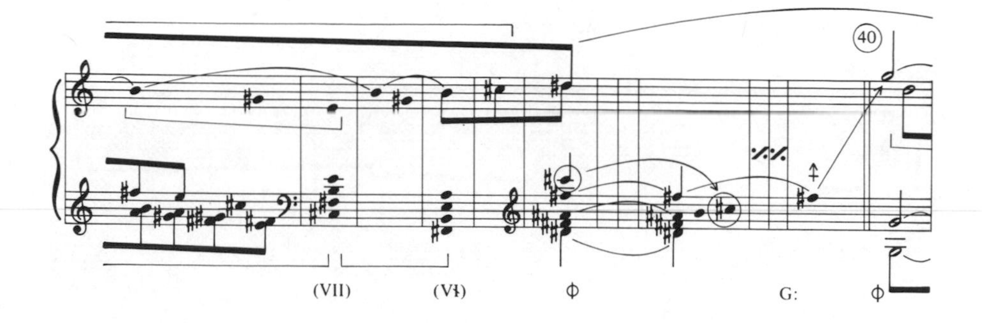

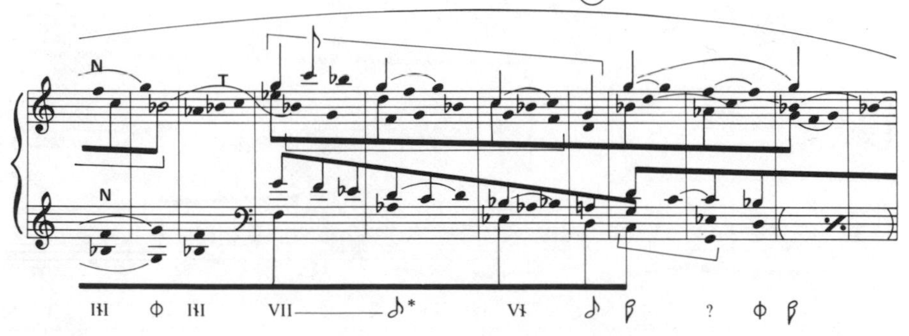

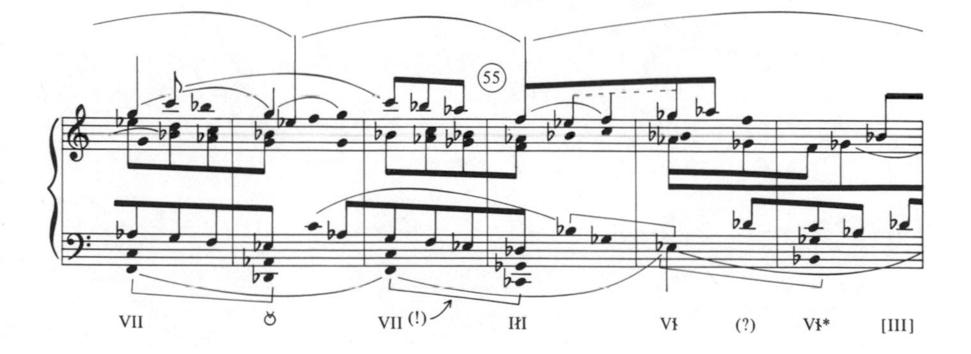

Example 7.6: *Continued*

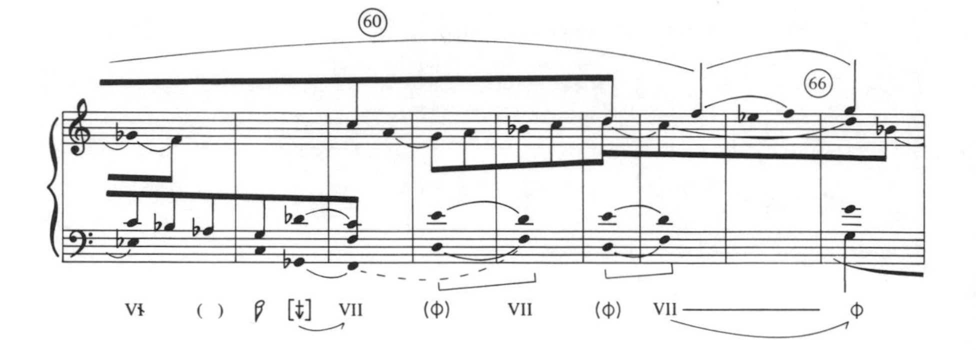

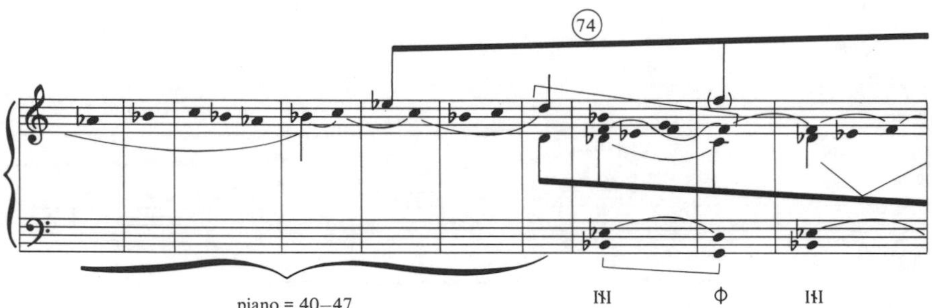

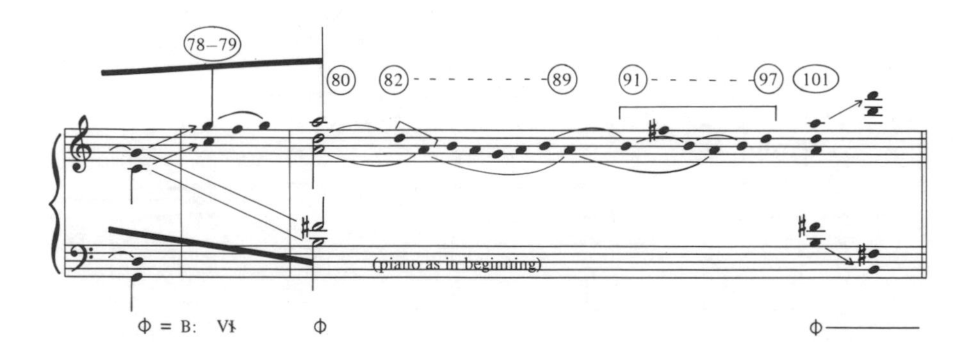

Example 7.6: *Continued*

The voice in section A offers two embellished arpeggiations of the pillar chord, ascending and returning within the octave established in the piano right hand in m. 1 (A4–A5): the first arpeggiation goes as far as F♯5 in m. 10, the second reaches A5 at "auf" (m. 13). In these first measures Hindemith carefully maintains a balance of chord values, using the opening minor seventh chord as the point of departure. In m. 2, a minor ninth is introduced (F♯–G), which aids the identification of the neighbor-chord figure through a pattern of relative dissonance: minor seventh, minor ninth, minor seventh. The poor definition of chord root is another factor: the strong bass motion plainly suggests ♪, but the correct chord root by Hindemith's method is ↕ on the first beat and perhaps ϱ on the third. (When the voice holds B4 against this figure in m. 11, the "correct" root would be ϕ !) An exact determination of root is overridden by the traditional nature of the chord: a dominant ninth with the fifth lowered (voice-leading from this chord is hardly traditional, however). The contextual function is very clear even if the root is not.

The prevailing sevenths in the piano introduction give way in mm. 8–9 to triads or open fifths. These, repeated and developed with step-progressions in the upper parts in mm. 17ff., effect the transition to section B and modulation to IłI. The harmony once again consists of simple linear chord embellishments.

The voice in section B presents even plainer arpeggiations than in A. The first is shaped as a broad arch whose high point is F♯5 in m. 26. The simple outlining of the pillar chord in the ascent is shifted down a whole step in the descent (and accompanied by quartal harmony) (ex. 7.7). Against the continuation of quartal harmonies, the voice rises again to D♯5, where the piano recovers its initial neighbor-chord figure. Note the very characteristic approach to the goal, D♯5, by means of step-progressions from above and below. The whole of section B is a much expanded harmonic prolongation: the seventh chord on IłI is the point of departure (m. 21) and the goal (m. 33)—the tonally ambiguous quartal chords are subsidiary. Despite the difference in figuration, a detail of the piano introduction complements this relationship: the highest register of the piano part circumscribes a tiny arch (C♯6–E6–C♯6 in mm. 22, 27, 33) a major third higher than A5–C6–A5 in mm. 1–6.

Section C (mm. 40–79) is the longest and has an internal ternary design. It also has the greatest variety in harmonies and the greatest number of active voices. Harmonies generally change once per measure and are

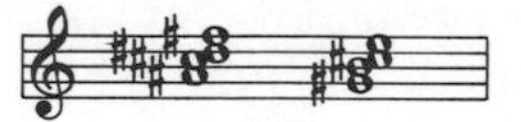

Example 7.7: Arpeggiations in the voice part, section B

usually defined by fifths in the two lowest parts, but more detailed changes take place within individual measures. The closing cadence uses the degrees of the piano's characteristic accompaniment pattern in this section (IƗI ϕ), but not the identical figure (unlike the other sections).

The upper register of the voice part in this song does not display the clarity in long-range connections one would expect of Hindemith in the late forties. Instead, the voice merely touches notes that are significant in the piano, for example, A5 in m. 13 and F♯5 in m. 26. Only section C works differently. In the piano, F♯5 moves directly to G5 in mm. 39–40, but the voice's upper register makes a connection (E♭ in m. 53 at "ach") to its own closing pitch (D♯5) in section B. E♭5 links to F5 in m. 64, and then the piano takes the line to its characteristic G5 again in m. 66 (at the internal reprise of section C). G5 connects directly to A5 in the pillar chord of the reprise (mm. 78–80). (Attachment of F♯5 in m. 93 to F5 or G5 in section C is dubious; Hindemith tried to make a clearer connection to F♯5 in the revision.)

The lack of clear step-progression patterns is not necessarily to be ascribed to the early date of the composition, but instead to the predominance of arpeggiations. As we have seen, some long-range patterns of step connection do exist, as do careful step connections at points of modulation or section change. The bass, however, has little original melodic character. Unlike the basses of Hindemith's later music, it seems to be mostly a carrier of harmony.

In the 1936 revision of "Geburt Mariä," Hindemith added a bass note (C4) to m. 9. The progression from m. 7 to m. 10 thus becomes ϕ–ꞵ–‡–ϕ, a sharper, harmonically more assertive motion. He also changed mm. 17–19, the transitional measures, primarily to effect a different modulation (to F♯), but also to clarify the harmony (the piano now has triads) and to tighten step-progression connections to section B in the voice. (See the analytic graph of the transition and section B in ex. 7.8).

The structural function of section B is quite different, even though it was shortened by only four measures. Clear tonal focus is gone, and though still distinguished by its figuration, the section has become what Hindemith called "a bridge between two more significant structural members." In the orchestral version, by the by, Hindemith accentuated this lightness of function by scoring the section for solo flute with upper strings. The characteristic neighbor-chord progression is retained but the degrees change, the minor-third shifts in the major-triad harmonies outlining a diminished seventh chord which reaches E♭ (= D♯, the original controlling degree in the section) at m. 32, where it is interpreted as G: VƗ. Arpeggiation in a transitional passage and the use of major triads with contradictory figuration above are both very typical of this period.

If the revision of B is understood as a modulatory extension of A, the structure of the song becomes tripartite:

1922:	A	B	C	A′
	mm. 1–20	21–39	40–79	80–104
1936:	A		B	A′
	mm. 1–35		36–77	78–102

In the new section B, harmonies and their progressions have been clarified and the texture simplified. Mm. 48–60 of the 1922 version (now mm. 44–56) were the most seriously affected, though elements of the original version are still visible in the piano in mm. 44–48 and in the voice from m. 50 (the latter a transposition up a fourth from the original line: the "Surrexit Christus" motive as reconstructed for section C). The exact tonal role of A♭ (‡), reached at the dramatic climax after m. 50, is not clear. Hindemith refers to the tonal symbolism scheme,[26] but that contradicts the chronol-

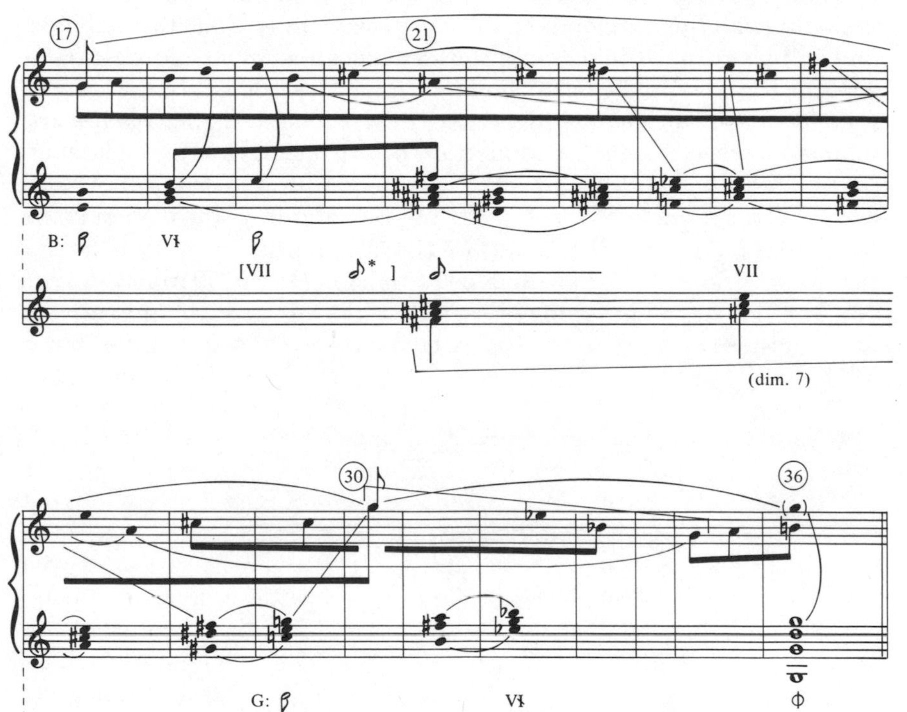

Example 7.8: "Geburt Mariä," (revised), mm. 17–36, Stage IV and V analyses (combined)

26. Hindemith, *Introductory Remarks*, 12.

ogy: if tonal symbolism had been a factor in 1936, Hindemith would not have reduced the role of the old section B (with its reference to Christ) and certainly would have retained the E-major triad at the words "the One." Apparently, A♭ was used as the mediant in a triadic pattern of pockets of tonal focus from mm. 44–63, C–A♭–F (G: ꝑ–↨–VII). Dramatic climax and tonal significance, then, do not coincide.

The demotion of the old section B in the tonal structure necessitates alteration of the Stage II graph (ex. 7.9). The background tonal pattern is now an echo of the pervasive neighbor-chord figures. This could be fairly interpreted as a background structure similar to the middleground in the first Piano Sonata (discussed in chapter 9), complete with possible voice-leading between the pillar chords and motivic connections to the surface.

The character of the bass has been altered very little in the new version, which is puzzling. This part is still concerned primarily with harmonic steps, not with the development of step-progressions. Equally puzzling is the complexity of the highest register. The neighbor-note figure A5–G5–A5—the top voice in the pillar chords of Stage II—seems to be the largest-scale feature of the piano's highest part even though higher pitches are sounded in every section. A connection by arpeggiation can be made between A5 (m. 11) and A6 (m. 24): A5–C6–C♯6 (m. 21)–F♯6–A6. A step-progression continues to D♭7 (m. 30), but this last note—the highest in the piece—has no continuation unless we consider register transfer in longer step-progressions: D♭7–E♭6 (m. 50)–F5 (m. 56)–G5 (m. 59 or 64)–A5 (m. 78). The very high notes in the piano's figuration are probably the result of local register transfers (ex. 7.10). A better connection to E♭6 (m. 50) is

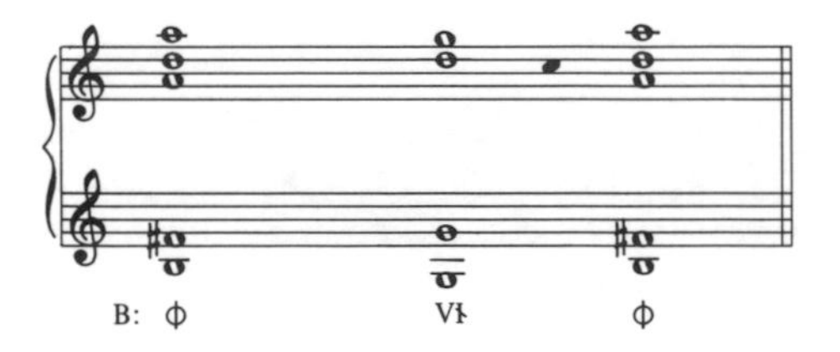

Example 7.9: "Geburt Mariä" (revised), Stage II analysis

Example 7.10: "Geburt Mariä" (revised), mm. 29–33, piano figuration, Stage V analysis

made from F♭6 in m. 33, a simple and typical case of step-progressions defined by registral specificity.

The voice has its own long-range step-progression connections. A5 is reached in section A and G5 at "dem Einen" (the One) in the transition. This latter note, not in the original version, could then connect to F♯5 in the reprise (m. 90); but the connection is still somewhat muddled by the shorter progressions from G5 in section B and because the piano also takes G5 (mm. 36ff.). In general, the step-progressions cannot be said to exhibit the long-range control of register that is typical in Hindemith's music in the forties.

"MARIÄ VERKÜNDIGUNG"

Nicht dass ein Engel eintrat (das erkenn),
erschreckte sie. So wenig andre, wenn
ein Sonnenstrahl oder der Mond bei Nacht
in ihrem Zimmer sich zu schaffen macht,
auffahren—, pflegte sie an der Gestalt,
in der ein Engel ging, sich zu entrüsten;
sie ahnte kaum dass dieser Aufenthalt
mühsam für Engel ist. (O wenn wir wüssten,
wie rein sie war. Hat eine Hirschkuh nicht,
die, liegend, einmal sie im Walde eräugte,
sich so in sie versehn, dass sich in ihr,
ganz ohne Paarigen, das Einhorn zeugte,
das Tier aus Licht, das reine Tier—.)
Nicht, dass er eintrat, aber dass er dicht,
der Engel, eines Jünglings Angesicht
so zu ihr neigte, dass sein Blick und der
mit dem sie aufsah, so zusammenschlagen,
als wäre draussen plötzlich alles leer
und, was Millionen schauten, trieben, trugen,
hineingedrängt in sie: nur sie und er;
Schaun und Geschautes, Aug und Augenweide
sonst nirgends als an dieser Stelle—: sieh,
dieses erschreckt. Und sie erschraken beide.

Dann sang der Engel seine Melodie.

The changes in "Geburt Mariä," although significant, were relatively few. But in "Mariä Verkündigung," one of the 1923 group and the third in the cycle, there were many. This song, in its various versions, provides an excellent vehicle for a closer examination of the stages of the revision process.

Hindemith's statement about the revision is somewhat misleading. In the "Introductory Remarks," he says that "the old version measured by the criteria just mentioned [chord value, tonal amplitude], could by no means bear serious examination. Accordingly, an entirely new one has been substituted for it."[27] In fact, he did take the old version seriously in 1937, because a completed revision of it is in the *Neukomposition III* set. In this revision, the original material is treated in much the same way that sections B and C of the 1922 "Geburt Mariä" were treated in 1936: melodic lines, harmonic organization, individual harmonies, and presentation are all clarified. Only in 1941 did Hindemith undertake to do a completely new setting, but it took three tries before he found what he wanted.

The original version of "Mariä Verkündigung" is based on a motto which is an acerbically harmonized quote from the chorale "Von Himmel hoch" (ex. 7.11). The voice's first phrase and the piano's counterpoint (which becomes the thematic motive in the following song, "Mariä Heimsuchung") are both of thematic significance. The song is written in a flowing 6/4 meter with occasional 9/4 measures and is marked "Erzählend" (in a narrative manner). The large parenthesis beginning in the eighth line of the text ("O wenn wir wüssten . . .") is set as a lyrical recitative above a sustained fifth C♯–G♯ in the piano. The thematic basis of the vocal line is the "Mariä Heimsuchung" motive. A much-condensed reworking of the opening follows, setting the repeated text of the fourteenth line ("Nicht, dass er eintrat . . .") and the following lines but is interrupted by an accelerando leading to a climax based mostly on motivic fragments, including a loose inversion of the "Von Himmel hoch" motive. The material of the opening is restored and the close is calm, reminiscent of the recitative, the last vocal phrase being a combination of the "Von Himmel hoch" and "Mariä Heimsuchung" motives (ex. 7.12). The formal scheme has four divisions: A, mm. 1–21; B (the recitative), mm. 22–24; C (including the accelerando), mm. 25–51; A′ (reprise and coda), mm. 52–67.

Although the poem has a rhyme scheme based on four-line groups, it is not really a series of quatrains. Instead it is laid out as two paragraphs: the

Example 7.11: "Mariä Verkündigung," mm. 1–2

27. Ibid., 7.

first contains six sentences in twenty-three lines; the second is one sentence in a single line. Hindemith sets the first two sentences in section A. The following two sentences are the extended parenthesis set by the recitative. The remainder of the first paragraph is placed in sections C and A′, except for the coda, which sets the single-line second paragraph shown in example 7.12.

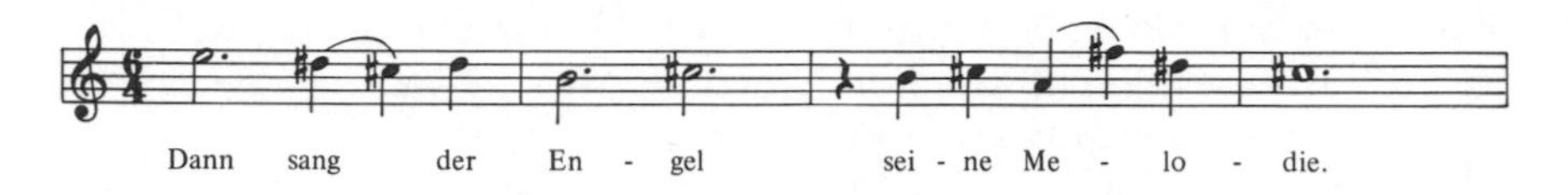

Example 7.12: "Mariä Verkündigung," final vocal phrase

This design follows the poem's sequence of thought very well. The text for the first section portrays the angel's entrance, which is not forceful but very quiet, a slight disturbance of the light and nothing more. The parenthesis sets forth traditional images associated with Mary: purity, light, the unicorn. The remaining text of the first paragraph describes the encounter between Mary and the angel, in the course of which they "erschraken beide." Only the final line—a most delicate image—touches on the angel's annunciation itself: "Dann sang der Engel seine Melodie."

The role of the accelerando in section C is closely text-related. The accelerando leads to (and intensifies) the climax, but it has a source in the text, the nineteenth line: "und, was Millionen schauten, trieben, trugen, / hineingedrängt in sie: nur sie und er." The pacing of the text suddenly picks up: four verbs in a row, ending with "hineingedrängt." All activity, all human action, at that moment is suddenly drawn into and contained in the two characters, Mary and the announcing angel. The accelerando, though it actually starts sooner, is the perfect mirror of this text.

The tonal orientation of the song is not easy to determine, since the logic in harmonic detail is not easily discerned. As a Stage I reading, I advance the following surmise:

Section:	A	B	C	A′
Key:	B—?—B	C♯	?—B	B—C♯

The harmony differs sharply from that of "Geburt Mariä." In section C especially, Hindemith exploited the indiscriminate harmonies of the linear-contrapuntal style. Still, the harmonies balance those of the recitative, where there is nothing but consonance, although a few mild clashes occur with the pentatonic figures of the voice.

The setting which appears in *Neukomposition III* was finished in July 1937 and is a straightforward revision in the spirit of *Craft I.* Example 7.13 shows how the chorale motive was reharmonized to remove the now inappropriate harshness and to clarify the progression. All the verticals are trichords built in major seconds, fourths, and fifths. The pitch center is plainly B and the mood more consistently tranquil because of the softer harmonies, a reduced pace of events, and generous rests in both parts. The first vocal phrase is retained, but the "Mariä Heimsuchung" motive is replaced with repetition of the chorale motive. Most of the recitative is also still there, though transposed up a step to E♭.

Example 7.13: "Mariä Verkündigung" (1937 revision), mm. 1–4

The "nicht, dass er eintrat" return is newly set (ex. 7.14). The tempo shifts abruptly to *ziemlich lebhaft* (rather lively), with almost constant repetition of a short thematic motive akin to the theme of the sixth song, "Verkündigung über den Hirten" (ex. 7.15). The pitch center is B. As in

Example 7.14: "Mariä Verkündigung" (1937 revision), beginning of section C

Example 7.15: "Verkündigung über den Hirten," mm. 18–22, voice part

Marienleben I, there is a return to the opening mood and material and a coda based on the recitative. The vocal line is retained, transposed down a step (ending on B), but the piano postlude closes on E.

The tonal design of the 1937 version is as follows:

Section:	A		B		C			A′	
Key: (B)	ϕ ——	IłI ——	IłI		ϕ ——	? ——	ϕ	ϕ ——————	ꝭ

The transposition of the recitative probably reflects Hindemith's bias during this period against step (especially whole-step) relations in favor of mediants. The modulation to E in the coda is a surprise and without any obvious larger function (the next song is in B again). There was a similar change in tonality at the end of the 1923 setting, of course.

This first revision, like the "Geburt Mariä" of 1936, is typical of the *Neukomposition* groups. Far more easily than "Geburt Mariä," though, "Mariä Verkündigung" (one of the 1923 linear-contrapuntal songs) allows us to observe Hindemith bringing a composition into line with his views in 1937: deliberately controlling harmonic tension (by no means always decreasing it) according to his harmonic fluctuation theory, utilizing whole-tone materials in ambiguous tonal situations, carefully planning the logic of melodic step-progressions, and generally diatonicizing the melodic lines (especially in the first calm section and in the voice). In other words, the criteria for revision are closely and obviously linked to a specific formulation of the *Craft* theory.

The next two revisions owe more to the 1937 version than to the original setting. Both are contained in the 1941–42 sketch notebook. The first is an incomplete sketch for a completely new setting; the second, also new, is the prototype for the second published version (a fair copy of this sketch is in *Neukomposition IV*). I will refer to these sketches as 41a and 41b, respectively. 41a begins on the page facing the key symbology scheme and is the first of Hindemith's essays to use this device. The opening is a quote of the motto phrase—a reworking of the "Surrexit Christus" motive—from the 1936 version of "Geburt Christi." The motto is placed on B, the key of Mary, and is followed by the opening section of text set to an entirely new melody, also in B (ex. 7.16). The first section breaks off before the paren-

Example 7.16: "Mariä Verkündigung" (revision 41a), beginning

thesis, but below it is a harmonization of the theme from "Verkündigung über den Hirten" for the piano alone. This theme is in A, the angels' key, with a 2/4 time signature (the first section is in 3/4) (ex. 7.17). No tempo is indicated, but as the section leads to the "Nicht, dass er eintrat" return it is probably meant to be faster than the first section. The theme is used in the voice (in A) to set text beginning with "Jünglings Angesicht" (referring to the angel). The setting is extended a bit and then breaks off.

Example 7.17: Harmonization of the "Verkündigung über den Hirten" theme in revision 41a

The key symbology at this early stage is utilized on a very broad, straightforward basis carefully tied to the cyclical use of thematic material: the births of Christ and of Mary are connected by the "Surrexit Christus" motive, and the two annunciations by the angels' theme. The key center, B, has passed from a tentative appearance without functional underpinnings in the motto phrase of the 1923 setting through solidification in the *Craft*-influenced 1937 revision to a position weighted by symbolic and thematic association in 41a. The pitch center, A, which did not appear in the *Neukomposition III* version, is now used for the announcing angel. The

"Verkündigung über den Hirten" theme, intimated in 1937 (but not all in *Marienleben I*), now becomes the second principal theme. There is a certain irony in this: the "Verkündigung über den Hirten" theme is quoted for the first time in a setting of "Mariä Verkündigung" in a form identical to its appearance in *Marienleben I,* but only at the service of the key symbology system, a rather arcane outgrowth of the *Craft* theories. This is by no means bereft of significance for the interpretation of the whole revision process.

The prototype for the published second version, 41b, draws on all the earlier versions. The first two sections, including the parenthesis, are the same as the published version except for insignificant differences of detail. The rapid third section exists in two forms, both complete—the second, final version of the section is a rewriting of the first, occasioned mainly by changes in the principal thematic material.

The key of B is no longer in evidence. The song opens with a long piano introduction which is a harmonization in A of the "Verkündigung über den Hirten" theme (ex. 7.18), the obvious source being 41a, though the harmonization is different. The compound duple meter and the calm pastoral mood of the 1923 and 1937 settings have been restored and the theme made to fit. The regaining of the original meter allows the use of some rhythmic configurations from the earlier settings, particularly the 1937 version. Some melodic configurations even recur with the same text; for instance, the setting of the fifth line ("auffahren—, pflegte sie an der Gestalt") and portions of the recitative. A recitative-like passage to set the parenthesis also reappears, with the sustained chord from *Marienleben I* and the key center E♭ from *Neukomposition III,* though the vocal line is substantially rewritten. In the key symbology, E♭ is associated with purity (= the unicorn).

The setting of "nicht, dass er eintrat" is in C♯, the key of the inevitable (Hindemith said it shows the "youthful determination of the angel"[28]). The idea of setting this text to a more rapid tempo stems from *Marienleben I,* which has the accelerando in this section. The tempo change, which was abrupt in the 1937 version, became somewhat less so in 41a, only to recover all its abruptness in 41b. The shape of the melodic line in this section owes a little to *Neukomposition II,* although the lines beginning "und, was Millionen" have a shape and emphasis obviously derived from the 1923 setting.

The long piano introduction is literally and completely restated at the close, effectively setting off the one line of text after it. Stephan claims that this recapitulation of the introduction is structurally weak and boring.[29] I disagree. The body of the text—the first paragraph—is a group of images

28. Ibid., 12.

29. Stephan, "Hindemith's *Marienleben,*" 285–86.

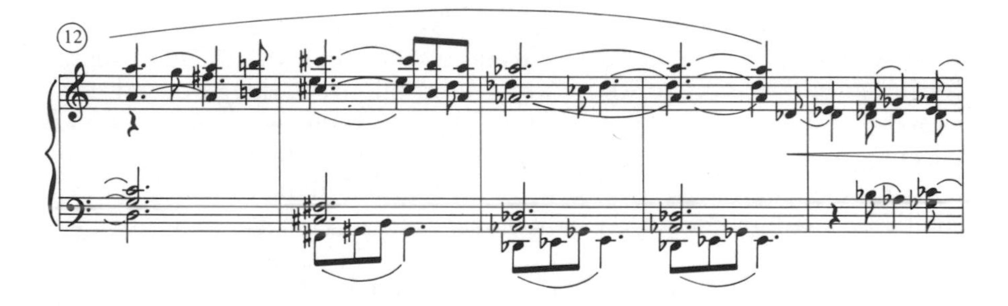

Example 7.18: "Mariä Verkündigung" (revised), mm. 1–22

centering on the look that the angel and Mary exchange and on the verb *erschrecken,* which suggests both surprise and fright. The poem's final line presents an image and action entirely divorced from the rest and properly isolated in the musical setting. If this passage is abstract, it is rightly so.

The formal plan of 41a cannot be entirely determined from the extant sketches. At best, it can be said that nothing contradicts the plan of the 1923 setting: A B C A′. The theme quoted in example 7.16 belongs to section A. B would be the recitative (not sketched, however) and C the section based on the angels' theme (ex. 7.17). The tonal plan, however, would certainly depart from the original:

Section:	A	B	C	A′
Key: (B)	ϕ	(?)	VII	(ϕ)

41b and the final version also use the formal plan of the original setting, though the tonal design differs:

Section:	Intro.	A	B	C	A′
Key: (A)	ϕ	ϕ ----------	ʊ ----------	IłI ----------	ϕ
Mm.:	1–20	20–47	48–71	71–99	99ff.

This sequence of tonal centers is unusual for Hindemith and may be due primarily to text expression through his tonal symbolism scheme.

The smooth combination of traditional sonorities, pentatonic-related discords, and a few sharper discords, as well as the fluidity of the diatonic-cell-based melodic activity—characteristic of the music of the forties—are apparent in the last versions of "Mariä Verkündigung" (41b and later). An analytic graph of the piano introduction, which is essentially the same in 41b and the final version, is shown in example 7.19. The melodic line of the right hand from m. 3 onward is the 1923 "Verkündigung über den Hirten" theme, a survivor from 41a. The combination of the pentatonic-related sonorities, accompaniment figuration in the bass, and a very slow tempo results in some obscurity in the harmonic surface. The short motive of the accompaniment, constantly repeated, could be understood to produce four chord roots in the first measure alone: ϕ–(♪)–ϱ–(♪). The last of these, whose root is not at all distinct, must nevertheless be taken seriously because of its half-measure length. An interpretation vertical by vertical is too narrow, though: a larger progression controls mm. 1–2, a neighbor-chord figure like those in "Geburt Mariä." There may be a connection. Recall that the "Surrexit Christus" motive was quoted in 41a. Like mm. 1–3 of "Geburt Mariä," a tonic, clearly defined, is embellished by a dominant, poorly defined. In several instances from m. 3 on, the angels' theme combined with the accompaniment figure alters the interpretation of the har-

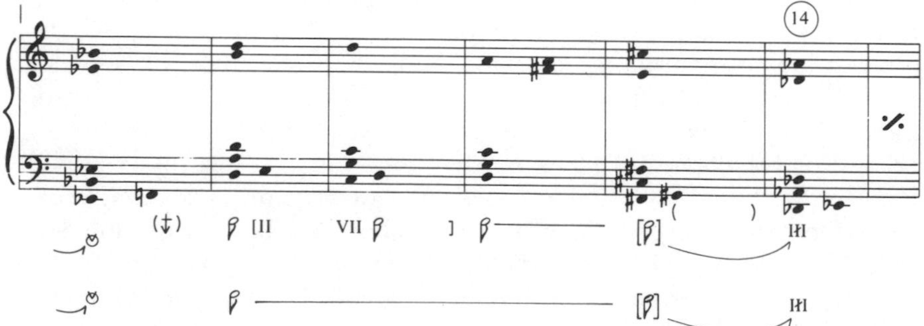

Example 7.19: "Mariä Verkündigung" (revised), mm. 1–22, Stage IV and V analyses

Example 7.19: *Continued*

mony. Twice, the neighbor chord acquires harmonic value when the resolution into the tonic is excised and the chord extended (compare mm. 6–7, 11–12). As is typical of very slow tempi, there are several levels of harmonic activity: the eighth note (vertical to vertical in m. 1), the half measure (the neighbor-chord figure of mm. 1–2), and the full measure. The latter two, being structurally superior levels, are the basis of the harmonic synopsis.

The intratonal plan for the piano introduction is nearly the same as the tonal plan for the whole song. The first phrase (mm. 1–9) moves from (A) ϕ to ʊ, the second (mm. 10–15) to IƗI, and the third (mm. 15–22) is simply ‡– ϕ, with expansion of ‡. This degree, though not prominent in the tonal plan, receives emphasis from the voice at the end of C (mm. 95–98). The introduction, then, in addition to presaging the birth of Christ (by virtue of its theme linking the two events in which announcing angels play a major role), is a kind of tonal overture (an obvious parallel to the Praeludium of the *Ludus Tonalis*). The tonal narrative is presented in miniature, its main features recounted in the abstract language of the key symbolism.

The final form of the second version of "Mariä Verkündigung" is a synthesis of all the preceding versions. Hindemith sifted and mixed elements from each, recalling some, rejecting others, inventing a few new ones. Organic connections exist between the various versions, published and unpublished, complete and incomplete—connections established for the most part deliberately, as the stages of the revision demonstrate.

EIGHT
CARDILLAC (1925–26)

Cardillac was Hindemith's first full-length opera and the first of his stage works to be truly representative of his gifts as a composer of dramatic music. Unlike the three early one-act operas, *Mörder, Hoffnung der Frauen, Sancta Susanna,* and *Das Nusch-Nuschi* (all premiered in 1921–22), *Cardillac* is a composition in which we find assembled and perfected all the techniques and stylistic idioms of Hindemith's early career.

With Alban Berg's *Wozzeck,* Ernst Krenek's *Jonny spielt auf!,* and Kurt Weill's *Dreigroschenoper, Cardillac* was the most successful and most characteristic German opera in modern style of the mid- and late twenties. (Though it was completed in 1921, *Wozzeck* is included in the list because it was not premiered until 1925.) Krenek's and Weill's operas are both special cases which are more readily compared with Hindemith's *Zeitoper, Neues vom Tage* (1929) or even his cinematic one-act opera, *Hin und Zurück* (1927). *Cardillac* is better compared with *Wozzeck* or with another opera of the same period, Busoni's *Doktor Faustus.*Of these three, only *Cardillac* represents the New Objective manner, but all are excellent examples of twenties-style formal constructivism in dramatic music, applications of the principle on a grand scale. Each is based on baroque or classical vocal and instrumental forms. Hindemith's opera is the extreme case because the traditional forms lie very close to the musical and dramatic surface. This must be ascribed to Hindemith's compositional and dramatic intentions rather than to an attempt to depict the milieu of late-seventeenth-century France, the opera's historical setting, since jazz elements are introduced into the tavern music of act 3.

The aesthetic and musical-technical issues in *Cardillac* are touched on in a multiauthor review of the premiere in the periodical *Melos,* a contemporary music periodical published by Schott. This review may be taken as a fair assessment of *Cardillac* from the point of view of New Objective music criticism:

> [The negative critics] seemed justified with respect to the opera's subject, which, not only in milieu but especially in its presentation of a plot dependent on [extended] dramatic tension, stands solidly on the ground of ro-

manticism. . . . But even in the shaping of this subject itself moments stand out which cannot be grasped with the older logic of the music-drama. . . . [An essential aspect of this] is the strongly formal layout of the book, which divides the material into closed scenes and . . . makes of it a libretto for a number opera controlled by musical formal principles.

So we meet with terms like "aria," "duet," "scene and quartet," and *Wechselgesang (Passacaglia)*. The manner in which the opera opens and closes—with choral scenes—, in which the second act is framed by the two arias of Cardillac, and in which the rapid and tranquil pieces are distributed, is all evidence of an architectonic scheme determining the plan of the whole.

This large structure of closed individual forms corresponds with Hindemith's purely musically oriented form-will, which first established itself in instrumental compositions of a polyphonic-concertante manner. This polyphonic-concertante style also rules the score of *Cardillac*, which, though it is constructed in accord with purely musical requirements, simultaneously succeeds in dramatic effect. Music and drama stand here in a new relationship: the music absorbs the dramatic content and lifts it to a higher level. What this may take from the work in immediacy, it gives back in intensity and concentration.

The individual numbers lack . . . most dramatic-psychological development in the sense of the music-drama. Instead, in their first measures they encompass clearly both character and situation, and they persistently maintain that basis throughout, with the thematic material sometimes worked out in a [purely] concertante manner. Accordingly, the great musico-dramatic intensifications and high points are also lacking. Because of this renunciation of any obvious dramatic structure, at first glance the impression is one of the [wholly] undramatic.

In fact, through the musical-formal principles powers are released that for the most part are overlooked in the music-drama. These powers are not subjective-psychological but objective-musical. The theme—clearly stated at the outset—is transformed in the most varied ways and always in a deeper-lying relation to the scene. . . . These [musical] means include the ostinato motive, the unison lines, two- and three-voiced counterpoint. Melody avoids *espressivo*, is more short-breathed and weak in tension than laden in emotion, avoids great interval spans but is controlled by a crisp diatonicism. The result: a constructed melodic progression which necessarily also controls the polyphony [ex. 8.1].[1]

It is significant that this is the subject for a fugato. . . . How would it look in a music-drama?! Here the music objectifies the spiritual content and at the same time expresses it completely. In this degree of stylization

1. In the review, all three examples (exx. 8.1–8.3) appear as melodic citations only. For exx. 8.1 and 8.2 I have given the piano reduction as well. Also, for ex. 8.1, the reviewers cite the form of the fugato subject first given in the orchestra (at 5 before E) but with the Daughter's text at 3 before F. The only difference in the latter statement beyond addition of text is that it lies a whole step higher.

Example 8.1: *Cardillac*, No. 10, at 6 before F

lies an essential characteristic of the opera. The example also shows that the voice is exploited less for its own dynamic and sonorial possibilities than as an equally rated factor in the instrumental texture. Despite such stylization, the voice part is still able to contain the emotional tension of the situation. [For example,] the excitement of the gold merchant as he discovers that Cardillac is the long-sought murderer is contained in a jagged, rhythmically displaced, but still tightly constructed melody [ex. 8.2].

To be sure, this principle of dramatic construction is not followed inflexibly or to [unreasonable] extremes. The swelling arioso line in the second aria of Cardillac is reminiscent of the romantic music-drama [ex. 8.3]. In other places, similarly pointed vocal lines are for the most part paralyzed by the orchestral thematic working.[2]

2. Review of *Cardillac* by Hans Mersmann, Hans Schultze-Ritter, Heinrich Strobel, and Lothar Windsperger, in *Melos* 7 (1928): 292–295; quoted in Christoph Wolff, ed., *Paul Hindemith: Sämtliche Werke* IV/1: *Cardillac* (Mainz: Schott, 1978), xxi–xxii.

Example 8.2: *Cardillac*, No. 15, beginning

Example 8.3: *Cardillac*, No. 13 at 7 after C

The opera's surprising juxtaposition of stylistic and expressive components, which is emphasized by the review's authors, is also brought out by Hans Heinz Stuckenschmidt in a review of a recent production in Berlin:

> More than a century ago, Cesare Lombroso pointed out the psychophysical connections between genius, madness, and criminality. His controversial researches—later partly disproved, partly extended by Sigmund Freud's psychoanalysis—had an equally strong effect on Thomas Mann and on the Expressionists. The essentially Romantic spirit [of his ideas] is rooted in the fantasies of E. T. A. Hoffman and related writers of the early nineteenth century. Through Hoffman's "Fräulein von Scudéri" moves the goldsmith Cardillac, who is under a compulsion to kill the buyers of his work and reclaim his jewels. It belongs to the true paradoxes of recent cultural history that this highly Romantic figure became the title role in a *Singdrama* of a designedly anti-Romantic style.[3]

Both reviews make abundantly clear the opera's essential musical and dramatic issue: the dichotomy between Hindemith's neo-baroque chamber music style, exemplified especially in the *Kammermusiken* series of concertos, and Ferdinand Lion's expressionistic libretto. Hindemith's task was not only to make the best possible dramatic use of this dichotomy, but also to reach a satisfying compromise between its elements. And at this he was very successful. As Ian Kemp states, "Hindemith's achievement in *Cardillac,* the major work of this period, was to reconcile the Baroque aesthetic with the demands of an expressionistic dramatic subject."[4]

The orchestral prelude to act 1 already suggests the separate musical and dramatic themes, yet implicitly unifies them: the music announces objectivity, but at the same time, through its slightly too rapid tempo and unnecessarily pointed rhythms and dynamics, provides a dramatic complement to the disquiet and confusion of the crowd in the chorus (no. 1). The music of the prelude also continues as the orchestral background for this chorus.

The prelude consists mostly of an extended fugato on the theme shown in ex. 8.4. This theme, which is given fortissimo in octaves, shows the most characteristic manner of melodic construction in Hindemith's New Objective linear counterpoint: cells of diatonic figures mixed without regard for key origins (that is, treated as independent motivic units almost in the manner of pitch-class sets), the half-step as a general leading tone, and sharply accented rhythmic motives. The harmonic framework is B–A♭, but as is often the case in Hindemith's early music, the cadence is almost a surprise, a seemingly arbitrary stopping point rather than the result of organically unfolded harmony. The effect reinforces the sense of deliber-

3. Review of the Deutsche Oper's production of *Cardillac* in Berlin, 1977, by Hans Heinz Stuckenschmidt, in the *Frankfurter Allgemeine Zeitung,* October 5, 1977; reproduced in the *Informationen* section of *HJB* 6 (1977): 180–183. The quotation is from p. 180.

4. *New Grove Dictionary of Music and Musicians,* ed. Stanley Sadie, s.v. "Hindemith, Paul."

Example 8.4: *Cardillac*, Prelude to act 1, beginning

ate constructivism and the impression that the melodic-rhythmic energy of linear counterpoint is Hindemith's real preoccupation. Effect and impression are confirmed as the fugato proceeds (see ex. 8.5). The traditional sense of voiceleading as a specific, consistent relationship between melodic

Example 8.5: *Cardillac*, Prelude to act 1, mm. 12–21

elements and distinct underlying harmonies is virtually gone. Harmony is radically demoted not only as functional syntax but even as "color."

Like other techniques, this is not followed "inflexibly or to [unreasonable] extremes" (as the *Melos* review has it). More detailed functional progressions do sometimes occur, as in the prelude's closing cadence (ex. 8.6), which has an expanded dominant-class sonority with two leading tones and a descending fourth in the bass (a favorite of Reger, inherited from Brahms). This cadence smooths the way for the opening bars of the chorus (ex. 8.7) with its tertian sonorities and simple neighbor-chord construction.

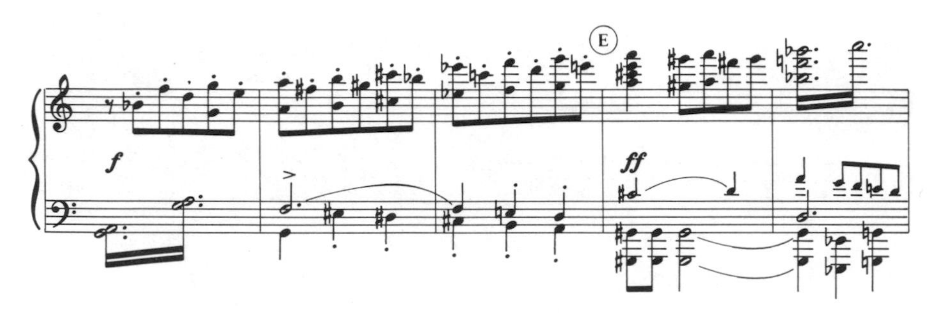

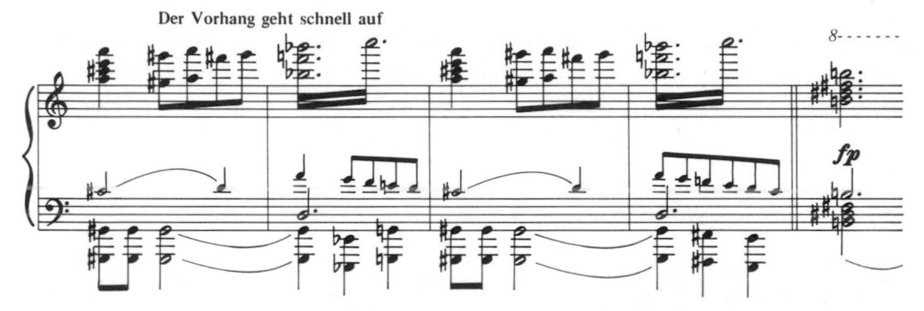

Example 8.6: *Cardillac*, Prelude to act 1, final measures

The structure of the prelude demonstrates the uneasy relationship between a functionally doubtful harmonic surface and a large-scale tonal-formal plan. The cadence of mm. 11–12 is repeated, motto-like, at two later points to provide formal definition for the otherwise free flow of contrapuntal lines. The resulting scheme is not far from a large two-part or binary structure:

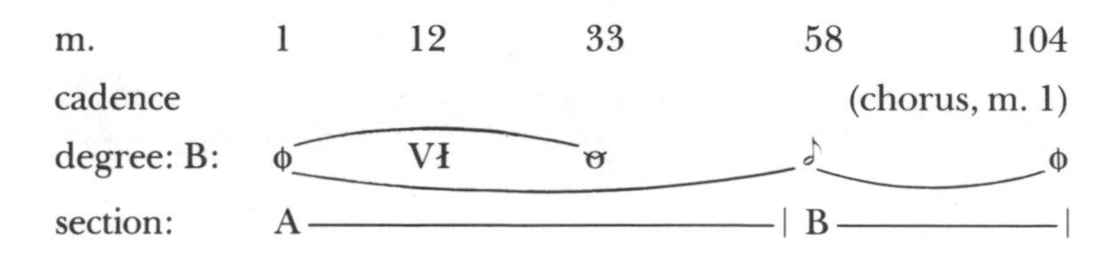

The likelihood that this cadence-articulated design can be translated in listening into a sense of harmonic progression (I–V–I) seems very small indeed. The design is less a large-scale progression (as it would be in traditional tonal music) than a neutral, abstract frame which the composer deliberately overwhelms with surface events; that is, "an architectural rather than an evolutionary scheme."[5]

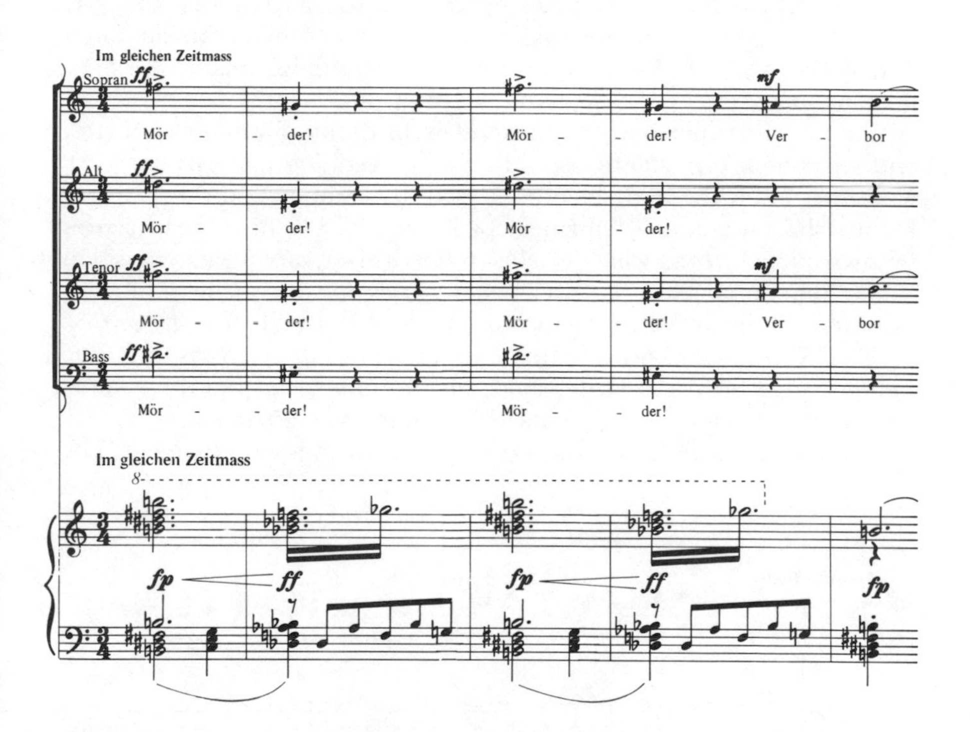

Example 8.7: *Cardillac*, No. 1, beginning

The arioso which begins act 2 introduces the opera's tragic hero Cardillac in his normal surroundings, his studio-shop (though in fact he had already appeared in a murderer's cloak at the end of act 1). The fatal character flaw is quickly revealed as he sings, almost passionately, to the gold on which he works. The ensuing duet with the gold merchant exposes the combination of fear and fascination with which the artist was viewed, as the merchant is challenged by the smith for having crossed himself before en-

5. Ibid.

tering the shop. The number which contains these two pieces is cast in the form of a dramatic *szena* with an orchestral ritornello as a frame:

Section:	Ritornello	Arioso	Ritornello	Duet	Ritornello
Tonic:	D	E	D	C♯	D

The ritornello is strongly reminiscent of the *Kammermusiken* concertos —specifically, of the first piece in that series, a chamber concerto from 1922 (Op. 24, no.1). A single motive controls the ritornello, but a miniature three-part design results from changes in its treatment. In the opening six measures, long notes in the bass acting like pedal points are set against staccato triplet figures consisting of thirds (usually minor), fourths, and seconds in consistently ascending or descending patterns (ex. 8.8). Measures 7–14, the middle section, give the seconds and thirds in the form of sharply pointed changing chords (ex. 8.9). The final two measures of this section are somewhat detached from the rest, serving as a transition to the "reprise" of mm. 15–24. The latter uses only the material of m. 1, however, gradually filtering it out to the pedal D itself (by m. 23; see ex. 8.10). The emphasis on winds, the bass and active upper parts with little middle-range filler, the fairly rapid staccato notes, and the throw-away sixteenth-note figure are all characteristic of the *Kammermusiken*.

Both recurrences of the ritornello depend on literal restatement. The

Example 8.8: *Cardillac*, No. 7, beginning

Example 8.9: *Cardillac*, No. 7, mm. 7–9

Example 8.10: *Cardillac*, No. 7, mm. 15–19

first signals the interruption of Cardillac's reverie and the entry of the gold merchant, as the ritornello's first twelve measures are combined with the two voice parts in the manner of a recitativo accompagnato. The third recurrence uses only the reprise (mm. 15–23), as Cardillac calls his daughter to watch his shop while he and the merchant leave to examine metals for the goldsmith's approval. In both cases, the music is well matched to the action: the first recurrence mirrors the obvious disquiet of the gold merchant, the second winds down and concludes the scene.

In the ritornello, tonal design and harmony (at least in the sense of clear fundamental tones) are carried entirely in the few bass notes, from which the active melodic lines of the upper parts are obviously detached. Under these circumstances, it is difficult to speak of pillar chords. Nevertheless, I have constructed a Stage II analysis in ex. 8.11 which does include some upper voice tones in closed notes, more to show the three points of consonance (mm. 1, 7, and 15) in the overall pattern of harmonic fluctuation of Stage III than to suggest that these are strongly defined harmonies. The pattern of the bass is almost symmetrical about these points of consonance (coinciding with section divisions): from D to A♭ and an extended F to F♯ (dissonant in m. 6, consonant in m. 7, where the second section begins), then returning to an extended F (mm. 8–13), and—bypassing A♭—to D in m. 15.

The beginning of the arioso brings an abrupt change of mood, tempo, and texture. Cardillac sings "Let the sunlight enter" as late afternoon rays turn the workshop a lurid, expressionistic gold-red, matched perfectly by the unusually rich tone of the tenor saxophone and by its angular, espressivo melody (ex. 8.12). Though Cardillac sings with intensity, even passion, the object of his love is not a woman, but his precious metal: "Stay in my hands, close, for it is you I love, / and whisper your wishes, / O Gold-work,

Example 8.11: *Cardillac*, Stage II and III analyses of the ritornello (No. 7, mm. 1–23)

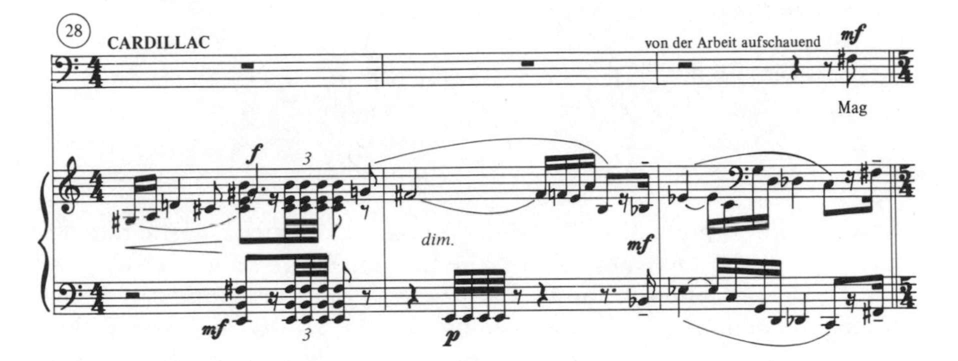

Example 8.12: *Cardillac*, arioso, beginning (No. 7, mm. 25–31)

in my ear."[6] Manner and means are closer to those of the late nineteenth century here than anywhere else in the opera, but Hindemith succeeds in maintaining a seemingly impossible balance between serious expression and personal distance from it—indeed, even a hint of parody. The ri-

6. "Bleibe bei mir, dicht, da ich dich liebe. / Und flüstre deinen Willen, / O Goldwerk, mir ins Ohr."

tornello, which is irrelevant (even obstructive) to the staging of the mood of the arioso, announces Hindemith's objectivity, his detachment from the emotion the scene calls on his music to generate. Even in the first measures of the arioso, the accompaniment is surprisingly sparse and given mostly to winds and percussion.

The formal design of the arioso is again three-part, the tonal design quite clear with considerable emphasis on the dominant (as ex. 8.12 shows, the saxophone melody closes on that degree: m. 31). The texture is strongly harmonic with clear division between the melody and the repeated or isolated chords of the accompaniment. The tonal-harmonic structure of the piece may be represented as follows:

m.25——31—32 33 34 35 38 49 50 51 53 57 || 58
E: ɸ 𝅘𝅥𝅮 ɸ ↕ 𝅘𝅥𝅮 ɸ 𝅘𝅥𝅮 ------ IɫI II/↕ ↕ ɸ ↕
D: ↕ ⌣ ɸ

In section B (mm. 38–52), the tempo picks up somewhat; the rate of harmonic change increases rapidly; the harmonies are richer, mostly triadic; and in the course of the section several degrees are emphasized, including the dominant and lower leading tone, II, IɫI, Vɫ, and later in the section the upper leading tone. The cadence which leads to the abbreviated return of the principal section would have been very comfortable in one of Hindemith's compositions from the forties (ex. 8.13). The two "dominant" dissonances are both poorly defined. The first shows the indefinite third relation, and the second is a whole-tone sonority with the lower leading tone as its bass (m. 51), while the tonic, although not a simple triad, is strongly defined by the harmonic fifth E–B in the bass and tenor and the doubling of the B in the upper parts (including the solo saxophone). The voice carries a strong step-progression downward to the tonic, using the upper leading tone with escape-note figure which is so common in Hindemith's later music (bracketed in ex. 8.13, mm. 52–53).[7]

7. In the revised version of the opera, the arioso and duet also open the second act, but the ritornello was excised along with the more declamatory transitional passages. The tonal plan of the number, then, is quite different from the original: E–C♯. In the arioso, only a few notes in the voice part have been changed, but the duet is much longer with considerable new material. Texts for both pieces, however, are entirely new.

The relationship between the original *Cardillac* (Op. 39) and the revision Hindemith worked on from 1948 to 1952 is, if possible, even more complicated than the relationship of the two *Marienlebens.* See Hans Ludwig Schilling, *Paul Hindemiths "Cardillac";* Dieter Rexroth, "Von der moralischen Verantwortung des Künstlers," *HJB* 3 (1973): 63–79 (esp. 69–75); idem, "Zum Stellenwert der Oper

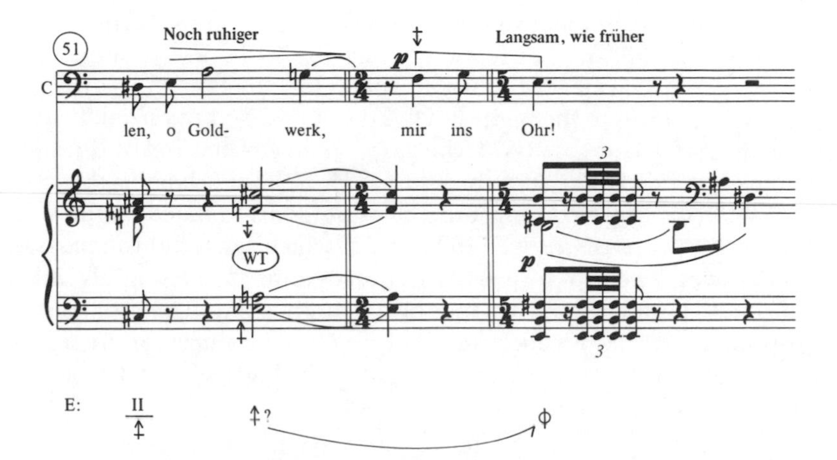

Example 8.13: *Cardillac*, arioso, cadence leading to reprise (No. 7, mm. 51–53)

The tenor saxophone's melody in the principal section is subjected to a Stage V analysis in ex. 8.14, which shows the entire line as given in ex. 8.12 plus the notes from the final measures of the ritornello which lead into it. The accompanying parts are not included. Despite the expressive angularity of the line, the step-progression patterns are surprisingly tight, the majority outlining chromatic steps and in several cases grouped in threes. An example is the C♯–C–B component of the first step-progression, mm. 24–25, which is isolated from the preceding tones by the minor ninth leap and from the concluding A♯ by the duration of the B. These chromatic groupings also suggest the melody's nineteenth-century provenance. Perfect fifth leaps also play a prominent role. In a Stage IV reading the harmonic

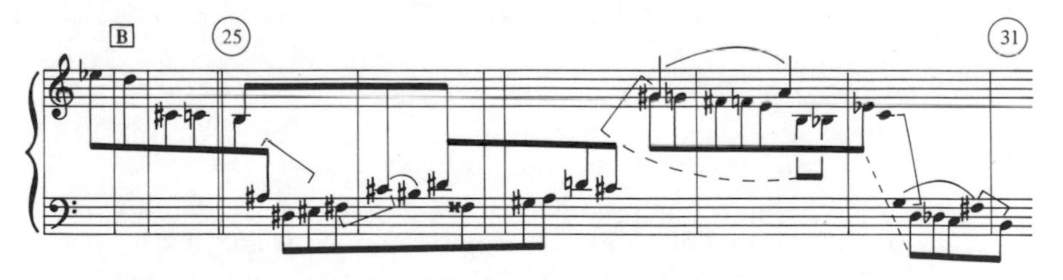

Example 8.14: *Cardillac*, Stage V analysis of tenor saxophone melody (No. 7, mm. 23–31)

Cardillac im Schaffen Hindemiths," in Rexroth, ed., *Erprobungen und Erfahrungen*, 56–59; Hellmuth Christian Wolff, afterword to *Paul Hindemith: Cardillac (Neufassung 1952)* (Leipzig: Peters, n.d.), 259–61.

stasis of the accompaniment would necessarily elevate these fifths to near-harmonic status. Still another feature, which ex. 8.14 does not show, is the grouping of tones by means of the octave interval: in mm. 25–26, the lowest tone, D♯3, moves to the highest, D♯4 (both notes emphasized by duration); in m. 28, G♯3 moves to G♯4, the latter again emphasized by duration.

In the second part of section A (mm. 31–38), the whole of the saxophone melody is repeated, but some of its notes are claimed by the voice part. A Stage V analysis is given in ex. 8.15, which separates the parts on different staves. The two-measure insertion in mm. 33–34 is tightly linked with the motivic and linear substance of the original line. The broken step-progression by means of which the voice reaches the climax of the section (mm. 34–35) is dramatically appropriate also: the highest tone, E4, is given to the word "Gold."

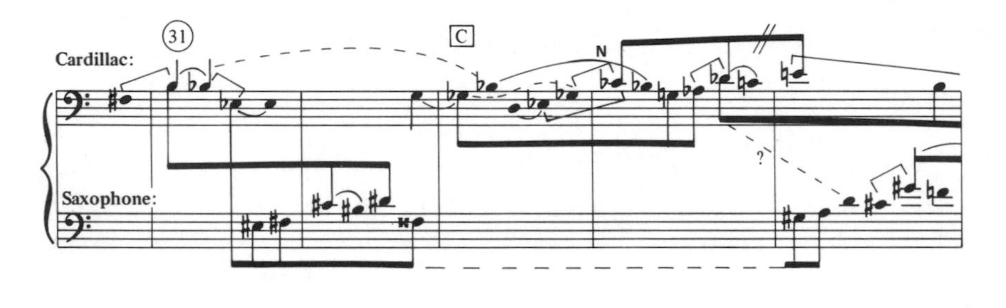

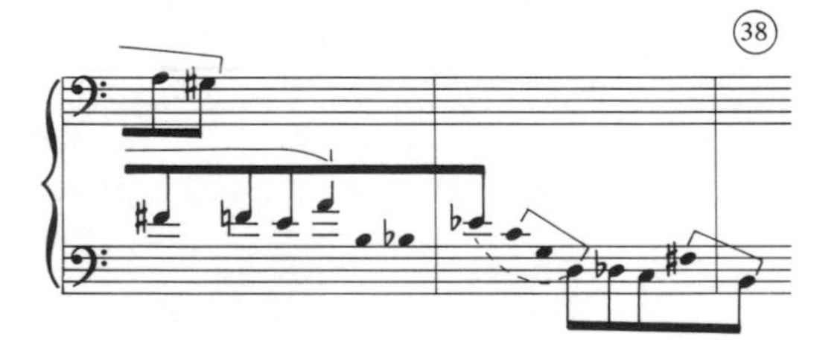

Example 8.15: *Cardillac*, Stage V analysis of arioso excerpt (mm. 31–38)

Of possible subjects he might have treated, why did Hindemith elect this paradox of the "fantastic and pathological case of the goldsmith" married to the "polyphonic-concertante" style? From one point of view, the motivation behind creating this tension—a tension in style and materials as great as any in the dramatic action—may be explained as a musical critique of expressionism and thus no contradiction of the New Objective ideology: "Examined more closely, this subject offered a consistent critical theme which many responsible artists of the twenties could not avoid—for what else do the murders Cardillac commits on the buyers of his work . . . say than that the total identification of an artist with his work must lead to his complete social alienation?"[8]

On the other hand, as the *Melos* review reminds us, it is a mistake to think that Hindemith followed the anti-emotional program to an extreme. According to Stuckenschmidt,

> For all its show of coolness and distance, Hindemith's score is a true cornucopia of inspired music. Born completely of a polyphonic spirit, wearing canon and fugue as emblems of all its impulses, it advances from instrumental thinking into the realms of the vocal. . . . In terms of mood, the music fluctuates between Hindemith's notorious coolness, occasional emotional outbursts, and wandering chordal background which reminds one of the manner of the Debussy or Berg operas.[9]

The risk Hindemith took in *Cardillac* was considerable. Had he overemphasized emotional detachment, the opera could have lost its serious tone and become a parody. Had he overemphasized its romantic qualities, it could easily have degenerated into pastiche. Indeed, the difficulties he overcame to achieve its synthesis were in many respects greater than those he later conquered in *Mathis der Maler.* As the pieces discussed in this chapter suggest, the two operas are more closely related in both style and technique than is generally conceded. Kemp's "reconciliation of Baroque aesthetic and . . . expressionistic dramatic subject" extended deeply into the musical materials themselves, so that, more than any other single work, *Cardillac* held the key to what became the *Mathis* style.

8. Rexroth, "Zum Stellenwert *Cardillacs,*" 57.
9. Stuckenschmidt, review of *Cardillac,* 181.

PART IV
THE MUSIC AFTER *MATHIS*

NINE

ECHOES AND THE AMERICAN YEARS (1935–50)

In *Mathis der Maler* and the works that followed from it in the late thirties, Hindemith employed relatively large harmonic and melodic blocks, with a full chorale texture as the starting point. In these works the triad is the harmonic point of reference, and harmonic phrases controlled by major or minor triads are often simply juxtaposed with phrases controlled by sonorities developed from augmented or diminished triads, as in the Grablegung from the *Mathis* Symphony or the first movement of *Trauermusik*. Large diatonic-modal melodic cells are treated in a similar manner, as in the first phrase of *Trauermusik* or the viola's first gesture (m. 13). Influenced by Hermann Roth and so by a tradition of harmonic theory which included Schenker, Hindemith in this period came closest to working in terms of a linear harmonic logic analogous to the older diatonic tonal system.

Only gradually did he work his way free of this manner of thinking. Some evidence of it is still present in the 1941 sketches for *Marienleben*, but in the *Ludus Tonalis* the change is complete. The texture is leaner, and harmony and melody are more clearly differentiated. The harmonic point of reference is now the fifth, which can expand in one direction to major and minor triads, in another to diatonic or pentatonic discords. Harmony is no longer merely a series of functions: it is a network which depends on strength of tonal association (the principal tonal functions) and on the kind of degree of activity (homophonic or polyphonic texture). The older, broader style of treatment does not disappear: it is still important in the interludes of the *Ludus Tonalis* and is essential to the *Symphonic Metamorphosis of Themes by Weber,* written in 1943. But the broader style has become a special case, an expressive tool or device rather than the principal means of stylistic or technical control.

The six compositions discussed in this chapter will serve to chart the course of the development just described, though in the main these brief essays are intended more to illuminate representative details of harmonic or melodic process and patterns of tonal and formal design than to make a general statement about this period of Hindemith's career. The compositions chosen represent only the smallest sampling (a few other pieces from this period have been analyzed in earlier chapters): the years after *Mathis* were very fertile despite the changing circumstances of Hindemith's life, and the number of successful and now well-known compositions is large.

DER SCHWANENDREHER (1935)

"Go forth, you old, long silenced songs, and make friends!"[1] One of the steadfast friends made by the songs in Böhme's collection *Altdeutsches Liederbuch* was Hindemith, who used the book as his source for the many older melodies he incorporated into compositions as early as Op. 41 (1926) and gave to students as cantus firmi for counterpoint exercises.

If *Mathis der Maler* is a grand Renaissance romance, the viola concerto *Der Schwanendreher* is a medieval romance—not in the sense of the literary genres of the era, but a free, picturesque period tale in a nineteenth-century manner: "A musician [*Spielmann*] comes among merry company and performs the music he has brought with him from afar: songs grave and gay and at the end a dance. According to his ability and inspiration, he expands and embellishes the tunes, preludizes, and fantasizes, like a true *Musikant*."[2] Hindemith uses four melodies from Böhme's collection in the concerto, whose design is shown in figure 9.1.

Mvnt. I:

Introduction	Sonata movement	Coda
Viola, then "Zwischen Berg und tiefem Tal"		(based on introduction)
C: ɸ ———————	ɸ	ɸ

Mvnt. II:

A	B	C	A′ + B
Viola and harp	"Nun laube, Lindlein, laube"	"Der Gutzgauch auf der Zaune sass" (fugato); add "Lindlein" near the end	("Lindlein" in horn)
A: ɸ —— ɸ	ɸ ———— ɸ	VƗ ———— (VƗ) ——	ɸ

Mvnt. III: Theme and 11 variations on "Seid ihr nicht der Schwanendreher?" (Details are given in Figure 9.2)

Figure 9.1: *Der Schwanendreher*, tonal-formal scheme

1. Böhme, *Altdeutsches Liederbuch*, xix.
2. Hindemith's foreword to the score (Mainz: Schott, 1935).

Schwanendreher takes the idioms of the *Kammermusiken* (Opp. 24, 36, and 46) and the *Konzertmusiken* (Opp. 48–50) (especially the two viola concertos Op. 36, no. 4, and Op. 48) and transforms them in the spirit of *Mathis* (see the opening flourish of the solo viola, ex. 9.1). Stage IV and V analyses are given in example 9.2, along with a Stage III reading that is frankly Salzerian, showing in particular the hierarchic treatment of the neighbor-note motive E–F–E. I offer this reading to underscore the point that with the style and manner of *Mathis* Hindemith showed a new willingness to employ nineteenth-century techniques he had avoided as part of the New Objective program: more varied and carefully differentiated timbres, richer harmonization using sonorities of traditional harmonic vocabulary (triads and seventh chords), and motivic development. Note especially (1) the short opening phrase (mm. 1–2) with its triads and ϕ–♪–ϕ progression but reversed chord qualities; (2) the progress toward ʊ in m. 7 and its simple prolongation for nine beats; (3) the preponderance of minor-third melodic motions in the long, unstable region from m. 4 to m. 10 (especially the diminished-triad outline in m. 9, which reminds one of the "gentle cadencing" Hindemith cited in his analysis of the "Angelic Concert" fragment in *Craft I*).

The third movement of *Schwanendreher*, a free set of variations on another old melody, poses some problems for analysis of formal design because of Hindemith's special conception of variation procedure. His attitude toward the process changed very little after emerging mature and

Example 9.1: *Der Schwanendreher*, I, opening measures

Example 9.2: *Der Schwanendreher*, I, opening measures, Stage III, IV, and V analyses (as harmony and voiceleading graphs)

complete in the Quartet, Op. 10, in Op. 11, no. 4, and in the passacaglia of Op. 11, no. 5. It drew on two broad traditions of variation composition, of which the first was elaboration (or diminution), the model familiar from the work of the English virginalists; the baroque composers who wrote variations, partitas on chorales, passacaglias or chaconnes; the classical composers; and the romantics of more conservative bent (Mendelssohn, Schumann, Brahms). The second tradition was the "free" variation, akin to the baroque toccata, but more obviously derived from the paraphrases and fantasies on opera tunes that were the stock in trade of the virtuosi of the 1830s and 1840s (for example, Liszt's *Don Juan Fantasy*). This notion of variation as a fantasy on (or even development of) motives of the theme rather than simple elaboration of the harmonic and melodic structure is closely related to thematic transformation and becomes a standard procedure for variation sets written in the later nineteenth century. Max Reger, Hindemith's most direct source, mixed the two types, strict and free, in his large variation sets on an original theme (Op. 73), on themes by Bach (Op. 81), Beethoven (Op. 86), Hiller (Op. 100), and Mozart (Op. 132). Reger's design is sectional (that is, one can usually tell where the joints between variations are), but some variations are by diminution, and others are fantasies on motives (or harmonic progressions) without the theme's formal design.

This view of the variation process can be clarified by analogy to Hindemith's conception of polyphonic texture in *Craft III*. In a passage cited earlier, he says that in contrapuntal writing, as long as the principal harmonic pillars are clear, the tonal or harmonic relationships between can be worked out in the weakest form. Between the pillars one can string multiple lines of melody with less concern for the value of the harmonies created, since the pillars will hold the strings up by themselves (the suspension bridge effect). In the variation set, strict variations create the listener's pillars: they are easy to follow, all components of the theme being more or less obvious to the ear and the form simply a reiteration of the design of the theme. Mixed with these are the free variations, improvisations controlled or contained in the structure of the whole by the strict variation pillars. (A similar process works internally in the free variations. The pillars of the principal motives from the different theme phrases emerge occasionally to organize the contrapuntal fantasizing.)

The theme of *Schwanendreher*, third movement, is in the traditional German *Bar* form (A A B), the only peculiar feature being the considerable length of section B, the *Abgesang* (see ex. 9.3). The twelve phrases are each two measures long: a b c / a b c / d d′ e e′ f f′. The closing cadence is something of a surprise: the emphasis on the fifth G–D suggests the Mixolydian mode, but the cadence is on C. The theme and eleven variations are organized in a tripartite structure (roughly ABA, or *Mässig bewegt-Ruhig bewegt-Mässig schnell*) (fig. 9.2). Note that the design is symmetrical: five short sections in A, two in B, five in A′.

The theme is set antiphonally, the orchestra taking a phrase or phrase pair, the solo viola its repetition. The first variation maintains the length and formal articulations of the theme but has a running commentary on the melodic line in the viola and occasional motivic quotes in the orchestra at different transposition levels—a type intermediate between the strict and free classes. Variation 2 is strict, the theme set simply and consecutively in the bassoons and lower strings with obbligato passagework in the viola. (In figure 9.2 it is five measures longer because a bridge passage to the next variation follows the cadence.) The third variation reverses the orchestra-soloist antiphony, the viola playing diminutions on the theme, the orches-

Example 9.3: "Seid ihr nicht der Schwanendreher?" as used in III

Theme	beginning to B	26 mm.	G–C
Var. I	B to 6 before D	26 mm. + 1 beat	C?
II	to 5 before F	31 mm. + 1 beat	G–C
III	to 4 before H	25 mm. + 1 beat	A–A
IV	to 6 before K (as if coda)	24 mm.	D–E
V	6 before K to M	30 mm.	F–D
VI	to 13 after O	33 mm. + 1 beat (with an interpolated cadenza)	F–D + modulating cadence
VII	to 4 before Q	20 mm. + 1 beat	B♭–B♭
VIII	to 4 before R	19 mm. + 1 beat	B♭–B♭ + modulating cadence
IX	to T	20 mm.	G–C
X	to 7 after U	21 mm.	G–G
XI	7 after U to the end (as a coda)	68 mm.	C–C

Figure 9.2: *Der Schwanendreher,* III, tonal-formal plan (based on numbering in Hindemith's sketches)

tra answering with an unelaborated statement. Variation 4 serves as a reflective coda to the first large partition of the structure and, to emphasize that function, generates a new melody from the last three notes of the theme. The second part of the variation quotes both opening and closing motives from the theme. In his scheme, Hindemith listed this as a variation, not an extension of the cadence of variation 3: it is nearly as long as the theme and preceding variations and has the same essentially two-part division (a a / b). Variations 5 and 6 are closely related, the latter being for the most part an elaboration of the former with an interpolated cadenza. Both belong to the category of free variations. Variation 7 is a cadenza whose relation to the theme is secured only by motivic pillars, but variation 8 is simple. The theme appears intact in the horn with obbligato viola, continuing in variation 9 as the orchestra plays the theme in canon. The tenth variation is quite free, a cadenza with short orchestral interpolations; some of the figuration is similar to that of the seventh variation. The final variation is a much longer version of the fourth. It opens with the new melody from that variation, then continues with an extended series of quotations from the theme (each part or phrase taken in turn) until the theme is expanded to about twice its original length.

To illustrate one way the free variation can work, I offer a partial analysis of the fifth variation (the first half of the Ruhig bewegt) in example 9.4a. The main function of this analysis is to trace the theme. The top staff gives the theme in the transposition appropriate to this variation; the system below shows which notes in the variation correspond to this transposed form of the theme. (The opening measures of the variation are shown in ex. 9.4b for comparison.) The most significant point about the use of the theme is perhaps the change of quality (from major to minor), which makes the Ruhig bewegt section analogous to the minor variation of classical sets. In the A section, Hindemith picks out individual notes from his model. (Observe, by the way, that he is careful to repeat the A section (in the orchestra), as the theme demands. This repetition is one of the strongest formal elements in the movement.) In the B section (phrases d, d′, e, e′), Hindemith picks out a motive and uses it alone; in phrases f and f′ he does the same, even though the motive is reduced to nothing more than two notes (B–A) or to the three-note close, D–B–D.

In the bottom system, I have shown a few selected step-progression patterns to illustrate two characteristic procedures in this period: (1) the tightly constructed bass voice; (2) the complex organization of the solo part in the short *einleiten* (introductory) passage just after letter L, where everything melodic converges on the D major triad five measures after L. In the solo part this happens three different ways: line from above, line from below, and diminished-triad arpeggiation. The bass is also involved, albeit over an open span of several measures (E♭2–D2).

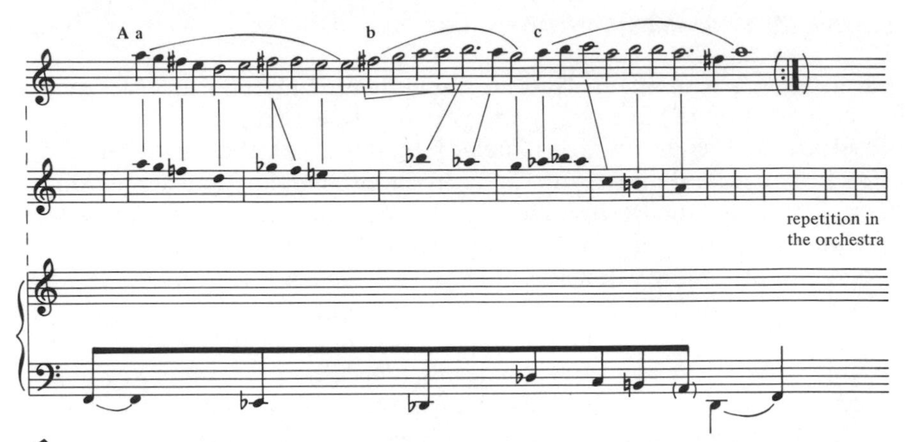

Example 9.4a: *Der Schwanendreher,* III, fifth variation, partial melodic analysis (Stage V)

Example 9.4b: *Der Schwanendreher*, III, fifth variation, beginning

TRAUERMUSIK (1936)

The history of the *Trauermusik* for viola and string orchestra demonstrates the richness of the compositional environment created by *Mathis*, and how near it lay to the surface of Hindemith's life during the late thirties. He traveled to London on January 19, 1936, to play a series of concerts (including a radio broadcast) for the BBC. King George V died the next day, which made the broadcast of the sometimes bumptious *Schwanendreher* inappropriate. Nothing else could be found, and Hindemith decided to write an occasional piece, which he did on the afternoon of the twenty-first. The new composition was performed over BBC radio on January 22nd.[3]

Hindemith wrote to his wife that the piece "is not exactly highly original, but—considering the speed at which it was done—I couldn't go off on voyages of discovery. . . . [It is] a little Mathis, a little 'Lindlein,' and at the end a chorale."[4] A modest assessment of a striking, enduring work—and a considerable compositional and technical feat. Hindemith often wrote quickly, in part because of a Mozartian ability to compose quantities of music in his head before committing anything to paper; but that he could produce in a day a piece as polished and as convincing in its expression as *Trauermusik* is due at least as much to the thoroughness with which the *Mathis* idiom had imbedded itself in his musical consciousness and the consequent ease with which he could draw on it for new creative endeavors.

Trauermusik is divided into four short movements (cyclically related) spanning about nine minutes; it resembles not a concerto but a baroque

3. Letter to Willy Strecker, 23 Jan. 1936, in Dieter Rexroth, ed. *Paul Hindemith: Briefe,* 159.

4. Letter to Gertrude Hindemith, 23 Jan. 1936, in Rexroth, *Hindemith: Briefe,* 160.

chamber sonata. The first two movements are in slow tempi of differing characters: the first combines qualities of sonata movement and slow march, the second is a rather solemn pastorale. The third movement expands the theme of the second in a few dramatic development-like phrases before ebbing away in a soft coda that prepares for the final movement's chorale, "Für deinen Thon tret ich hiemit," given by the orchestra with cadence elaborations by the solo viola.

"A little Mathis" refers to the first movement in particular, which owes a great deal to the Grablegung of the Symphony. The rhythmic relationship is evident in the opening phrases (ex. 9.5). A less obvious relationship

Example 9.5a: *Trauermusik*, I, beginning

Example 9.5b: *Mathis der Maler* Symphony, II (Grablegung), beginning

is to the first phrase of the chorale (ex. 9.6). Hindemith used the theme again for the "Trauermusik" of the Trumpet Sonata (1939), where the melodic succession is the same in the first phrase, but the rhythms have been changed (though the broken legato style is maintained). There is also a debt to the 1936 *Trauermusik*: the Trumpet Sonata ends with a chorale, "Alle Menschen müssen sterben."

"A 'little Lindlein' "—by which Hindemith means the second movement of *Schwanendreher*—refers to the construction of the chorale movement, which is the same as that of the first statement of the Lindlein tune in *Schwanendreher* (II, mm. 35–63). More than that, the reference to *Schwanendreher* means the rhapsodic, personal voice of the viola solo. If it was the medieval Musikant telling bright tales in *Schwanendreher*, here the viola is the subdued voice of the mourner. One further reference Hindemith did not mention is his letters: *Trauermusik* was a tribute to Britain's dead king, but it was equally a homage to its living composer laureate, Ralph Vaughan Williams. The ease and sureness with which Hindemith blends his own personal style with that of the English folklore symphonist is to my mind the crowning grace of this composition.

The tonal design of the whole is given in figure 9.3. This design unites the movements in a single large gesture. Motion is away from the tonic through other degrees, returning in the third movement though not stabilized, and resting in the chorale (the only movement with a closed tonal structure). There are also cyclical references: the upper leading-tone goal of the first period of I is the tonal point of departure for III (and permits

Example 9.6: *Trauermusik*, IV, beginning ("Für deinen Tron tret ich hiemit")

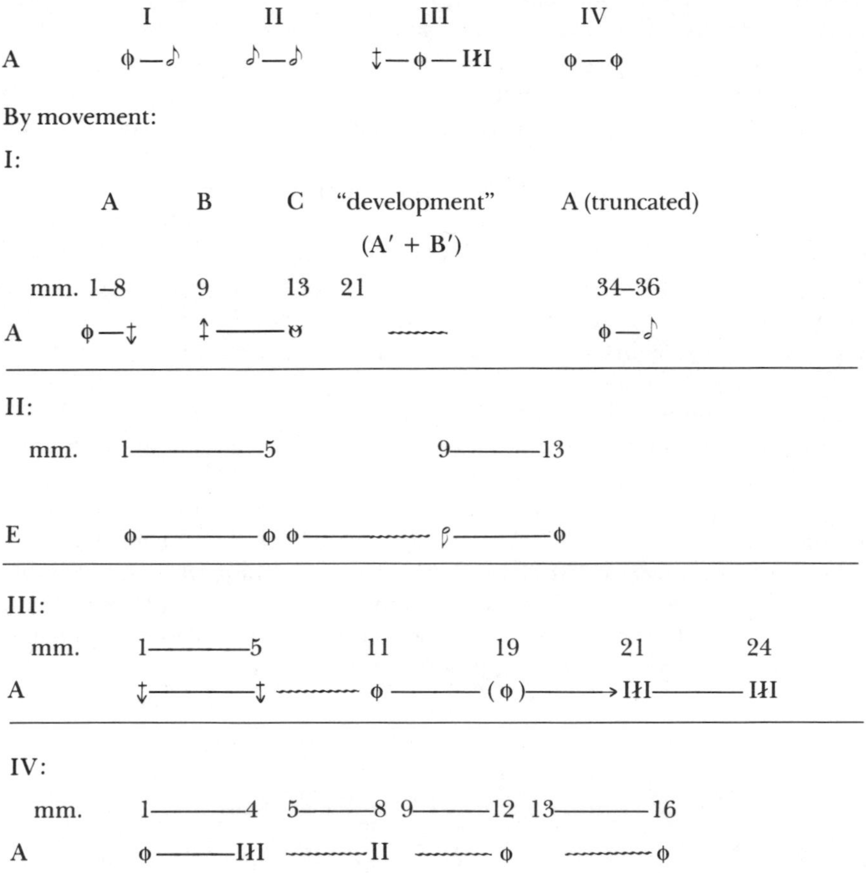

	I	II	III	IV
A	ϕ—♪	♪—♪	‡—ϕ—IƗI	ϕ—ϕ

By movement:

I:

	A	B	C	"development" (A′ + B′)	A (truncated)
mm.	1–8	9	13	21	34–36
A	ϕ—‡	‡———	℧	--------	ϕ—♪

II:

mm.	1———5		9———13	
E	ϕ———ϕ	ϕ——------	ꝭ———	ϕ

III:

mm.	1———5	11	19	21	24
A	‡———‡ --------	ϕ———	(ϕ)———→	IƗI———	IƗI

IV:

mm.	1———4	5———8	9———12	13———16
A	ϕ———IƗI	--------II	-------- ϕ	-------- ϕ

Figure 9.3: *Trauermusik*, tonal-formal scheme

statement of the theme at the level of the viola in I); the tonic reappears in II as ꝭ of the new key; the degree IƗI, reached at the end of the third movement and acting there in the old functional role of mediant substituting for tonic, returns as the goal chord of the first phrase of the chorale.

Cyclical thematic connections take place as well. I have already mentioned the possible derivation of the main theme of the first movement from the opening of the chorale. The principal theme of II is derived directly from a motive in the viola's opening gesture in I (ex. 9.7). The third movement is essentially a development-like variation of II.

Example 9.7: *Trauermusik*, I, viola entrance

In details of harmonic and melodic usage, Hindemith draws freely on the *Mathis* style, including relatively large (four-to-six note) diatonic sets, with frequent modal associations; subtle chromatic coloration of scale-tones, as evident in the viola's first gesture quoted in ex. 9.7; the rich mixture of triads and pentatonic and seventh chords; dramatic or developmental positioning of sonorities and melodic patterns based on the diminished or augmented triads; and preference for modal cadences, especially those involving the upper leading tone.

PIANO SONATA NO. 1 IN A (1936)

The appropriateness of a more-or-less traditional Schenkerian analysis of the opening viola flourish in *Schwanendreher* has already been mentioned, as has the hierarchical use of a neighbor-note figure. This motivic parallelism—binding the different structural levels by means of recurrent motives—was extremely important to Schenker;[5] and it would seem reasonable to expect that in this period, when Hindemith reimposed something like a functional harmonic system by means of the *Craft* theory, he would also pay more attention to the idea of motivic working and development, including its use on different structural levels. An excellent example of such use is found in the first movement of the first Piano Sonata,

5. Charles Burkhart, "Schenker's 'Motivic Parallelisms,'" *Journal of Music Theory* 22 (1978): 145–75.

where a detail gives the clue to interpretation of a plausible middleground and retroactively to the voiceleading structure of the main theme phrase.

The movement is in a binary form with coda in which the two parts are kept thematically distinct:

	A	B	coda
mm.	1–21	22–39	40–51
A:	ϕ—ϕ	♪—I♮I ┈┈┈┈	♪

The entire B section consists of variants of a single two-note motive, B–B♭ or A♯ (ex. 9.8). The harmonic support of the B by its lower fifth and the repetitions of the motive lend a strong leading-tone quality to the B♭, which is further emphasized at the end of the first phrase (ex. 9.9). In mm. 29–30, the motive comes to rest on A♯, which generates statements of the complete motive a half-step lower (making B♭ the main tone and A the leading note) (ex. 9.10). But at the climax of the section, mm. 32ff., the B natural is reinstated and strongly emphasized by octave doublings (ex. 9.11). The middleground representation of this section is obvious: it mimics the foreground motive (ex. 9.12).

Example 9.8: Piano Sonata No. 1 in A, I, mm. 23–24

The relationship between the openings of the two main form sections should now be clear. In both, a neighbor-note motive in the principal upper voice is embellished by subsidiary tones (above) while an alto voice moves down stepwise through a third. See example 9.13a, which gives the

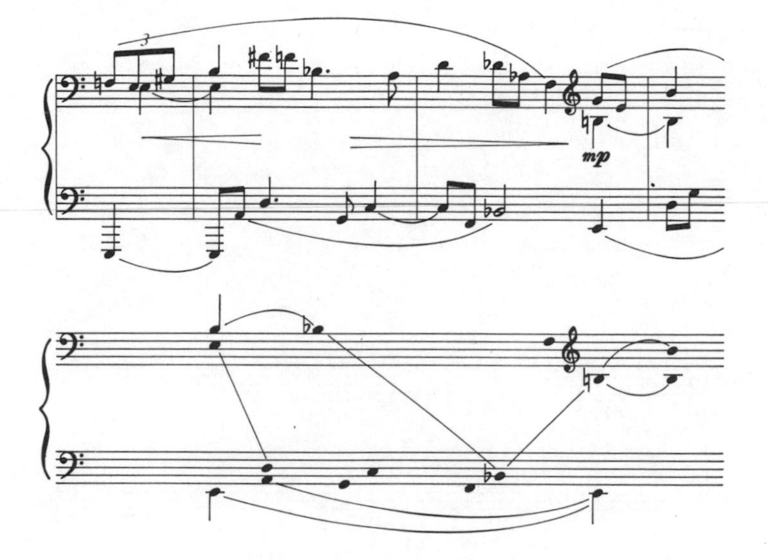

Example 9.9: I, mm. 25–27

Example 9.10: I, m. 30

Example 9.11: I, mm. 31–32

Example 9.12: I, mm. 23–39, harmony and voiceleading graph

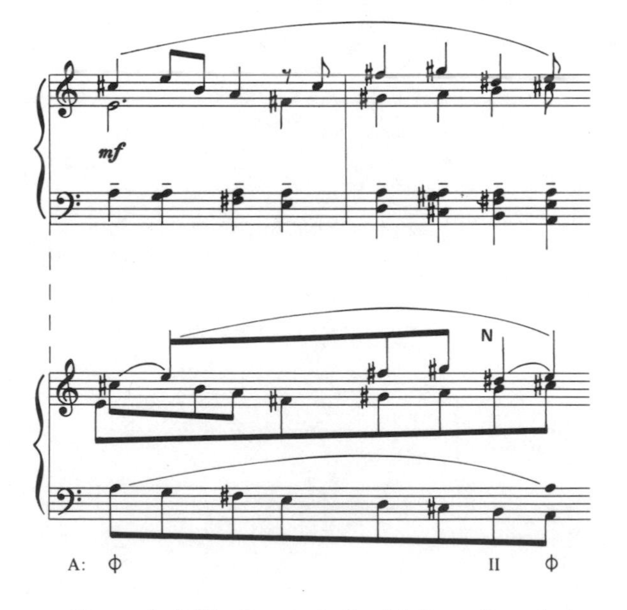

Example 9.13a: I, mm. 1–2, with Stage V analysis

opening of section A. The neighbor note is shown in the analysis E–D♯–E. The alto moves from C♯ quickly through B to A. See also example 9.13b, which gives the corresponding measures of section B. Here the neighbor-note figure is B–B♭–B, given twice, and the alto's third line is G–F♯–E. In both examples, a pedal point lurks in the lower parts, but the descending bass of section A is lacking in B, and other factors keep the two distinct: the clear period articulation, a more differentiated texture in B, and contrast of register and chord quality (tonic major in A, but dominant minor in B).

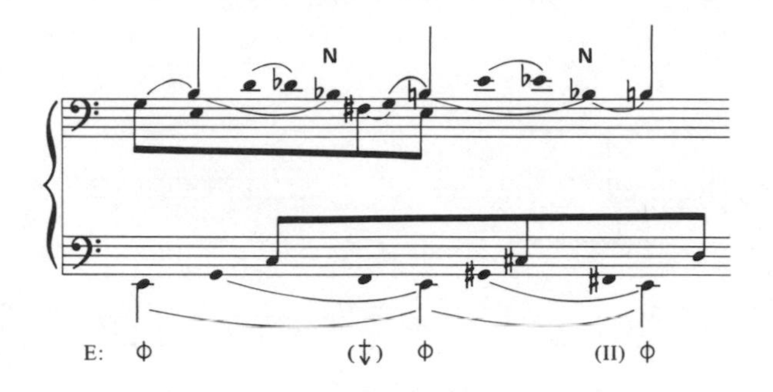

Example 9.13b: I, mm. 23–25, with Stage V analysis

Support for this reading comes from the fourth movement, which is essentially a varied recapitulation of the third. Here, however, the order of the principal sections is reversed:

	B	A	coda
mm.	1–23	24–46	47–58
A:	𝅗𝅥-----	𝅗𝅥-------	-------𝅘𝅥𝅮

The original B section is transposed down a whole step, so that the motive becomes A–G♯. The harmonic character of the motive is consistently emphasized by the addition of the fifth—below the A, but above the G♯ (ϕ – ʊ, not ϕ – ‡ relation, as before). The middleground neighbor-note area (mm. 29–32 of the first movement) is gone. In its place is a sequence built on the motive phrase but reversing the motive's direction (ex. 9.14). This leads directly to a climax which is a varied repetition of the B-section climax from the first movement (mm. 33ff.), now of course on A. The bass this time is more active. It traces a familiar whole-tone bass pattern while the right hand remains stationary (ex. 9.15). The whole-tone pattern depends from the initial A3 (A–G–F–E♭), but that E♭ is not the true goal, for it serves as the upper leading tone to D3 in m. 24, the pitch center for the first phrase of the reprise of the main theme. The A3 acts as a prolonged dominant, although the patterns that prolong it are not typically diatonic. There is

Example 9.14: IV, mm. 13–17

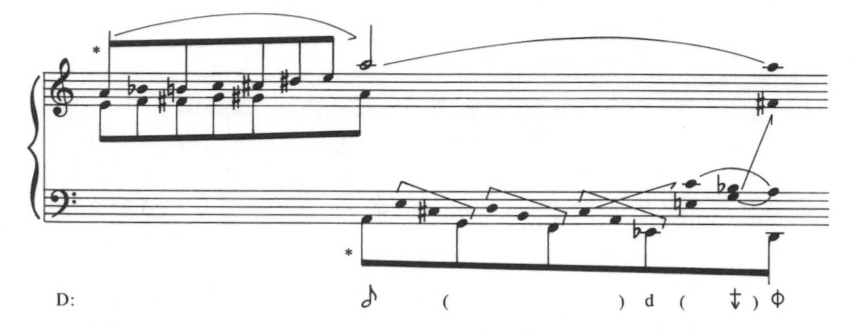

Example 9.15: IV, mm. 13–24, partial Stage IV and V analyses

also a special intervallic relationship between the soprano and bass figures in example 9.15: the bass line is the inverse of the soprano, starting from the same pitch (shown with asterisks).[6]

The transpositions Hindemith employs in the fourth movement resolve the differences between the levels of the middleground motive in the principal sections of the first movement. In sections B and A both, the motive is A–G♯–A. Like the first movement, however, the motive reverts to B–B♭–B later and closes on ♪.[7]

6. These form the pc set 5–24. For more on the set structures in this passage, see Neumeyer, "Early Music of Hindemith," 247–48.

7. The neighbor-note motive may have a connection to the sonata's tonal plan as well, which in its final form is:

	I	II	III	IV	V
		trio			
A:	ɸ–♪	IłI [IłI] IłI	‡–‡	♪–♪	ɸ–ɸ

Movements I and IV act like introductions to the more substantial II (a slow march) and V (finale). In this scheme, the upper leading-tone tonic of the scherzo (III) has the role which is usually assigned to the tritone: the point of greatest distance from the overall tonic of the Sonata, A.

Finally, I draw attention to three characteristic details of tonal-harmonic usage in the closed first section (A) of the first movement. The harmonic plan is:

mm.	1–4	5–10	11–16	17–22
A:	ф–ф–[VII] II	–[VII] ʊ	ф ··················	↕IłI ʊ VII ф
A:	ф ———— II	ʊ	ф ··················	↕ ф

First, ʊ and ↕ are used as intermediate harmonic goals—a device that also plays an important role in *Mathis, Schwanendreher,* and *Trauermusik.* Second, the three clear cadences in the section are all from VII, or distinctly modal. Chord quality in each is different, however: in m. 4, a major-major seventh; in m. 9, a minor triad (with an embellishing escape tone);[8] in m. 21, a half-diminished seventh. The last of these is particularly interesting. The pattern is relatively complex because of upper-voice motion, and Hindemith presents the chord (E–G–B♭–D) in its traditional first inversion, so that G (fifth G–D) is the root, not E (ex. 9.16). An upper leading tone appears in the soprano and a whole-tone tetrachord is outlined in the bass. Third, an even more typical combination of leading tones and chord outlining is used for the approach to the ↕-level statement of the opening phrase in mm. 17 and following (ex. 9.17). Here a diminished seventh chord appears in the upper parts (upward-facing stems beneath the bracket in the example), while a diminished triad (A–C–E♭, not bracketed) and then a secondary ↕ major triad appear in the bass. In addition to the upper leading tone, the chord at the end of m. 16 has "leading tones" to the other members of the B♭ triad: C♯–D, F♯–F. Hindemith used this device of di-

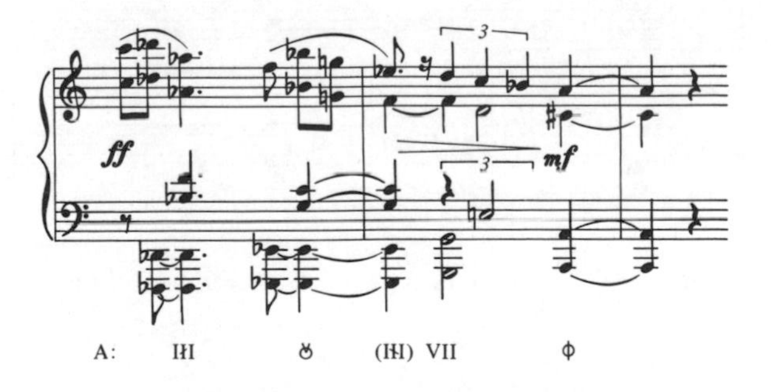

Example 9.16: I, mm. 20–22

8. This has been called an "incomplete cambiata" figure; see Friedrich Neumann, "Kadenzen, Melodieführung und Stimmführung in den *Six Chansons* und *Five Songs on Old Texts* von Hindemith," *HJB* 8 (1979): 52.

Example 9.17: I, mm. 11–18, Stage IV and V analyses

minished triad or seventh chord arpeggiation on a much larger scale and in a more complex manner to create the development section of his second sonata, first movement.

PIANO SONATA NO. 2 IN G (1936)

The first and third piano sonatas are large virtuoso pieces—"grand sonatas." The second really belongs to the Spielmusiken and has much in common with the Sonata in E for Violin (1935) and the sonatina-like set Three Easy Pieces for Cello (1938). The link to the Spielmusik is more specific than just mood or level of performance difficulty: the main theme of the first movement is fashioned from the opening of the 1928 cantata *Frau Musica* (ex. 9.18).

Example 9.18a: Piano Sonata No. 2 in G, I, beginning

Example 9.18b: *Frau Musica*, I, beginning (melody only)

Felix Salzer supplies harmonic and voiceleading graphs of the first movement in *Structural Hearing*.[9] Apart from the sorts of problems with tonal and formal hierarchies discussed in chapter 2 above, his analysis is quite serviceable. My observations will be confined to one remarkable aspect of the Sonata's structure: design by harmonic proportions.

Each of the three movements is cast in a traditional form: the first a sonata design, the second a scherzo and trio (with an unusually long reprise), and the third a slow introduction and nine-part rondo whose final refrain is excised to make way for a restatement of the last measures of the introduction (giving the movement something of the flavor of a French baroque overture). Tonal design outlines a minor triad arpeggiation from G to G:

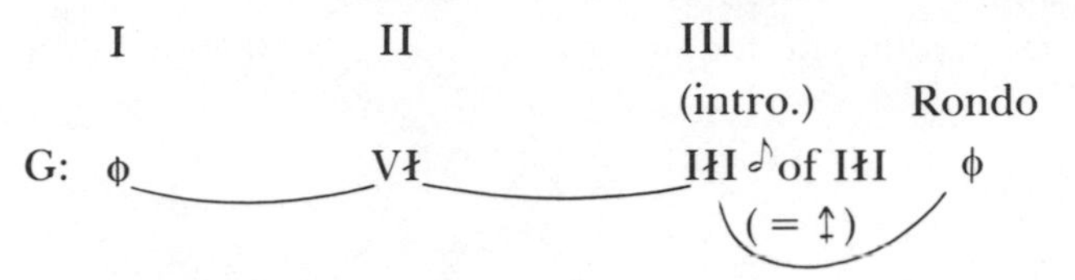

In the first movement, the one unusual feature (for the traditional sonata and for Hindemith as well) is the placement of the second theme in the key region VII:

	main theme	transition	second theme
mm.	1–26	26–30–33–36	41–63
G:	ɸ – ɸ	(ɸ – II – ʚ – VII)	VII – VII

	development	reprise (MT)	(ST)	(coda)
mm.	63ff.	95–107	117	130
G:	(VII – IłI – ↨ – IłI – II – VII)	ɸ – IłI	———	ɸ

The subdominant (rather than ɸ) in the reprise balances the structure to some extent, though we might have expected II, since Hindemith was more inclined toward symmetrical arrangements like that in Beethoven's Waldstein Sonata, first movement, where the second theme occurs in both mediants. In Hindemith's Flute Sonata (1936) and Horn Concerto (1949), first movements, the second theme appears in the two leading-tone degrees. (See also the mediant pairing in the episodes of the third movement, below).

9. Felix Salzer, *Structural Hearing*, vol. 2, fig. 505.

The formal design of the first movement blends the sonata plan with a proportional and symmetrical structure using primary and secondary golden section divisions (fig. 9.4). At both articulations, an error of about 1.5 percent must be allowed for: the secondary golden section falls midway in m. 61, the primary golden section midway in m. 96. Without other evidence, this discrepancy might cast doubt on the interpretation, but harmonic proportions are used throughout the Sonata, reaching their most complex and most convincing expression in the last movement.

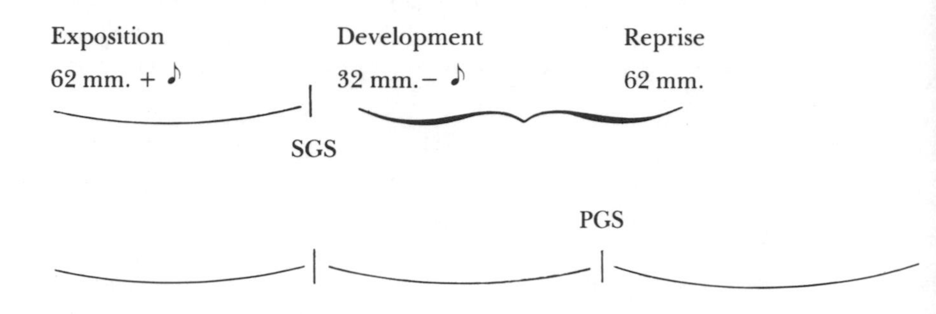

Figure 9.4: Piano Sonata No. 2 in G, I, proportions

The proportions of the first movement and its tonal action are reflected in condensed form in the first period. The period is harmonically and thematically closed:

mm. 1——10 11——16 17——26
a b
1–6 7—10 (measure totals:
G: ф–ф ♪?—II ----- IłI ----- ф——ф 10–6–10)

An alternative reading is produced if the phrases are combined slightly differently:

mm. 1—6 7——16 17——26
G: ф–ф ♪?—IłI----- ф – ф (measure totals:
6–10–10)

The symmetrical axis falls halfway through the five-eighth-note duration of the right hand's octave B4–B5 in the middle of the unstable central phrase. Even melodic shape is symmetrical: a series of eighth notes rises toward the B with a crescendo and somewhat uncertain pitch orientation on E and A (held tones); B is the climax point (forte), followed by a descent and decrescendo, the pedal point B surrendering only on the last quarter of m. 16 to a cadential ‡. Both golden section divisions for the period occur in this passage but do not coincide with points of formal articulation. The correspondence with the proportions of the whole movement is not precise, yet the impression is very much the same: a balanced musical unit with an unsettled central section framed by two thematically unified outer members governed by the tonic G.

In the second movement, the measures total 144, a number of the Fibonacci sequence. This is certainly coincidental, since the primary golden section is not articulated at all, and the secondary golden section—though at a point of strong dramatic emphasis, m. 55—does not articulate large form sections. The effect is not balance but sharp disjunction (perhaps in character for this waltz parody). The movement is nearly divided into halves:

	A	(trans.)	B	A′		
mm.	1–26	27–31	32—68	69—		—144
		(68 mm.)			(76 mm.)	
E:	ϕ – ♪	~~~~	II ~	ϕ	–	ϕ

The first half has a clear secondary golden section division: the end of section A, m. 26. In A′, primary and secondary golden sections occur within the only two fortissimo passages in the section (mm. 97 and 115–116). The result might be described as internal balance within sections set into a large structure that is ironically skewed.

The third movement has the most complex design: interlocking patterns of both golden section divisions (fig. 9.5). The calculation is based on a relation between the slow introduction and the Rondo of ♪ = 𝅝, or 138, 177, and 54 units. This does not coincide exactly with the metronome

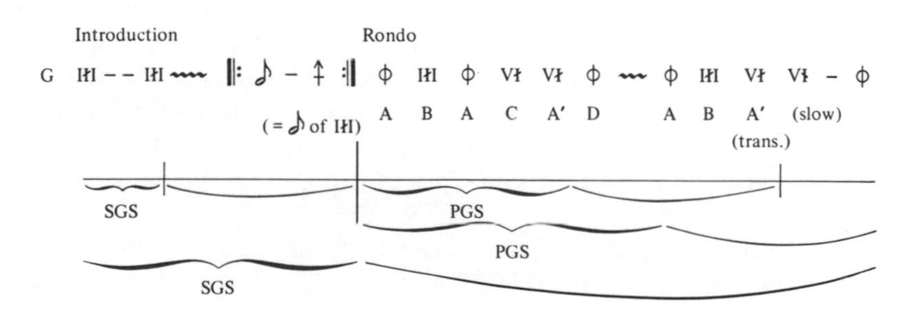

Figure 9.5: III, tonal-formal scheme and proportions

markings (♪ = 69; 𝅗𝅥 = 100–108), but does reflect a common performance tendency to take the introduction slower and the Rondo faster than indicated. In several cases, also, errors of up to two percent had to be allowed for. The symbolic (or abstract) relationships between the proportions and the tonal structure finally come clear. The secondary golden section is associated with motion away from the tonic, the primary golden section with motion toward it. In the first movement, this corresponds with the end of the exposition and beginning of the reprise. In the third, the secondary golden section divisions are in the introduction, the primary divisions in the Rondo. The high dramatic and tonal climax of the Sonata comes in the Rondo's episode D, where the theme of the introduction is given in the tonic key, and the two proportions are reconciled.

PIANO SONATA NO. 3 IN B♭ (1936)

The opening two-phrase period of the third Piano Sonata was discussed under the Stage V heading in chapter 3, including a critique of Felix Salzer's analysis of the passage. The third Sonata, like the first, is laid out on a broad canvas. Its tonal scheme is quite reserved, however:

	I	II	III	IV
B♭:	ϕ	ϕ	℘	ϕ

The first movement is a sonata design of moderate length, with a main theme whose pentatonic arpeggiations, rhythms, and chords emphasizing major thirds combine to give it a vaguely English and folk quality. The second theme uses the first as its accompaniment and in the reprise returns first, creating a symmetrical design:

	Exposition	Development	Reprise	Coda
	MT trans. ST		ST PT (and PT + ST)	
B♭:	ϕ ------- ↕—	(VII) -------	↕ --- ϕ ————————	ϕ

As the diagram shows, the tonal scheme pairs the two leading tones in parallel positions in exposition and reprise, another aspect of the symmetry. The return of the main theme is altered considerably to take advantage of the contrapuntal possibilities suggested by the combination of main theme and second theme. After a short canonic passage (as if a stretto) there follows a bit of invertible counterpoint that puts the main theme above and the second theme below.

The second movement, a scherzo, is as substantial as the first. Its tonal argument is direct and, with its closed sections related by mediants, typical of the traditional scherzo and trio:

	A: scherzo			B: trio	A (truncated)
	a	"b"	a		
B♭:	ɸ – ↥	-----	ɸ – ɸ		
	ɸ ———		ɸ	I♮I ——— I♮I	ɸ ——— ɸ

The tonal plan of the scherzo proper is also typical, not in degree succession but in placement and definition of tonal areas. This is more serious a piece than many of the clever, but slight, scherzi of the forties, though it does not have the massive proportions or Chopin-like somberness of the first Sonata's scherzo, which tends to dominate that work.

Like the first Sonata, the third has a slow march, but this is less funereal. There is more motion and variety of texture and color and a more complicated structure:

	A (march)	B (fugato)	C trans.	A	C coda
	(coda)			(extended)	
E♭:	ɸ – II ↧ – II ——↥	♪ ---------	♪ -------	ɸ	ɸ (V♮) ɸ

The final movement, which has the only grand fugue in Hindemith's solo piano music, uses the whole of the B section from the march as its second subject:

	Subj. 1	episode	Subj. 2	Subj. 2	Subj. 1	Coda:
				+ episode		Subjs. 1 and 2
B♭:	ɸ	↥	ɸ ——— ↧	↧ -----------	♪	ɸ ——— ɸ

Notice the cyclic use of degrees in this tonal scheme: the leading tones from the first movement, the ♪ from the march. This is a device Hindemith used frequently, and it is related to the microcosmic presentation of the tonal design of a movement in its first period. When expanded to the scale of this Sonata, the hierarchical system of tonal references is not far removed from the abstract tonal symbolism of *Ludus Tonalis* or *Marienleben II*.

TONAL-FORMAL SCHEMES IN THE SONATA SERIES AND CHAMBER WORKS AFTER 1935

At the head of the sketches for the second Organ Sonata, first movement (1937), is the tonal scheme: e c h / as / a f e. This can easily be correlated with the main divisions of the published score of the movement, which has the character of a baroque organ concerto allegro:

Key areas:	E	C	B	/ A♭	/ A	F	E
Measures:	1–31	32–49	49–71	72–98	99–125	126–153	154–184
Material:	A	B	A′	A″	A‴	B′	A (literal reprise)

The key successions reflect Hindemith's preference, which grew stronger in the forties, for symmetrically balanced groups of keys (here, 3–1–3) and for symmetrical interval patterns (here E–C–B, which leads from E, is balanced by the transposed pattern A–F–E, which leads to E). In *A Composer's World*, he says that the successions of tonalities in a piece form a sort of "background melody" (though he doubts it can be heard).[10] He was probably alluding to patterns like the one in this movement.

The sketches for the Clarinet Quartet, first movement (1938), contain a similar scheme based on inversion: F E Cis D / F Fis A Gis / F. The score of the movement is laid out as follows:

Keys:	F	E	C♯	D /	F	F♯	A	G♯ /	F
Rehearsal numbers:		[3]	6 after [5]	[8]	4 before [12]	[13]	[14]	6 after [15]	*langsamer*
Number of measures:	35	33	32	47	19	12	16	32	31
Material:	Th1	Th2	Th3	Th2 (Dev.)	Th1 ——		Th3 ——		Th1 and 2

As we have seen in the piano sonatas, Hindemith routinely used a hierarchic network of degrees within a movement or across a multimovement composition. This procedure remained characteristic throughout his career, but the kind and degree of patterning varied. In the thirties, he employed all degrees fairly freely but gave emphasis in structural positions to the dominants and mediants.[11] After 1940, Hindemith rarely used VII and II, which appear in the Harp Sonata (1939) and the second Piano Sonata, first movement. In the forties and fifties, he gradually came to prefer the six principal tonal functions in structural positions. Some examples of his procedures:

In the first Organ Sonata (1937), the tonal scheme is:

Movement:	I	II
Key:	E♭	E — E♭
E♭:	ɸ	↧ —— ɸ

10. Hindemith, *A Composer's World*, 93.

11. In a study of sonata movements from 1935–40, Ronald Rodman has found the leading tones to be more common than I suggest here (Hindemith seminar, Indiana University, summer 1984).

The second movement is divided into three clear sections emphasizing the leading tones:

Section:	sehr langsam		phantasie		ruhig bewegt	
Key:	E ————	E	~~~~~~	D	E♭ ————	E♭
E♭:	↧ ————	↧	~~~~~~	↥	ϕ ————	ϕ

The second part of the first movement is the source of the upper leading tone:

Section:	mässig schnell		lebhaft	
Key:	E♭ ————	G	E♭ ————	E — E♭
E♭:	ϕ ————	IŁI	ϕ ————	↧ — ϕ

The third Organ Sonata (1940) similarly emphasizes the upper leading tone:

Movement:	I		II	III
Key:	A♭ ————	B	A	A♭
A♭:	ϕ ————	IŁI	↥	ϕ

There is no obvious internal justification for the tonal design of the first movement, which is in two parts, a small five-part rondo whose theme moves from A♭ to C (ϕ – IŁI) followed by a setting of "Ach Gott, wem sollt ich's klagen?" in the manner of an organ chorale.[12] In other pieces, Hindemith used an open tonal design to accentuate cyclic connections—as in the *Trauermusik* and the Trombone Sonata (1941), a thumbnail tonal sketch of which appears in his sketchbook (ex. 9.19). This scheme, which appears after all the sketches for movements I–III, but before any sketches for movement IV, is in part an analytic retrospective on the movements already completed. It also suggests that the Sonata was originally intended to have only three movements, with the *Lied des Raufbolds* as the finale. Movements I–III form a complete tonal unit—I is not tonally closed, II is closed but in D, and III mirrors I, beginning on the dominant, ending on the tonic. These movements form a strong tonal cycle to which the thematic recurrences of movement IV are appended (based on themes of I).

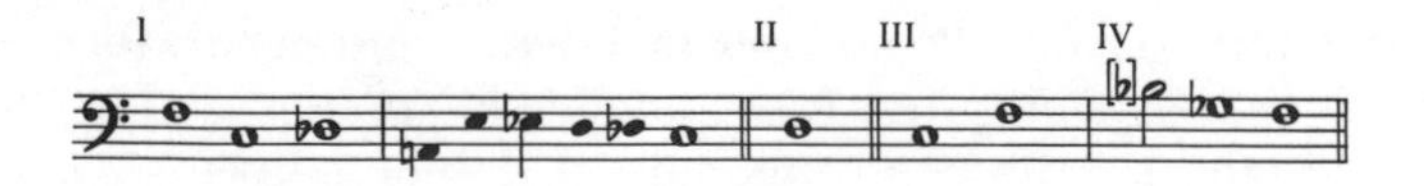

Example 9.19: Tonal-formal scheme for the Sonata for Trombone (from Hindemith's sketchbook)

12. The melody appears in *Craft II*, 158.

The three sonatas which do not end in their initial key require three different explanations. The first, the Harp Sonata (1939), has an anomalous tonal design: E♭: ɸ, II, ɸ⟶VƗ. The tonal motion of the third movement might have its source in the poem which Hindemith sets as an "instrumental recitative." The English Horn Sonata (1941) is cast in the form of a double variation set, and the tonal contrast between the themes becomes the design of the whole:

Section:	Th1	Th2	V1—Th1	V2—Th2	V3—Th1	V4—Th2
Key:	C♯	F	C♯	F	C♯	F
C♯:	ɸ	IƗI	ɸ	IƗI	ɸ	IƗI
	(ɸ	————	————	————	————	IƗI)

In the second Organ Sonata (1937), whose three movements are in E, E, and A, the first movement shows evidence in the sketches that it may have been intended to begin at the present m. 99—that is, in A.

The three sonatas from 1938 have quite similar designs. The bassoon and oboe sonatas each have two movements, the second opening in a non-tonic key region (the third movement of the Piano Duet Sonata (1938) does this, too). The Oboe Sonata, whose second movement is like a miniature *sonata da chiesa*, uses an arpeggiation pattern like that of the second Piano Sonata:

Movement:	I	II			
Section:		sehr langsam	lebhaft	sehr langsam	lebhaft
Key: G:	ɸ	VƗ	IƗI	IƗI	II —— ɸ

The design of the Bassoon Sonata shows symmetrical patterning of two mediants around the tonic:

Movement:	I	II		
		(slow)	(march)	(pastorale)
			(trio)	
B♭:	ɸ	IƗI	ɸ (VƗ) ɸ	------- ɸ

The Duet Sonata scherzo similarly uses the VƗ of VƗ in the trio.

Some sonatas stay close to the tonic. In the Viola Sonata (1939), Clarinet Sonata (1939), Two-Piano Sonata (1942), and Alto Horn Sonata (1943), only one of four or five movements is in another key. In the most common design for a three-movement work, Hindemith employs a mediant or leading-tone degree for the second movement, as in the Flute Sonata (1936; B♭–A–B♭), Horn Sonata (1939; F–D–F), Violin Sonata (1939; C–E–C), and Cello Sonata (1948; E–C♯–E). This design is used as well for the closely related final pair of sonatas in the series, the Double Bass Sonata

(1949; B–A–B) and the Tuba Sonata (1955; B♭–C♯–B♭). The final movement of the latter—a variation set—is based on the same degrees:

Section:	Th	V. 1	2	3
Key: B♭:	ϕ (or I‡I / ϕ)	I‡I	?	ϕ

Except for this parallelism, the tonal design of these sonatas is not characteristic of the period. The Sonata for Four Horns (1952) is more typical:

Movement:	I	II	III: Th	V. 1	2	3	4
B♭:	ϕ—♪	ϕ—ϕ	ϕ–♪	‡	ʊ	♪	ϕ

The keys for the four variations in the third movement are those given by Hindemith in sketch notations. Here there is some parallelism (movement I and the theme of III), restriction to the principal tonal functions, and symmetry in the tonal patterns of III.

A more strikingly symmetrical design is the one used in the Wind Septet (1948):

Movement:	I	II	III	IV	V
E♭:	ϕ	ϕ→‡	II	‡→ϕ	ϕ

The symmetry is brought out by the fact that IV is a literal retrograde of II.

If we can generalize about Hindemith's planning of large-scale tonal design, we might say that in the thirties he sometimes used a tight structure and sometimes allowed development in the course of composition. In the forties he gradually controlled the design more and more closely, so that by 1950 a tonal design which does not exhibit both parallelism and symmetry is unusual.

WHITMAN REQUIEM ("WHEN LILACS LAST IN THE DOORYARD BLOOM'D" [1946])

In the *Symphonic Metamorphosis of Themes by Weber* (1943), Hindemith expanded variation technique even further than in the *Four Temperaments* or the English Horn Sonata. This orchestral piece, whose popularity rivals that of the *Mathis* Symphony, is a grand fantasy on several short piano and orchestral pieces by Weber—variation and elaboration on a large scale. The second movement, the "Turandot" scherzo, is a cosmopolitan tour de force: a Chinese melody quoted by Rousseau and used by Weber for incidental music to an oriental play by Schiller is used by Hindemith in America to create, among other things, a fugato with a jazzlike subject!

The evident power of reflection on historical musics on Hindemith's creative imagination in *Mathis der Maler* carries over into, and is gradually refined in, the later music quite as much as any specific technique of melody or harmony. In the second movement of Sinfonia Serena (1946), he applies the Weber technique to Beethoven, making a brilliant paraphrase for winds out of a small march. But it is fair to say that he tends more and more to turn the eye of reflection onto his own music—in the revisions of the forties especially. This technique is of course closely related to the "immediate" contemplation by means of which the final tableaux of *Mathis* were written; that is, building larger structures on the basis of earlier pieces of his own. In *Harmonie der Welt,* Hindemith followed the same procedure as in *Mathis,* and several years earlier (1946) he had used it to generate the Whitman Requiem from a song written in 1943 ("Sing on there, in the swamp," no. 8 in the collection *Nine English Songs* [1944]), which was itself a reworking of a German-language setting from 1919.[13] The "Lilacs" Requiem, as it is often called, was commissioned by Robert Shaw and is Hindemith's only profoundly American work, written at the time when his feelings for his adopted country were strongest (he and his wife became naturalized citizens in the same year). He chose a text from Whitman's *Memories of President Lincoln* appropriate to his purpose—a musical elegy for war dead—and his sensitive reading of that text achieves a masterful synthesis with the musical design (fig. 9.6).

The mezzo-soprano arioso (section 5) is an orchestration of the song from the 1944 collection transposed down a whole step. The analytic graphs of example 9.20 give a complete five-stage reading of the arioso. The essential harmonic motions are very few: an extended tonic prolongation at the opening, an arpeggiated degree progression leading to an area of uncertain tonal definition settling on IłI (with fifth doubling to keep the tonal orientation clear while the chord values fluctuate with the melodic activity), then returning more quickly by arpeggiation to the tonic. If we accept the F of m. 8 as a harmonic center, the arioso is split into two parts with mirroring arpeggiations: mm. 1–8, A–D–F; mm. 9–16, C♯–E–A.

The very slow tempo permits considerable harmonic nuance, but Hindemith did not exploit this to produce complex surface-chord progressions. Instead, as in the opening of the revised "Mariä Verkündigung" from *Marienleben,* he concentrated on fine shadings of the pentatonic sonorities (ex. 9.21). The falling minor third in this example is an ancient musical emblem for a birdcall, used here for the poem's thrush.

The melodic progress through the arioso is an excellent example of the technique of opening registers (E4, A4, E5) associated with notes of the tonic chord and notes of those registers associated with harmonic and expressive events: chromatic movement upward from the fourth E4–A4 to B♭4–E♭5, then C5–E♭5 in m. 8, regaining E5 (with B4) in m. 9, and B4 closing to A4 in m. 13 (upper register) or 14 (middle register).

13. This setting is the second of the Drei Hymnen, Op. 14 (1919), which have been published in Kurt von Fischer, *Klavierlieder I.*

Text Incipit	No. of Lines	Whitman's Section	Hindemith's Section	Music
—	—	—	—	orchestral prelude
"When lilacs"	6	1	1	baritone arioso
"O powerful"	5	2	—	chorus
"In the dooryard"	6	3	—	baritone arioso
"In the swamp"	8	4	2	mezzo-soprano arioso
"Over the breast"	7	5	3	March, part A
"Coffin that passes"	11	6	—	part B
"Here, coffin"	11	6, last 2 lines; 7	—	baritone arioso
"O western orb"	11	8	4	baritone and chorus
"Sing on there"	5	9	5	mezzo-soprano arioso
"O how shall"	3	10	6	baritone song
"Sea-winds"	2	—	—	chorus
"These and with"	5	10, last 2 lines; 11	—	baritone song
"Pictures of"	3	—	—	chorus
"With the sweet"	5	—	7	introduction and
"Lo, body and soul"	10	12	—	fugue
"Sing on, sing on"	9	13	8	mezzo-soprano song
"Now while I sat"	11	14	—	baritone recitative
"And I knew death"	4	—	—	Hymn: "For those we love"
"I fled forth"	12	—	—	baritone recitative and mezzo-soprano song: "Sing on, sing on"
"Come lovely and soothing Death"	28	—	9	Death Carol
"To the tally"	8	15	10	baritone arioso
—	—	—	—	(orchestral interlude)
"And I saw"	3	—	—	baritone arioso
"And carried"	3	—	—	chorus
—	—	—	—	(orchestral interlude)
"I saw battle"	4	—	—	baritone arioso
"They themselves"	4	—	—	chorus
—	—	—	—	(orch. interlude: "Taps")
"Passing the visions"	20	16	11	baritone arioso
"Lilac and star and bird"	2	—	—	chorus, baritone, mezzo-soprano

Figure 9.6: Whitman Requiem, Hindemith's and Whitman's plans reconciled

On the largest structural level, the arioso supplies the principal tonalities for the Requiem, though the relation of A and C♯ is reversed:

Nos.	1	2	3	4	5	6	7	8	9	10	11
keys:	C♯ ——			A ——			A–E	C	F	?–F♯-B♭	C♯

The material of the first mezzo arioso (no. 2) is based entirely on no. 5 (though the effect in performance, of course, is exactly the opposite). The thrush motive is present, but harmonized by C♯, not A, and the English horn offers the opening material of the original song transposed to C♯ (ex. 9.22). The whole step of the song, A4–B4–A4 (mm. 2–3 of example 9.21), provides the first gesture of the voice part G♯–A♯–G♯ in example 9.23, which is expanded in the following measure. This expansion forms the basis for the opening figure of the mezzo's other thrush song at the beginning of no. 8 (ex. 9.24).

Despite the change of key, the registral framework of no. 2 is the same as that of no. 5, with the addition of C♯4 below (a register exploited in no. 2

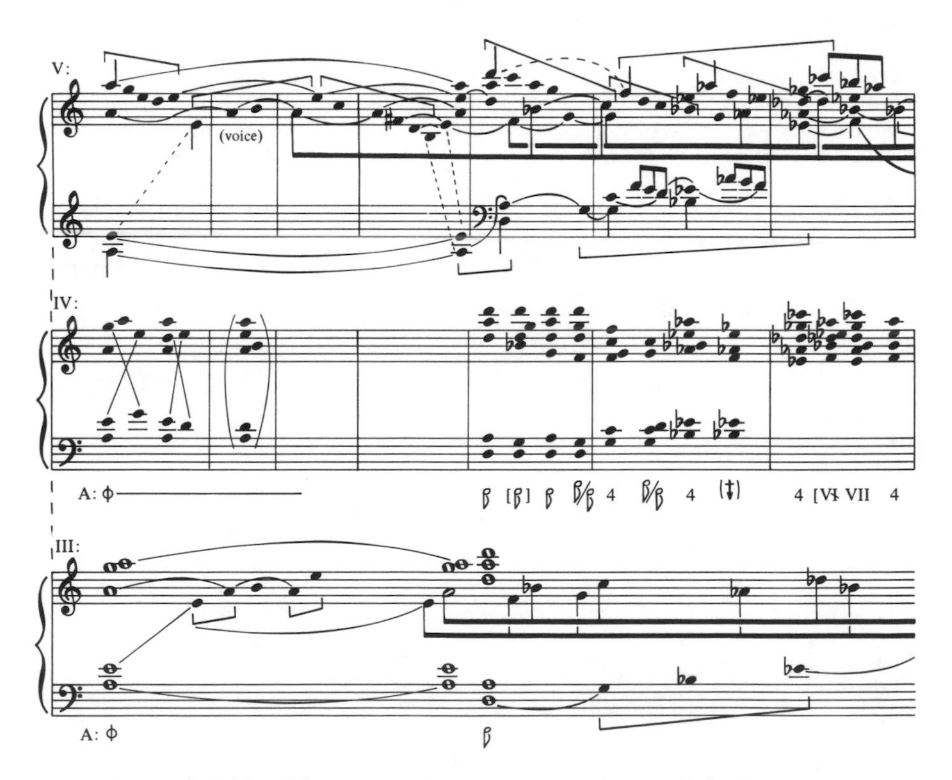

Example 9.20: Whitman Requiem, No. 5, complete analysis (Stages I–V)

Example 9.20: *Continued*

but not in the original, though its source is B3 in m. 4). The high register in both numbers is E5.

The materials of no. 2 can be traced in no. 1 (again, opposite to the perception in performance). The first baritone arioso has two distinct sec-

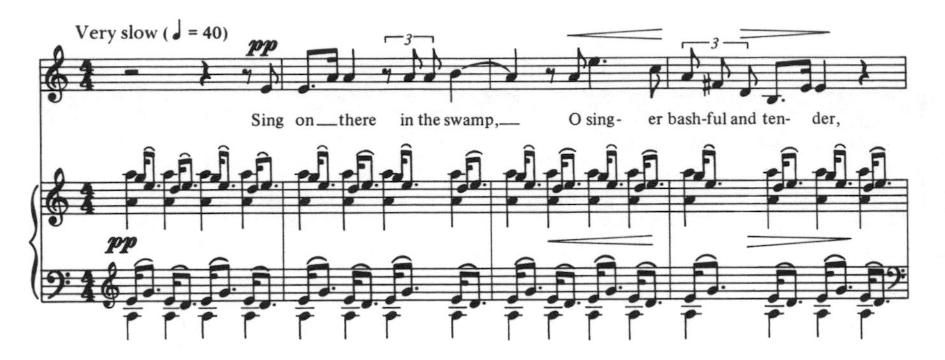

Example 9.21: Whitman Requiem, No. 5, mm. 1–4

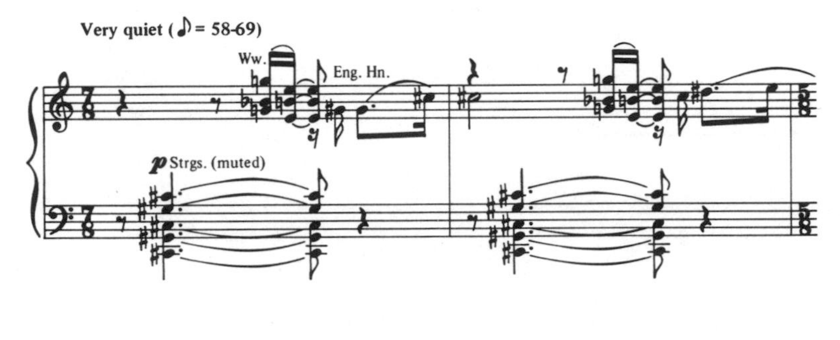

Example 9.22: Whitman Requiem, No. 2, mm. 1–5

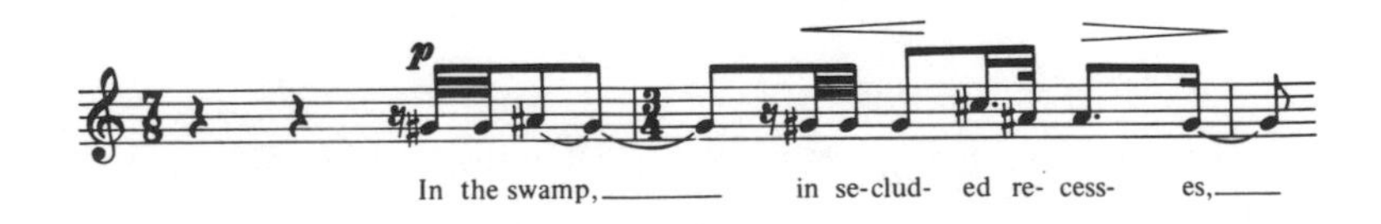

Example 9.23: Whitman Requiem, No. 2, mm. 5–7 (voice part)

Example 9.24: Whitman Requiem, No. 8, beginning (voice part)

tions: mm. 1–10 and 11–14. The first section is in C♯, though ending indefinitely; the second is in E. The minor third motive is first introduced in the second section (ex. 9.25), gradually prepared by the orchestra in mm. 6 and following. The baritone states but does not emphasize this interval in these measures, which serve as the source material for the later recitatives and ariosi of the baritone-narrator. The minor third becomes increasingly important in the process (see the end of no. 8 and nos. 10 and 11). The baritone gives the whole step C♯–B to stress the relation of the three words "lilac," "star," and "thought," and concentrates almost entirely on the tones E3–G3–B3–C♯4. In the reprise of this material at the close of no. 1, the orchestra plays a C♯-minor triad below, resulting in the figure which opens no. 2 and the indefinite third relation $\frac{\text{IƗI}}{\phi}$.

Going back one step further, in the Prelude the indefinite relation is exploited as the basic tonal-harmonic procedure. A pedal point C♯ sounds throughout the fifty-four measures. A repeated F major triad ($\frac{\text{IƗI}}{\phi}$) is sounded against it first; when other parts are added, the resolution tone E (the whole melodic figure in A–C–F–E)[14] is usually harmonized by a chord whose root is A. For the first formal section (mm. 1–22), then, the harmonic control is a compound indefinite relation: $\frac{\text{VƗ}}{\frac{\text{IƗI}}{\phi}}$. At m. 30, after an

Example 9.25: Whitman Requiem, No. 1, m. 11

14. This reappears in the baritone arioso to set the words "the western sky" (m. 4).

extended crescendo with trills, dissonant sonorities, and major-triad outlines in the upper part at minor-third transpositions, C♯ is given alone (with multiple doublings), forte-fortissimo (reminiscent of the climax of the first movement of Bartók's *Music for Strings, Percussion, and Celesta*). In the following measure, an E minor triad is sounded against the C♯ by the brass producing the $\frac{I\nmid I}{\phi}$ relation and the essential sonorities of the baritone arioso.

The rhythm of the minor third motive has its own role later in the composition, notably in the middle section of the mezzo-soprano's song "Sing on, sing on," where it appears in the orchestra as ($\frac{12}{8}$) 𝄽 ♪♩ 𝄾 𝄽 ♪♩ 𝄾| linked to half steps. At the end of the "Death Carol" (no. 9), the chorus uses the broken legato and short-long rhythm with falling fourths and half steps for "with joy to thee, O death" (followed by an orchestral coda of eight measures). In the final passage of the Requiem (the second part of no. 11), the rhythmic figure is used for "Lilac and star and bird."

The falling thirds of mm. 3–4 in the original song have motivic significance in no. 2, as we might expect, and also much later, in the opening section (mm. 1–49) of no. 10 (ex. 9.26).[15] These "iso-interval" chains may derive from a passage in the Grablegung movement of the *Mathis* Symphony (mm. 14–16), but they also appear in earlier pieces.[16]

The melody with which the baritone opens no. 1 begins as a combination of the Prelude's arpeggiations and the cadence figure of the first section of the original song (ex. 9.27) and is developed on the basis of this material. This is the principal theme of the first main division of the Requiem (nos. 1–3); anything not based on the mezzo-soprano arioso is derived

Example 9.26: Whitman Requiem, No. 10, beginning

15. Even the figure minor-third perfect-fourth (D4–B3–E4) with the rhythm ♩. ♬ ♩ (or elsewhere ♪♩) is important and is reused in no. 1, mm. 2 and 24–26; no. 4, m. 8; no. 6, mm. 8ff., 40–41, and in other places.

16. *Iso-interval chains* is a term used by Hans Ludwig Schilling, *Paul Hindemiths "Cardillac"*.

Example 9.27: Whitman Requiem, No. 1, mm. 1–2 (voice part)

from it. In no. 1, the chorus repeats the theme as section B (on I-I), and the orchestra gives it in the third section, the baritone catching up after two measures. The March (no. 3, part A) uses the opening motive (less the cadential fourth) in the same key. The second (choral) section of no. 3 is based on a new theme which is a combination of the March's fifth figure (G♯–C♯–G♯) and the major second of the arioso (ex. 9.28). This new theme, in turn, is the basis for the theme of no. 4 and eventually the fugue subject of no. 7.[17]

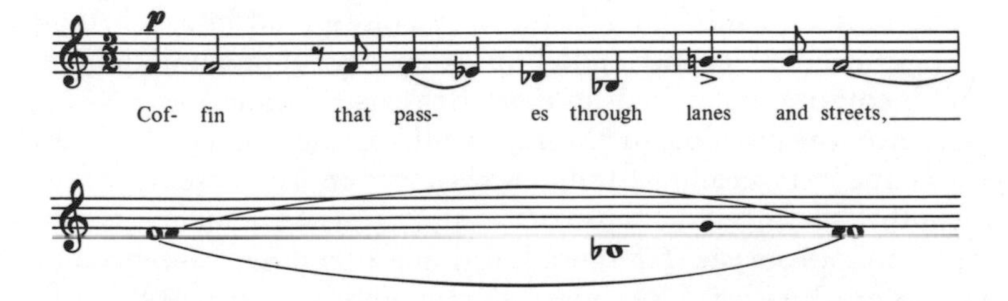

Example 9.28: Whitman Requiem, No. 3, theme of part B

The uncharacteristically tight motivic-thematic integration of the Requiem is a compound of the generative method Hindemith used in its composition and the consistent mood and recurrent imagery of Whitman's text. The Requiem is the last stage in the refinement of this aspect of the romantic reconciliation of *Mathis*. In later works, Hindemith adds nothing essentially new. Even here in his American masterwork, this refinement represents a special case. Organic unity as motivic integration, like expressionistic techniques Hindemith had used twenty-five years earlier, was a tool, not a fundamental aesthetic outlook.

17. In the march-like orchestral interludes of no. 10, this theme is gradually transmuted into "Taps."

TEN

THE PLAY OF TONES: ON THE *LUDUS TONALIS*

The *Ludus Tonalis* stands at the center of Hindemith's career. It was composed in 1942, twenty-one years after his great success with the String Quartet, Op. 16, at the first Donaueschingen contemporary music festival, and twenty-one years before his final work and death in 1963. The fluid and beautiful contrapuntal writing, expert craftsmanship, and convincing structural logic of this fugue cycle have made it for many people the quintessential Hindemith. Its connection to his views on compositional technique and its theoretical underpinnings, furthermore, is especially intimate. The *Ludus Tonalis* began as a simple collection of small three-voice keyboard fugues,[1] but once Hindemith decided that the key sequence would be based on his Series 1, the work blossomed into a large-scale, tightly organized cycle, and a much more successful practical demonstration of his compositional theories than the revised *Marienleben*.

The usual translation of the Latin title as the "Game of Tones" or "Tonal Game" is misleading. A high wit is never entirely absent from any of Hindemith's works, but the sense of "game" as an amusement—something trivial—is inappropriate. Hindemith did not intend his composition to be humorous or whimsical.[2] He chose *ludus* from the numerous titles used for medieval liturgical dramas. Thus, *Ludus Tonalis* is "Play of Tones," not a game but a musical drama whose tensions derive from those Hindemith understood as inherent in the dynamic interaction of degrees with a governing tonic: a sixty-minute musical dramatization of his notion of intratonal relations. The narrative is the working out of these tensions in the successive fugues, each of which personifies one of the twelve chromatic

1. Bernhard Billeter, ed., *Paul Hindemith: Sämtliche Werke* V/10: *Klavierwerke II* (Mainz: Schott, 1981), xii.

2. On the other hand, the little unpublished piece for clarinet and cello called "Ludus minor" (1944) suggests that "ludus" can be equated with the German "Spiel" and carry connotations of all three senses of "play": musical performance (Vorspiel or Spielmusik), theatrical play, and game. See also the *Ludi Leonum*, an exemplar of the published *Ludus Tonalis* decorated with drawings by Hindemith (two pages appear in facsimile in *Zeugnis in Bildern*, 72–73).

degrees. The interludes, like entr'actes, are positioned between the fugues, and the whole argument is summarized in prologue and epilogue, the Praeludium and Postludium.

Hindemith's own subtitle—"Studies in Counterpoint, Tonal Organization, and Piano Playing"—is also misleading insofar as it draws attention away from the dramatic character of the cycle toward the relatively mundane technical problems of counterpoint and piano playing. The fugues may be contrapuntal studies, the toccata-like interludes may be studies in pianistic idioms, each individual piece may be a special study in tonal organization; but the true subject of this fugue cycle is the translation of Hindemith's theoretical conception of tonal order and tonal dynamics into the language most suitable to him—into music itself. That he chose a relatively colorless medium like the piano for this endeavor shows his determination to avoid the "merely colorful" and to concentrate on essentials: the generation of musical motion and tonal order, the reconciliation of melodic activity and harmonic basis, of pitch design and formal structure.

Ludus Tonalis consists of twenty-five individual pieces: twelve fugues, eleven interludes, Praeludium, and Postludium. The fugues, one for each chromatic degree, are the core of the cycle, their sequence determined by Series 1 (with C as tonic). The types range from "single" (not employing any unusual devices) to stretto, double, triple, and mirror fugues.[3] Three fugues (A, E, E♭), like the mirror fugue (D♭), use the inverted subject. The fugue in B♭ uses various transformations of the subject (inverse, retrograde, retrograde inverse, augmentation) in stretti. The fugue in B is actually an accompanied two-part canon. None of the fugues has a consistently maintained countersubject, although in the fugue in C the second subject serves as countersubject for the third, and in the fugue in F♯ statements are paired and overlapped in such a way that the subject tail takes on the character of a countersubject.

FUGUES:

C: triple fugue; second subject is countersubject to the third; closing section combines the three themes.

G: uses stretto.

F: mirror fugue; retrograde—the second half is the first half in reverse with no melodic inversion.

A: double fugue; first subject inverted; closing section combines the two themes.

3. Hindemith listed his contrapuntal devices in the sketches; see Billeter, *Klavierwerke II*, xiii.

E: inverted subject.
E♭: inverted subject.
A♭: simple fugue; closes on degree IłI.
D: simple fugue.
B♭: stretto fugue; inverse, retrograde, retrograde inverse, augmentation of subject, combined in several stretti.
D♭: mirror fugue; second half is first half with texture inversion and melodic inversion of individual parts; coda added.
B: accompanied two-part canon.
F♯: stretto fugue.

Formal structures and expressive character in the fugues are as varied as the procedures used, in keeping with Hindemith's attitude toward fugue.[4] He particularly rejected the academic fugue, that "whole miserable collection of unmusical formulas—the dreary and lifeless pasting together of 'expositions' and 'episodes,' " and insisted that "there is no single hard-and-fast style that must be followed in fugues any more than in other musical forms."[5]

The interludes are generally constructed so that they modulate from the key of the preceding fugue to that of the one following, but they are also designed to complement the character of the fugues and to move the broad dramatic argument forward. Although we could extract several fairly convincing baroque-like prelude-and-fugue pairs, the interludes are meant as much to flow out of the fugue before as to prepare the way for the next.

The Praeludium and Postludium pair provide the dramatic prologue and epilogue. To a considerable extent the success of the composition as a cycle depends on the striking foreshadowing of its essential tonal argument in the Praeludium and the spacious, serene denouement of the Postludium. The focus of this essay is the relationship of these two pieces.

The Praeludium and Postludium, although they are associated with the interludes in the sketches for the *Ludus*, have quite a different part to play in the cycle. The Praeludium functions more nearly like an opera overture than a baroque prelude, in that it is a true prologue, giving the listener an idea of what is to follow, revealing in concise form certain essential arguments of Hindemith's "play." It provides a capsule view of the tonal space covered in the twelve fugues: the first two of the Praeludium's three sections are in C (ɸ), the third is in F♯ (ʊ). The relative status of

4. The best synopsis of formal design and fugal process in the fugues is in Günter Metz, *Melodische Polyphonie in der Zwölftonordnung* (Baden-Baden: Valentin Körner, 1976), 450–57.

5. Hindemith, *Traditional Harmony II*, 54.

these key areas is revealed by quality of tonal definition and even by the kinds of pitch materials used: diatonic pitch groups appear with the tonic, ambiguous whole-tone related sets with the tritone. The tonic is supported by its principal tonal functions, but the tritone is established through duration and position, not by tonal cadence. The end of the Praeludium is thus left open, allowing the dramatic action to proceed. That the first fugue immediately returns to C does not indicate an error in the tonal plan;[6] the Praeludium is an outline of the whole argument of the *Ludus*, and it leaves us where the fugues will eventually leave us—at the tritone.

It would be incorrect, however, to regard the Praeludium as containing the Series 1 sequence in microcosm. No orderly progression takes place from C through the various keys to F♯. The central Arioso begins and ends in C, and the shift to F♯ happens abruptly in the following cadenza (m. 33), which is an elaboration of successively smaller intervals used to move from C6 to F♯1 (diminished and perfect fifth are interchanged, however) (ex. 10.1). (The first interlude (C→G) traces the same route with almost equal abruptness in its first section, mm. 1–7, and defines the principal tonal regions the same way: C (ⴔ) with triads and clear progressions, F♯ (ʊ) with weak chord values, poor definition, and no clear cadence.[7])

Example 10.1: *Ludus Tonalis*, Praeludium, m. 33

These opening and closing pieces are cast in the shape of a multisection baroque toccata.[8] The opening section of the Praeludium has the character of a cadenza, signaling Hindemith's intention to deal with pianistic as well as tonal problems. The central Arioso strictly maintains a three-voice texture that has some contrapuntal qualities, presaging textures in the fugues, which are all in three voices. The closing section begins with a short

6. As Kemp has it: *Hindemith*, 49.

7. For more extended comments on this interlude, see my article "Hindemith's *Ludus Tonalis*," 95ff.

8. Franzpeter Goebels, "Interpretationsaspekte zum *Ludus Tonalis*," *HJB* 2 (1972): 157.

cadenza-like flourish, followed by a passage tentatively presenting the theme of the ensuing ostinato passage, essentially an extension (with harmonic embellishment) of the F♯ major triad.

Twenty pages of sketches are devoted to the Praeludium and Postludium, with fragments mingled and many sections reworked.[9] Though the general plan seems to have been determined from the outset, the parts were fitted together in several different ways, a highly unusual procedure for Hindemith. The disarray of the sketches is obviously related to the arduous compositional task Hindemith had set himself: the Postludium score, turned upside down and played backwards, was to be identical to the Praeludium score. The sketches reveal two salient points about Hindemith's experience with this unusual procedure. First, he had to experiment to make the procedure work. Second, he did not write one piece and then adjust it till it worked in reverse; he wrote both versions of the music simultaneously, line by line, measure by measure.

As is suggested by the term I adopt for this procedure, *modified retrograde mirror*, the basis is the combination of retrogradation with mirror inversion (the latter properly means texture inversion plus melodic inversion in individual parts). Hindemith, however, wanted a true mirror effect, demanding that the Postludium look the same as the Praeludium turned upside down and played backwards. The only precedents for this were certain types of canons. Texture inversion does result, but since accidentals must be retained, the melodic inversion is only by lines and spaces; exact interval sizes cannot be preserved. Pitches are moved into the opposite clef and placed on the opposite side of the staff in relation to the central line, but keep their accidentals; for example, G4–B♭4 in the treble clef becomes D♭3–F3 in the bass (ex. 10.2).

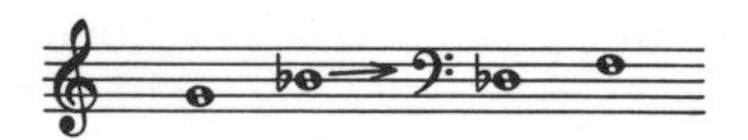

Example 10.2: Effect of the modified retrograde mirror device

Many decisions about pitch structure in both pieces were made not to secure a miniature Series 1, but to take advantage of the possibilities of this modified retrograde mirror procedure. In particular, Hindemith exploited the fact that certain pitches or pitch classes and the pitch-class (pc) content of certain intervals will remain invariant. In the first category (pitches) is C4, in the second (pcs) are all Cs, in the third (intervals) are all

9. All the sketches are reproduced in facsimile in Billeter, *Klavierwerke II*, xv–xxiv.

octaves on C and the thirds and sixths formed by D and B (in this category, the notes must have accidentals of the same type). These invariants stand out in the opening measures of the Praeludium and closing measures of the Postludium (ex. 10.3). To facilitate comparison with the Praeludium, all measure numbers in the Postludium have been calculated from the *end*, less the added measure containing the final C-major triad. The penultimate measure of the Postludium, then, is m. 1. In the example, all pcs 0 (C) remain pc 0; C5 in the right hand in m. 2 becomes C3 in the left; C2 in the Praeludium becomes C6. In the second chord of the Praeludium (m. 2, beat 2), soprano and bass form the compound sixth D♭–B♭, which is duplicated in the analogous Postludium chord. The major sixth D♭–B♭ which is the outline of the short descending run marked *x* is transposed into the fifth octave in the Postludium.

Example 10.3a: Praeludium, mm. 1–3

Example 10.3b: Postludium, mm. 1–3 (reverse numbering)

The first two notes of the two earliest versions of the opening measures also show the emphasis on invariants in the modified retrograde mirror. In both a short, sharp gesture precedes the cadenza later used to begin the final version[10] (ex. 10.4).

In addition to pitch or pc invariance, the contents of certain diatonic

10. Billeter, *Klavierwerke II*, xvi, Facsimile 4; xvii, Facsimile 6.

Example 10.4: A figure from the sketches for the Praeludium and Postludium

major scale sets (and sometimes subsets, as well) can be held invariant through the modified retrograde mirror. Although the use of diatonic scale sets seems to contradict Hindemith's insistence on the primacy of the complete chromatic scale, the evidence indicates that these sets were important factors in the composition of the Praeludium and Postludium. Of the twelve diatonic major scale sets, five hold their complete pc content invariant under the modified retrograde mirror: A♭, A, C♭ (not B), C, C♯ (ex. 10.5). The major scale is understood here as a pc set only, not as a scale belonging to a particular key or having a tonic. The letter name and mode are no more than convenient labels, implying nothing about the tonal-harmonic structure of the scale or of any passage in which one appears. This is the spirit in which Hindemith used these scale sets. They were familiar traditional formulas to which he could return as easy references for pc content.

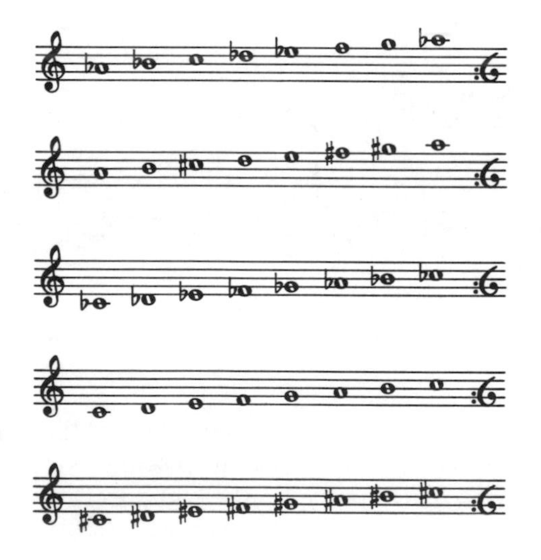

Example 10.5: Scales whose pc content remains constant under the modified retrograde mirror

Although major-scale sets or significant subsets (e.g., A♭ scale set in mm. 3–6, beat 1) are used in the opening section, compelling evidence that Hindemith treated them as references lies in the Arioso. This calm central section of both Praeludium and Postludium is constructed exclusively with the complete major-scale sets C, A♭, and A (not subsets), as the first nine measures demonstrate (ex. 10.6). In the continuation, the C major set claims mm. 23–25, beat 1, and mm. 31, beat 3, to the end, the A♭ major set taking the intervening measures. The B3 in m. 31 (D4 in the Postludium) is an anomaly, but the sketches show that these notes were originally flatted.[11]

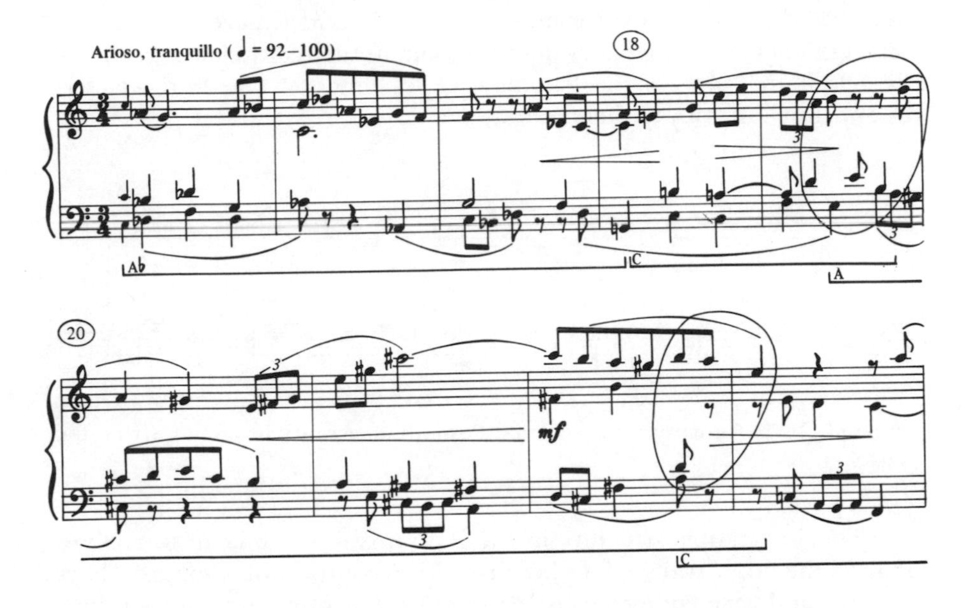

Example 10.6: Praeludium, mm. 15–23

A remarkable feature of the presentation of the sets is that shared subsets join each scale set with its successor. This interweaving occurs in both versions, so that the subsets used are also held invariant through the modified retrograde mirror. The trichord on the first half-beat of m. 18 in example 10.6, pc set (5, 7, 0), consists of all the pcs shared by the A♭ and C major sets. In the Postludium, the sonority is even identical, a quartal chord on G3. The pitches circled in m. 19, and again in mm. 22–23, form the pc set (9, 11, 2, 4), all the pcs shared by the C and A scale sets. In the

11. Billeter, *Klavierwerke II,* xx, Facsimiles 11 and 12.

Postludium, the pc content is preserved. Mm. 25 and 31 have simple chromatic steps rather than subsets to shift from the C to A♭ scale set and back.

Hindemith apparently did not begin composition of the Arioso with these scale sets as a constructive principle, but gradually arrived at them over a series of three sketches. The three are for the Postludium version, which was obviously the original.[12] A fourth sketch is the final version reversed; that is, the Praeludium Arioso. The first sketch (ex. 10.7) has the outer voices only and few hints of the diatonic character of the final version appear. The second sketch gives all but the last measures (16–14); the outer voices were composed first and the alto added. Numerous places were reworked to improve the musical substance and achieve the modified retrograde mirror. The latter intent is plain in the many changes of accidentals; in that process, the diatonic scale sets emerge. The third sketch is essentially a fair copy of the second.

Example 10.7: An early version of the Postludium Arioso, beginning (from the sketches)

Tonal-harmonic structure in the Arioso is more difficult to analyze than in the other two sections because of the contrapuntal texture, short phrases, and veiled or inconclusive cadences. The task is made easier if we recognize that the Postludium version has precedence because it was the one directly before Hindemith as he composed.

The Postludium Arioso is 19 measures long (mm. 32–14). The structure is two-part, with characteristic elongation of the second part: 8 measures and 11 measures. The same cadence and approach are used for each part, as in some traditional binary forms. The cadence is rather mild: IHI‿ϕ. Stage I is thus very straightforward.:

Measures:	32——————25	25——————14
Tonal focus:	C: ϕ	IHI‿ϕ ············ IHI‿ϕ

Harmonic movements within this tonal plan are not so clearly defined, but the short upper-voice phrases (five in each section) allow the construction

12. Billeter, *Klavierwerke II*, xix–xx, Facsimiles 9, 10, and 11.

of a workable analysis (Stage III in ex. 10.8). The most distant degree is reached about two-thirds of the way through (ʊ in mm. 21–20), a typical plan of tonal amplitude. The most characteristic feature of the surface harmony is the indefinite third relation, especially involving ♪ or ꞵ. Tonal harmonic organization can be described as exhibiting mild tension between the stability of the tonal outline (ϕ to ϕ) and clear two-part form on the one hand, and the mild cadence formula and indefinite third relations on the other. Over all this, melodic movements maintain a diatonic character based on segments of the three major-scale sets.

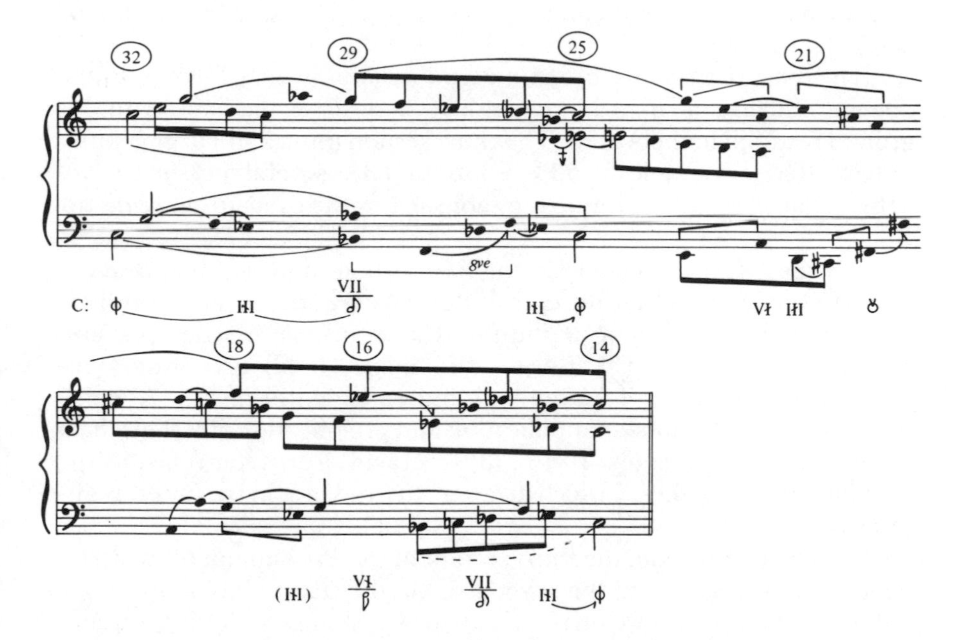

Example 10.8: Postludium, Arioso, Stage III analysis

The reversal of section durations in the Praeludium Arioso to 11 measures and 7 measures is a significant factor for analysis, as is the fact that the parallel closing cadences change position, becoming parallel phrase openings (mm. 14–17 and 25–28). The tonal-formal interaction (Stage I) thus varies considerably from that of the Postludium version (note in particular that the longer first section is now subdivided):

Measures:	15————	——19	20————	——25	26————	——32
Tonal focus:			(altern.)			
	C: ϕ	[VII] Ⅰ̶Ⅰ̶I	ϕ ꞵ		ϕ	ϕ

The surface harmonies do not exhibit such free use of the indefinite third relation; instead, more weakly defined chords and groups of secondary relations are combined with clearer intermediate cadences. As we would expect in any retrograde mirror procedure, harmonic-tonal organization is less stable than melodic activity. Chord roots and qualities and their local harmonic contexts suffer greater and more obvious change from reversal of soprano and bass and shifts in attack points and phrase lengths than do step-progressions from inversion and retrogradation (so long as both outer voices are clear, as they are here). In the Arioso, Hindemith makes few attempts to preserve harmonies under the modified retrograde mirror; it is his attempts to do so in the other sections that are of particular interest.

The Stage I structure of the entire Praeludium is as follows: in the opening cadenza, a circular progression C: ϕ—ϕ is the basis, with this ground retraced in the Arioso. The third section (mm. 33ff.) begins with a cadenza that moves quickly to F♯ (ʊ), but it takes several measures of indefinite harmony before the ʊ is established by the ostinato at *solenne* (m. 40).

A Stage III interpretation of the first section (mm. 1–14) appears in example 10.9. Its special features include: (1) concentration at registral extremes (also by duration or position) on "reproducible" pitches, pcs, and intervals: C4, C2 ↔ C6, B♭ ↔ D♭, F ↔ G; (2) diverging step-progressions in mm. 3–4 (elaborated and extended in mm. 4–7) which effect a sonorous harmonic amplification and prolongation of VII in which its third, ↕, participates (ex. 10.10); (3) several measures controlled by the indefinite third relation $\frac{♭}{\text{II}}$ which give way to a cadence in the lowest register: C♯1–C1 = ↕——ϕ.

Like the first section, the third section of the Praeludium (mm. 33ff.) exploits all the registers of the keyboard, but the changes are more rapid and more numerous. Two turns and an arpeggiation elaborating a transfer of C5 to C6 at the beginning of m. 33 are followed by a rapid descent (by means of a figure compounded of a neighbor note and a third leap) from C6 to F♯1 (see ex. 10.1). Harmonic activity is not a strong factor in this measure; the ʊ is established by position (at the end) and duration. Harmony and tonality are left deliberately ambiguous, inconclusive. F♯ gradually emerges as a tonicized degree through mm. 34–40, where the tentative announcement of the ostinato bass (which follows the equally tentative introduction in mm. 34–35 of the theme of the solenne) is coupled with pitch materials drawn from the group of whole-tone related pc sets (ex. 10.11). The cadence, when it comes, is again mild: F♯: VII‿ϕ.

The solenne section itself is essentially a series of short circular chord progressions effecting a more extended prolongation of the F♯ major triad. The difference between this section and the first in manner of tonal definition is remarkable. In the opening, C is unquestionably the tonic, yet the C

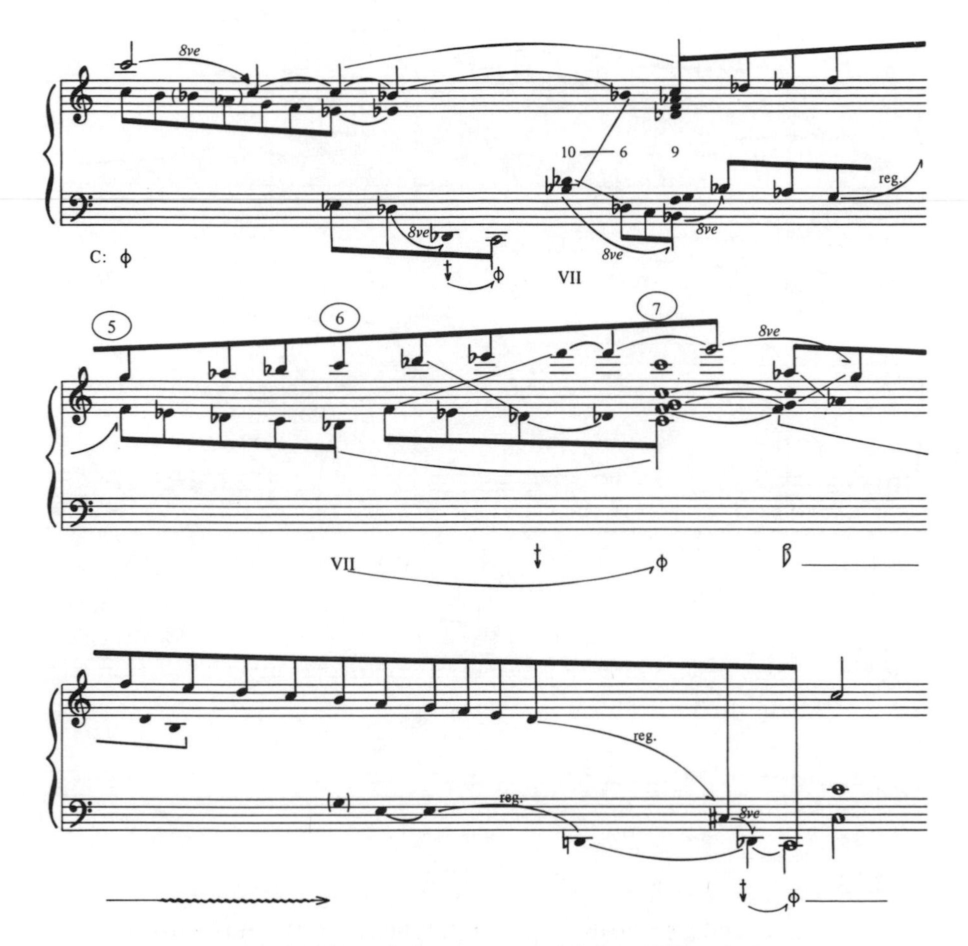

Example 10.9: Praeludium, mm. 1–14, Stage III analysis

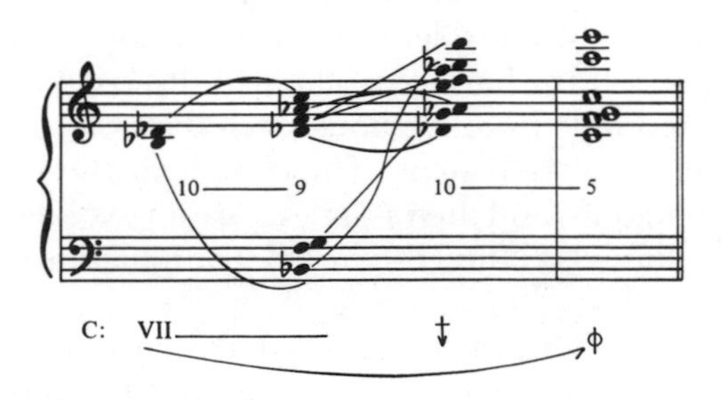

Example 10.10: Praeludium, mm. 3–7, condensed harmony and voiceleading graph

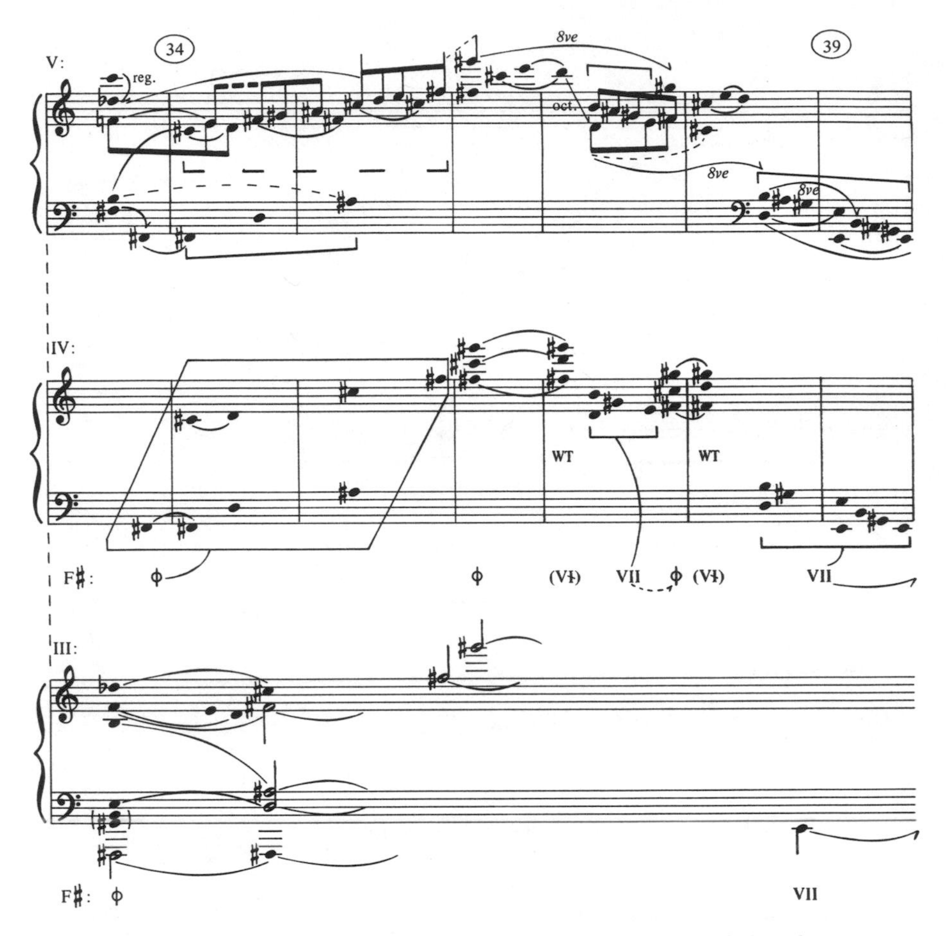

Example 10.11: Praeludium, mm. 33–39, Stage III, IV, and V analyses

major triad is never sounded (it appears in the Arioso). Supporting C is a welter of chromatic figures based on fragments of a limited group of diatonic major scale sets. The solenne ostinato prolongs a major triad in the most obvious way, but the harmonic status of this triad remains doubtful, and it is supported only by ambiguous pitch materials. The opening unfolds vigorously; the close is static. The complexity and richness of these compositional situations and their relations are an excellent mirror of Hindemith's compositional skill and the varied manipulation of elements of his theory.

The ostinati in both Praeludium and Postludium versions generate seven-note pc sets which are equivalent under transposition—the set of the ascending melodic minor scale (ex. 10.12). Hindemith also reproduced a five-note motive (marked x in ex. 10.12). Interval sequence and direction are identical, though rhythms differ slightly.[13]

The emphasis on major-scale sets is gone in the solenne ostinato, but the F♯–G♯ dyad in mm. 34ff. is due to the modified retrograde mirror. The repetition of C♯ in several octaves, descending from C♯6 to C♯2 in mm. 45–47, is cleverly placed: the same figure opens the Postludium (inversion would reverse the direction of the figure, but the retrogradation restores it). With the ostinato pattern, this figure greatly increases the likelihood that the listener will immediately recognize the derivation of the Postludium.

Since the last fugue of the cycle is in F♯ and is reserved and quiet, the transition to the Postludium is very fluent. Hindemith emphasized the relationship between the pieces by placing the last episode of the fugue so that its prominent repeated C♯6 (mm. 34–35), whose register is then abandoned for the coda by a long step-progression to F♯4, is plainly heard as linked to the first note of the Postludium (also C♯6). The fifth F♯–C♯ of the Praeludium becomes C♯–G♯, however, and the F♯ major triad becomes a C♯ major triad. Because of the context—the key of the preceding fugue—it is difficult to say if the solenne passage in the Postludium is in C♯ or F♯ (with C♯ as a prolonged ♪ without resolution). In mm. 39–34, the sound of the major-minor seventh chord prevails and the quality of C♯ as dominant seems particularly strong; yet the cadenza passage (m. 33) places C♯ in a new context (affirmed by the Arioso): C♯ as ↕ of C. The broad structure of tonal movements and formal design in the Postludium, then, is: (solenne)

Example 10.12: Praeludium and Postludium ostinatos (mm. 40ff.)

13. There are two ascending melodic minor scale sets (A and A♭) which remain invariant under the modified retrograde mirror, but Hindemith does not use either one. His replicated minor-scale set is achieved at some cost: B2 in the Praeludium ostinato acquires a sharp as it becomes D♯5 in the Postludium (the same changes occur in the transitional measures 34–39).

F♯: ♪ (or C♯: φ ?) becomes C: ‡ , (Arioso and conclusion) C: φ to φ repeated.

The descending arpeggiations in mm. 8–14 also appear in mm. 14–8 of the Postludium and tonal definition is equally weak. The chords are not so complex, but the tonal orientation is uncertain. IłI and II are emphasized, at last giving way to three chords, each containing three or four principal tonal functions and having functionally strong roots (ex. 10.13). The prominent, harmonically significant pitches F1–G1–C1 (= ꞵ–♪–φ) in m. 7 give the first clear signal of the approaching end. Additional evidence is provided by the arpeggios of mm. 7–4, which formerly diverged, but now converge on C4.

The Praeludium and Postludium summarize and complete the tonal drama of the entire cycle. Their central point is to illustrate the essential concept of intratonal relations, harmonic and tonal relationships not as function in the traditional sense, but as tension and balance of variously defined, often competing degrees revolving about a tonic. The role of the large circular progression φ to φ in the opening cadenza and Arioso is to present the principal character about which the others move. The abrupt shift to F♯ in m. 33 provides the broadest outline of the "play's" argument, the motion through Series 1 from φ to ʊ. Then the Postludium rather quickly draws the sphere of tonal and dramatic action back from the realm of the ʊ to the φ in the solenne ostinato and following transitional passage and once more presents the φ in the two circular progressions of the Arioso and closing cadence. In many ways, this ending is Hindemith's masterstroke in the cycle: the spacious reaffirmation of the tonic is worlds removed from the hammered reiterations of closing cadences or chords so common in nineteenth-century music. Here there is great serenity, balance achieved, drama ended.

Example 10.13: Postludium, m. 8, chord roots and degree content

ELEVEN

THE LAST MUSIC (AFTER 1950)

By Hindemith's earlier standards, the last decade of his life was a dry period. It is true that he wrote music totaling more than eleven hours, but a larger portion of his time and creative effort was focused on conducting rather than composing. There are three main reasons for this. First and foremost, he had reached a plateau, "the melancholy of success": he simply had difficulty refining or developing his compositional language beyond the point it had reached with the American works of the mid- and late forties. A symptom of this fact is that, in 1952 and 1953, his major products were revisions of two earlier operas, *Neues vom Tage* and *Cardillac*. In 1954, he got no further than work on the libretto of *Die Harmonie der Welt.* He must also have recognized that the next step for him might well be his own Art of Fugue; that is, a music at once abstract but highly personal that would contradict the ideals of musical community he had just forcefully rearticulated in *A Composer's World.* Second, he had increasing doubts about his compositional theory, though not (as is usually said) because he thought he had to concede to his critics and give up the physical basis of the theory and the compositional principles derived from it. His doubts arose because he had come to equate the three principal elements—melody, harmony, and rhythm—a process which, as we have seen, was complete by the mid-forties. But he was unable to find a satisfying way to integrate a rhythmic theory into the *Craft* pedagogy.[1] Third, Hindemith became a conductor in order to promote his own music.[2] In America he could still depend on his reputation as an "atonal" composer, but when he returned to Europe the avant-garde edge had worn off, and he became a "grand old man," increasingly isolated from the stylistic trends of new music. After a short period of adulation at the end of the war, his music encountered criticism more open and more severe than at any time since the twenties. His revisions of earlier works were by and large rejected, and his masterworks from the thirties threatened to become passé. In the 1950s, the work he

1. Briner, *Hindemith,* 321–22.
2. Schubert, *Hindemith,* 117ff.

intended to be the apotheosis of his career, *Die Harmonie der Welt*, failed, and commissioned works like the *Pittsburgh* Symphony (1958) and the Organ Concerto (1962) were given no more than a polite reception.

Though he had difficulty constructing a rhythmic theory, Hindemith looked for ways to accommodate some of the harmonic and melodic materials of the most recent practice, an aim already apparent in the Double Bass Sonata (1949). He sought a place for these accommodations in his compositional theory as music for "the cultivated listener."[3] In the German translation of *A Composer's World* (1959), he added a passage that explains his new orientation toward atonality:

> It has recently become a habit with composers to use almost exclusively the more complex relations and to avoid the simpler, more easily manageable relationships. This trend seems logical in view of the relatively small amount of exploitation of these complex relationships in the past. Yet, composers nowadays believe that in this way they have escaped the laws of tonality and reached an area of unlimited freedom. . . . What is held to be "atonality" necessarily turns out to be another aspect of tonality—the only difference being that the "atonal" work fixes the sequences in another of the various corners of the full tonal area.[4]

Within these wider limits for the mature *Craft* theory, it is possible to explicate the technical processes of the later music; but we must allow for broader and subtler harmonic-tonal structures, greater chromaticism in melody, and greater dissonance levels (as well as poorer chord definition) in harmony.

The first phrase of the Latin motet "Vidit Joannes Jesum" (1959) presents a characteristic melody harmonized in a way not at all typical of Hindemith's many earlier pieces in the "ruhig bewegt" tempo (ex. 11.1). In a piece from the forties, the opening chord would probably have been

Example 11.1: Motet "Vidit Joannes Jesum venientem," mm. 1–3

3. Hindemith, "Hören und Verstehen," 187.

4. Translated by Andres Briner, "A New Comment on Tonality by Paul Hindemith," *Journal of Music Theory* 5 (1961): 112.

diatonic (fifth, triad, or pentatonic) or, if meant to be poorly defined, a diminished-chord construct without the minor ninth or major seventh. The whole-tone construct of m. 2 would have been less likely to contain a diminished octave. The cadential dissonance of m. 3 is not unusual, but the cadence chord itself is pentatonic (although the root is clearly defined by a harmonic fifth). In the short second phrase, the approach to the cadence is simpler. The cadence chord is again pentatonic, and the root is now defined by the outer voices (ex. 11.2). In the final phrase of the introduction, all the sonorities are complex. Minor-second, major-seventh, and tritone intervals stand out (ex. 11.3). The cadence chord itself is an open fifth spiced by a piquant F♯. (The motion to C is misleading, incidentally. Hindemith now permitted considerable ambiguity in the definition of the principal tonality, just as he permitted complex and poorly defined chords.) The principal key is C♯, though we cannot be sure of that yet. The tonal-formal design of the entire motet is:

	intro.	A	B	C	A	B	C	A′	intro.′ (as coda)
m.	1–8	9–19	20–34	35–48	49–59	60–76	77–89	90–94	95–110
C♯:	(ϕ)–↕	—ϕ	—?	—𝅗𝅥	↕—V♮	—?	—𝅗𝅥	↕—II	𝅗𝅥—ϕ

Each of the devices of this first section is possible in the earlier music; it is the concentrated emphasis that is different.

The transposed setting of the opening phrase, on which the final ca-

Example 11.2: "Vidit Joannes," mm. 4–5

Example 11.3: "Vidit Joannes," mm. 6–8

dence of the motet is based (mm. 104ff.) is in familiar Hindemith style (ex. 11.4). The functional hierarchical distinctions could hardly be more obvious: the prolongation of a complex, tritone-rich dissonance in the first three measures versus the three chords of *Craft I*'s Group A; and the tritone-spanning step-progression of the first measures versus the leading-tone cadence with its escape tone E5 forming a minor third drop to the last note (and its counterpoint of strong intervals).

Like many other composers, Hindemith experimented with serial methods in the 1950s. He had repeatedly criticized and rejected such methods earlier, often using sharp language that has usually been construed—for the most part erroneously—as a personal attack on Schoenberg, but the notion of music for the cultivated listener and the acceptance of the atonal "corner of the full tonal area" brought with them the possibility that serial methods might find some place among Hindemith's compositional tools. His experiments were extremely limited, but they are interesting nevertheless. Sketches show that the principal themes of the first and third movements of the Tuba Sonata (1955) were arrived at after trials with a number of fully chromatic melodies apparently intended as tone-rows. Neither movement shows any further hints of serial procedures. In the *Pittsburgh* Symphony (1958), Hindemith wrote an ostinato movement (the finale) whose theme combines characteristics of an eight-note row, a passacaglia subject, and a ground bass, but whose procedures

Example 11.4: "Vidit Joannes," final measures, with Stage IV and V analyses as harmony and voiceleading graphs

suggest a highly personal interpretation of the notion of "perpetual variation." At the end of the movement, the theme does become a clear ostinato, but it is used to accompany a Pete Seeger tune, "Pittsburgh is a great old town." All in all, as a serial piece, this movement is hard to take seriously.

In the mid-forties, Hindemith's attitude toward Schoenberg was admittedly antagonistic, though it had not been earlier (despite the anti-twelve-tone rhetoric of *Craft I*). In the fifties, his attitude changed considerably. He read Schoenberg's essay on twelve-tone composition in *Style and Idea* and at least part of Josef Rufer's book on the same subject.[5] He analyzed the Schoenberg Fourth String Quartet (probably in 1956) and the Webern Symphony, Op. 21 (probably in 1961). His final act as a university teacher was to give a series of lectures on the Schoenberg string quartets (December 1957). It is entirely possible that Hindemith, in company with a good number of other composers, felt freer to explore Schoenberg's legacy after his death in 1951, since they would now be less threatened by any association with its ideology. It is also worthwhile noting in this connection that, far from being "the bitter old retiree," Hindemith now showed a breadth of interest in musical repertory greater than at any time since the late twenties. His concert programs ranged from Gabrieli and Monteverdi to Webern and Petrassi, with special nods in the direction of Haydn and Bruckner. If there was any compositional crisis for Hindemith as he allowed his style to develop in a way that would not divorce him entirely from newer fashions (or so he thought), that obstacle was passed over remarkably easily—somewhere between the initial melodic sketches and the first full sketch for the Tuba Sonata. The lecture "Hearing and Understanding Unfamiliar Music" (1955), shows more irritation than anxiety at the state of things and makes the passage to acceptance of the atonal corner with astonishing ease (and little comment). The pessimism of the Weinheber Madrigals (1958) noted by most writers on Hindemith's late music has little to do with a supposed collapse of his compositional theory and of the world-view on which it depended and much more to do with his personal disappointment at the failure of the first production of *Die Harmonie der Welt* (Munich, 1957).

The idea for an opera on the life of Kepler was one of several Hindemith considered in the early thirties. Although he chose to use Mathias Grünewald instead (for *Mathis der Maler*), Hindemith came back periodically to Kepler. By the late forties, he had assembled a substantial amount of material for a libretto. The compositional history of the opera is much like that of *Mathis*. The symphony *Harmonie der Welt* came first (in 1951), while Hindemith was still working on the libretto (intermittently from

5. Hindemith's personal copies of these books, with marginalia, are in the library of his home in Blonay, Switzerland.

1948 to 1956), but most of the music was composed in 1956. It was not in the revisions of his earlier works that Hindemith intended to make his statement to his contemporaries, but in *Harmonie der Welt*. The opera draws together strands from throughout Hindemith's life: the concept of a noble, ethical music; the notion of musical community; symbolism inherent in the *Craft* theory, thanks to Hans Kayser's influence; the early opera projects; even some sympathetic concession to his wife Gertrude's bent toward mysticism. According to Ian Kemp, Hindemith "believed that the element of divine revelation was not confined to the music of the spheres. It can be present in music as we know it. In the opera he used Kepler's life to dramatize this visionary idea."[6] Though the first production was not successful, the opera is the equal of *Cardillac* (first version) and *Mathis der Maler* as a dramatic stage piece. Both libretto and music are compact and consistent, and the opera boasts what is surely one of the most complex systems of tonal symbolism in any music of this century.[7]

During the first post-*Mathis* period (including the American years), Hindemith favored instrumental composition, in part because of the nature of commissions he received, but also because the musical ideas he was working out suited instrumental media better. After 1951 vocal composition seemed more congenial. This may appear odd for a conductor who favored symphony concerts and a composer who was beginning serious exploration of dissonant chromatic harmonic materials and weakly defined tonality, but he had insisted for years that the most perfect instrument is the human voice and that priority be given to choral singing. In the forties, works for voice tended to be confined to classroom and occasional pieces, with the important exceptions of the Whitman Requiem (a commissioned work) and the revised *Marienleben*. After 1951, Hindemith wrote or revised four operas—*Cardillac, Neues vom Tage, Die Harmonie der Welt*, and the *Long Christmas Dinner*—and composed *Ite, angeli veloces*, a large three-part cantata for UNESCO, *Mainzer Umzug*, a cantata for the two thousandth anniversary of the city of Mainz, a set of twelve five-part madrigals, nine of the thirteen motets for soprano or tenor with piano, and a Mass. Andres Briner regards most of this as "composing from within" to compensate for what he had lost without, but I prefer a different interpretation. Hindemith had blamed the excesses of later nineteenth and early twentieth-century music on the hegemony of instrumental media and techniques. For his own limited, strictly personal accommodation with the newer style in the fifties, he turned back to the stricter controls of vocal composition, insuring that any development of style or technique would not lose sight of their requirements, just as any exploration of the atonal corner would not

6. Kemp, *Hindemith*, 52.
7. See D'Angelo, "Hindemith's Opera *Die Harmonie der Welt*."

lose sight of the more fundamental principle of tonal organization, the whole tonal field or *Gesamttonalität.*

The Mass for mixed chorus a cappella (1963) is Hindemith's last completed piece. It is at once deeply personal and abstract, highly expressive but insistently concerned with musical and religious universals. In the Mass, more than in any of the other late works, we can see Hindemith the craftsman writing directly and without pretense, handling both historical references and the new stylistic elements with ease and clear purpose. The many emblems of his style and technique are set here in a traditional genre which does not require the external assistance of narrative or staging. Yet the Mass is not an easy work to perform or to grasp in listening. It was intended for *Spitzenchöre* (the most skillful professional choruses), the third in a series of three mass settings of progressive difficulty. Hindemith was partway through the Credo of the second setting at the time of his death.[8]

The tonal design of the Mass is symmetrical and involves tonal successions in arpeggiation shapes:

	Kyrie	Gloria	Credo	Sanctus[9]	Agnus Dei
F♯:	Φ	♪	I+I	♪	Φ

The Kyrie and Agnus Dei are closely linked: they are built on the same theme, have the same number of measures (31), and their formal designs are based on harmonic proportions.

In a framework of the "cultivated" chromatic manner appear traces of nearly every one of Hindemith's stylistic traits: the sound of early music in the Kyrie, Benedictus ("in the manner of a fauxbourdon"), and Agnus Dei; the newest chromatic angularity in passages of the Kyrie and Agnus Dei, in the glissando gestures of the Credo, and in the dramatic and dissonant structures which open the Sanctus; recollections of his own earlier manner (especially the choral style and melodic shapes of "Ite, angeli veloces" and *Die Harmonie der Welt*); and some nineteenth-century elements such as the consecutive construction of the Gloria and Credo, tempo and mood changes, and the rich chordal coloration (including parallel seventh chords at "Jesu Christe" in the Gloria). There are also hidden symbols, the most powerful of which refer simultaneously to early music, the period of

8. Briner, *Hindemith,* 302. Hindemith completed the Kyrie, Gloria, and part of the Credo of this intermediate member of the series. Excerpts appear in facsimile in *Paul Hindemith: Die letzten Jahre,* 72–73 and Rexroth, *Hindemith-Zyklus Nordrhein-Westfalen 1980–81,* 58.

9. The Sanctus is more complicated in design, but it ends clearly in C♯:

"Sanctus"	"pleni sunt" + "Hosanna"	"Benedictus"	"Hosanna"
F♯: (on) ♪	Φ—Φ	(in) ♪—♪	♪—♪

Mathis, medieval cosmology, and a religious interpretation of universal harmony: the golden section proportions in the Kyrie and Agnus Dei (figs. 11.1 and 11.2). Note that the beat count in the Agnus Dei yields numbers from the Fibonacci sequence, in this context unlikely to be coincidence.

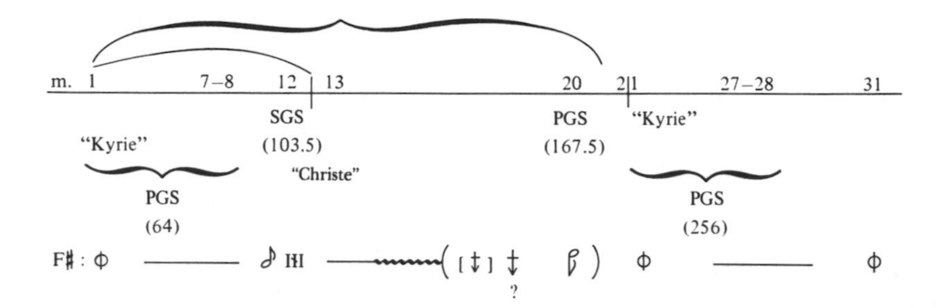

Figure 11.1: Mass, Kyrie, tonal-formal plan and proportions

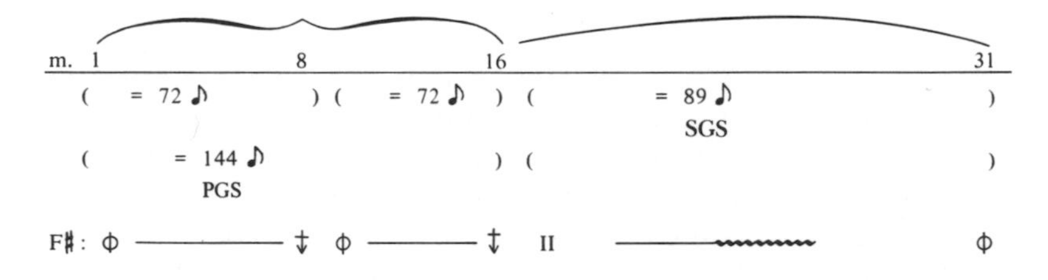

Figure 11.2: Mass, Agnus Dei, tonal-formal plan and proportions

The most private set of symbols in the Kyrie intertwines cross motives with letter-name mottoes.[10] In example 11.5a, the opening theme phrase, a motto derived from Hindemith's name (pAul HinDEmitH), is wound about the tonic-tritone interval, F♯4–C5. In the example, the notes forming the interval are circled and connected with a line. The tritone itself can be taken as representing the cross: the *diabolus in musica* appearing to displace the perfect fifth as the Devil appeared to displace Christ through the Crucifixion. But a more characteristic use of Renaissance and baroque musical symbolism is the cross motive formed by the first four notes: F♯–B–E–A, which create the four points of the cross. Yet another subtlety lies in the fact that the first note of the motive (and the tonic degree of the movement) is F♯, "sharp" in German being *Kreuz*, "cross."

10. Hindemith had used these mottoes almost forty years earlier in a wedding cantata. See my article "Letter-Name Mottoes in Hindemith's 'Gute Nacht,' " *HJB* 6 (1977): 29ff.

Example 11.5a: Mass, Kyrie, mm. 1–2 (soprano)

In example 11.5b, the cross motive reverses direction, the parallel rising fourths separated by a falling fifth in m. 1 becoming parallel falling tenths, G5–E4 and D5–B3, separated by a rising minor seventh. Thus, Hindemith's favorite falling minor third is expanded to a Webern-like melodic gesture. The four tones in this motive are those of a letter-name motto derived from Gertrude Hindemith's name: GErtruDE HinDEmitH. The remaining tones of example 11.5b repeat elements of the motto with one exception—C♯, the dominant of F♯, and the only note in this passage with a sharp sign (Kreuz). In addition, the second beat of m. 16 is the symmetrical axis of the movement in both measure and beat counts, and the final note of the "Christe" figure (B3) falls at the primary golden section of the "Christe" form division. These mottoes and motives as a group may be taken as signifying, "Lord, have mercy (on us [two] sinners)"; that is, on Paul and Gertrude. In the second section of the Agnus Dei, mm. 9–10, the two motives are combined: ex. 11.6. The "Kyrie" theme lies in the tenor, and a recomposed version of the "Christe" figure is in the soprano and bass.

Example 11.5b: Mass, Kyrie, mm. 15–18 (soprano)

The three sections of the Agnus Dei are apportioned at eight, eight, and fifteen measures. The first is based on the first Kyrie and the second on the final Kyrie; the third is essentially new, though its opening is a "diatonicized" elaboration of the Kyrie theme (ex. 11.7). A tonal and formal summary (Stage I) is given in example 11.8, along with a Stage II analysis of the first section. Analyses of the harmonic and melodic details of the first section (Stages IV and V) appear in example 11.9. In the first two sections,

Example 11.6: Mass, Agnus Dei, mm. 1–2

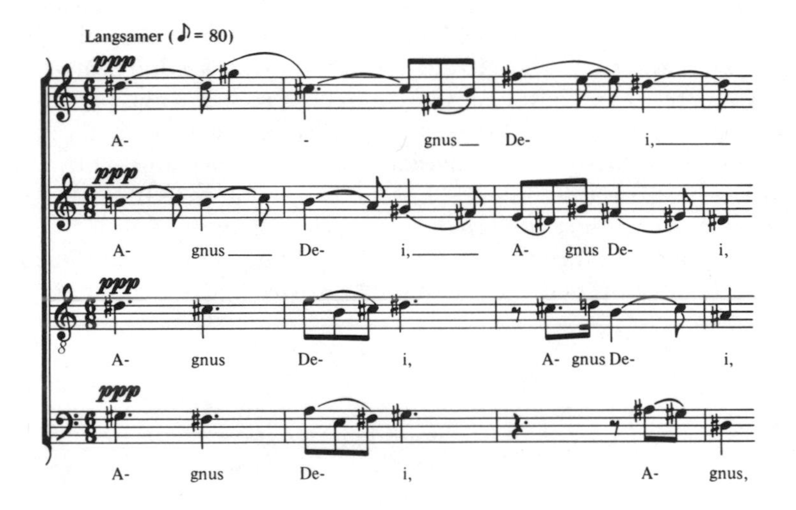

Example 11.7: Mass, Agnus Dei, mm. 17–20

large-scale tonal motion approaches the upper leading tone. In the third section, movement is from II through two prolonged whole-tone sonorities to the "dona nobis pacem" setting with its small dominant-tonic (= dissonance-triad) pairs and subtly colored VI♮ –♪– ϕ cadence (S–D–T!). Local harmonic usage shows Hindemith's late-period tendency to use more complex sonorities where he would earlier have employed pentatonic chords or triads (as in m. 5 or m. 7) and his sharper minor second-major

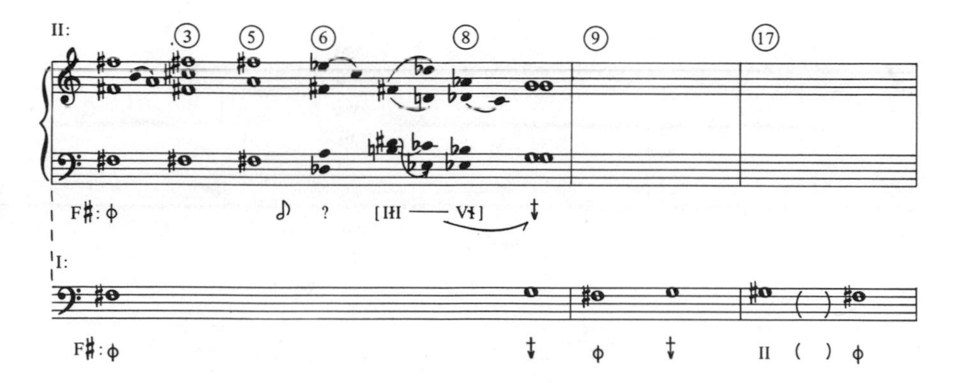

Example 11.8: Mass, Agnus Dei, Stage I analysis (for mm. 1–8, also Stage II)

seventh coloration of diminished and augmented-chord constructs (as in m. 6, m. 14, and mm. 22ff.).

The coherent long-range treatment of registral extremes is, in effect, an extension of the patterns of the Kyrie. In the Kyrie, the D5 of the opening phrase is extended to E5 in m. 3, but then that register is left until the close of the first section (mm. 10–12), where F5 is reached. The highest tone (G5) is reached at the "Christe" in m. 16, midway through the movement (ex. 11.5b). A retreat to F♯5 follows in the third section (m. 21), with another half-step descent (to F5) in m. 27. After this, the register is abandoned for the closing passage. The lower extreme (bass) in the Kyrie begins relatively high (C♯3), descending to G♯2 at the end of the first section, but returning and maintaining its original register throughout the "Christe." F♯2 is reached in m. 21 (as the soprano takes F♯5) and becomes F2 in m. 23, the last note in this register until the final F♯2.

In the Agnus Dei, the two registral extremes are given immediately in the doubled F♯s of soprano and bass, while the Kyrie theme flows between in the alto. The registers close somewhat in mm. 6–8. In the second section F♯5 moves upward to G5, and F♯2 down to E2 (D2) (ex. 11.6). In mm. 13–15 (parallel to mm. 6–8), the bass again moves upward, but the soprano splits the upper register into two components by means of a step-progression down to D5. At the beginning of the third section, D♯5 articulates this upper-middle register, while G♯5 reaches the highest point of the upper register (m. 17). Two steps carry G♯5 down to F5 in m. 21, this note being touched only once more, in m. 27. The bass again reaches F2 and E2 in mm. 25–26, but in the last passage the registers become much more compact.

In the final section, the soprano develops four distinct registral posi-

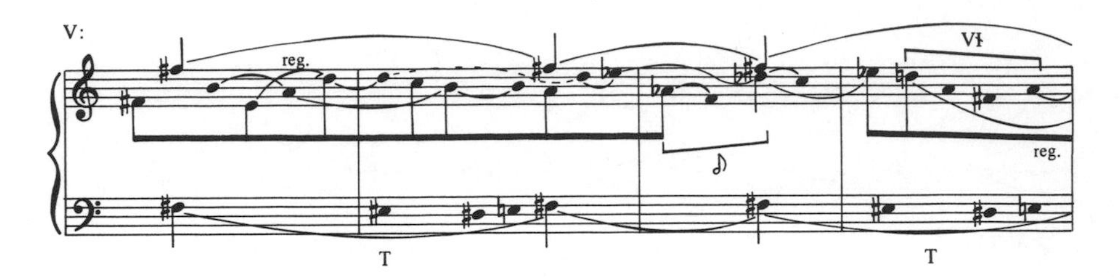

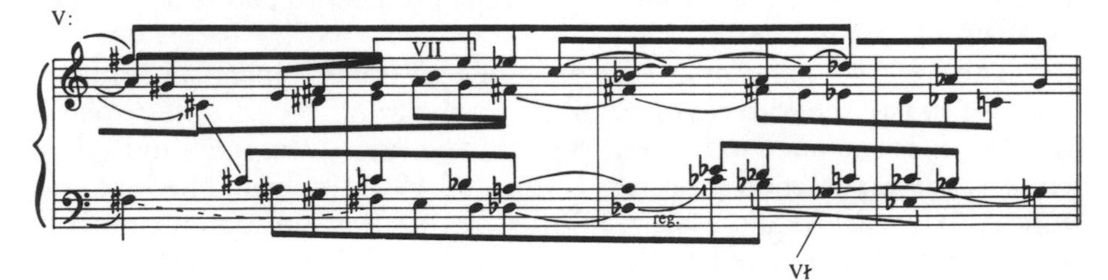

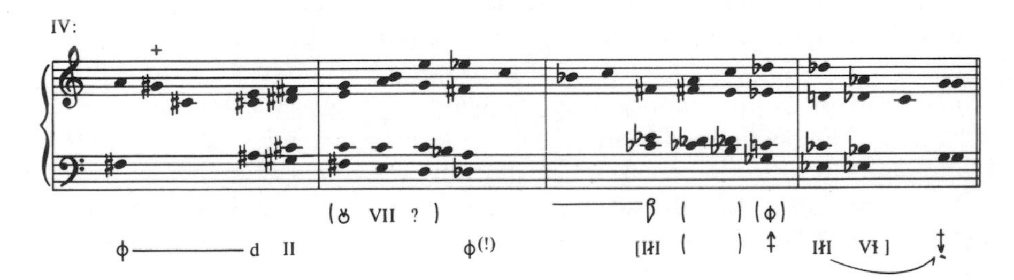

Example 11.9: Mass, Agnus Dei, mm. 1–8, Stage IV and V analyses

tions, articulated by the descending minor third (F5–D5) of m. 21 and the rising minor third (E♭4–G♭4) of m. 24. The higher pair represents the upper-middle and upper-extreme registers described above, the lower pair the position of the final cadence. In the descending chain that leads to the close, all four registers are struck again (ex. 11.10)

Example 11.10: Mass, Agnus Dei, mm. 27–28 (soprano)

This analytic glimpse at the Mass does not support the view that Hindemith abandoned his theoretical principles in the last music, nor even that he compromised them for the sake of remaining fashionable. I find changes in employment of some materials—especially details of melody and harmony—amounting to a change in style, but no fundamental change of principle. This is not a music of doubt or confusion, for by then Hindemith had passed through the last decade's crisis of materials and style. Nor is it a music pessimistic or cynical—that stage, too, he had passed through (in the Weinheber Madrigals [1958]). The Mass is an autobiographical document, a personal confession of faith, a gift to his wife Gertrude (a devout Catholic with whom Hindemith would often attend mass at a small church a half-mile down the hillside from their home in Blonay, Switzerland), and it is an abstract, contemplative music.

APPENDIX

THE WORKS OF HINDEMITH

A Chronological Listing

Compiled by Luther Noss, Curator, Hindemith Collection, Yale University

PREFACE

Unless otherwise noted, all of the works listed have been published, with the copyright date and name of the publisher enclosed in brackets. The following abbreviations have been used:

Schott	Schott & Sons, Mainz
AMP	Associated Music Publishers, New York (which served as a surrogate for Schott in the United States during World War II)
Schott-London	London branch of Schott & Sons, Mainz.

Only the date of the first edition is given. Details of format (full score, study score, reduction, etc.) or of any subsequent editions have been omitted. In many cases, this information can be obtained from the catalogue *Paul Hindemith: Werkverzeichnis* (Mainz: Schott, 1969).

Scores marked "unpublished" exist in the archives of the Paul-Hindemith-Institut in Frankfurt, West Germany, and will be included in the complete edition now being published (*Paul Hindemith: Sämtliche Werke,* general editors Kurt von Fischer and Ludwig Finscher [Mainz: Schott, 1975–]). About twelve volumes have already appeared, and at least ten more are in preparation as of this writing (1983). There is no fixed schedule for their publication, since too many variables are involved. Meanwhile, it is not possible to obtain photocopies of these unpublished compositions, for the directors of the Hindemith Foundation recently voted to prohibit any further distribution of materials now that the complete edition is under way.

Scores marked "refer to the preface" do not exist in the archives and are presumed lost. However, rumors of their existence persist; if found, they will be published. Scores marked "lost" are irrevocably lost. Most of them are known to have been destroyed in a bombing attack on Frankfurt during World War II which severely damaged Hindemith's tower apartment. Hindemith had left all his early scores in the apartment after moving to Berlin in 1927, for his mother and sister continued to live there.

Hindemith used opus numbers only from 1914 to 1930. Works from this period which are listed without a number were not given one by the composer. There is no Opus 42, for reasons unknown today. Exact dates of composition are given if known; otherwise only the year is noted. Data relating to the place (or places) where the work was written have been gathered from wherever they could be found, including the original scores, Hindemith's personal papers (letters, logs, journals), publishers' files, and articles written about individual compositions. The composer's place of residence during the year is noted in parentheses at the head of each section. Where performance times are given, they have been taken from Hindemith catalogues published by Schott and by Associated Music Publishers and cannot be guaranteed for accuracy. Statements in quotation marks are from Hindemith's work logs.

This list contains all Hindemith's published compositions and almost all those not published. Missing from the latter are a few small entertainment pieces for piano from the early 1920s (fox-trots, marches, rags, shimmys, etc.), experiments with phonograph recordings and mechanical instruments in the late 1920s, parodies for string quartet, some thirty small vocal canons written for special occasions, and a few slight pieces done as classroom demonstrations. No attempt has been made to list them here, for complete information about them is not yet available.

Hindemith kept very complete records of his compositions in notebooks, now all in the archives, and there is no valid reason to believe that he purposely omitted anything of significance. Officials of the Hindemith Foundation and Institute and all others who have been working closely with the composer's estate are fully convinced that all of his major works have been accounted for and that there are no masterpieces lying undiscovered.

1913 (FRANKFURT)

Theme and Variations in E♭ Major for Piano (lost)
Student work, written in Arnold Mendelssohn's composition class at the Hoch Conservatory, Frankfurt. "It had to be reworked continually; I could not seem to please the old man."

Rondo in B♭ Major for Clarinet and Piano (lost)
Student work, written under Mendelssohn. "I never quite finished it; had to fuss around with it too much."

Sonata in D Minor for Violin and Piano (only fragments exist)
Student work, written under Mendelssohn. "I did not like it even when I was working on it, but the old man made me finish it."

The Cousin's Visit (lost)
A musical play; text by Wilhelm Busch
Student work, written under Mendelssohn; Hindemith's first orchestral score.

1914 (FRANKFURT)

Nähe des Geliebten (unpublished)
Solo voice and piano
Student work, written in Bernhard Sekles's composition class at the Hoch Conservatory, Frankfurt.

Andante and Scherzo for Clarinet, Horn, and Piano, Opus 1 (only sketches exist)
Student work, written under Sekles. "Sekles thought the Scherzo was first rate."

1915 (FRANKFURT)

String Quartet in C Major, Opus 2 (unpublished)
Student work, written under Sekles. Awarded the Conservatory's top composition prize for the year. "Composed by Sekles; I soon hated the first movement because it was so old-fashioned, but I was especially proud of the last two movements."
Begun fall 1914, completed spring 1915

1916 (FRANKFURT)

Concerto in E♭ for Violoncello and Orchestra, Opus 3
"I liked this piece very much, particularly the first movement; the other two do not seem to me to have come off so well. I soon found out that I would have to try something else." There is evidence that this concerto was written without the direct supervision of Sekles. Although Hindemith was nominally still a student at the conservatory during the time he wrote opp. 3–9, he seems to have been regarded as a "graduate" student and allowed to work more or less independently. He continued to show his scores to Sekles but rarely accepted any advice for making changes.
Begun summer 1915, completed Apr. 1916. [c. 1976, Schott; in the complete edition. A piano reduction is available separately.]

Lustige Sinfonietta, Opus 4 (unpublished)
Small orchestra, in three movements
Mar.–Aug. 1916. [First performed in 1980]

Seven Merry Songs in the Aargau Dialect, Opus 5 (unpublished)
Solo voice and piano
"Probably never performed."
Summer 1916

Seven Waltzes for Piano, Four Hands, Opus 6 (only fragmentary sketches exist)
Subtitle: "Three Beautiful Maidens in the Black Forest"
Summer 1916

Sonata in G Minor for Solo Violin, Opus 11.6 (unpublished)
Opus number arbitrarily assigned by the Hindemith Institute.

March in F Minor for Piano, Four Hands (lost)
"This was only a kind of experiment."

1917 (FRANKFURT)

Piano Quintet in E Minor, Opus 7 (lost)
Begun late 1916, completed Jan. 1917

Three Pieces for Violoncello and Piano, Opus 8
Capriccio in A
Phantasiestück in B
Scherzo in C Minor
Feb.–Mar. 1917. [c. 1917, Breitkopf und Härtel, Leipzig]
(The first work by Hindemith to be published.) Performance times: 3 min., 6 min., 7½ min.

Three Songs for Soprano and Large Orchestra, Opus 9 (unpublished)
"With this 'mighty' achievement I thought I had overcome all difficulties and had become a very confident fellow."
Spring 1917, completed in June. [First performed in 1974]

Sonata for Ten Wind Instruments, Opus 10a (only fragments exist)
Opus number arbitrarily assigned by the Hindemith Institute.

1918 (With the German army in France)

String Quartet in F Minor, Opus 10
Known as the *First String Quartet*
"At the front" (France), Feb.–May 1918. [c. 1921, Schott]
Performance time: 29 min.

Wie es wär, wenn's anders wär (unpublished)
Soprano, flute, oboe, bassoon, string quartet
"At the front," spring 1918

Sonata in E♭ for Violin and Piano, Opus 11.1
"At the front," May 1918. [c. 1921, Schott]
Performance time: 9 min.

Sonata in D for Violin and Piano, Opus 11.2
"At the front," Sept.–Nov. 1918. [c. 1920, Schott]
Performance time: 18 min.

Two Pieces for Organ (refer to the preface)
"At the front, Douai, France, 18 Aug. 1918."

1919 (FRANKFURT)

Sonata in F for Viola and Piano, Opus 11.4
Between 27 Feb. and 9 Mar. 1919. [c. 1922, Schott]
Performance time: 16 min.

Traumwald, Opus 13 (unpublished)
Soprano and string quartet; texts by Christian Morgenstern
Die Primeln blühn—Frankfurt, 10 July 1919
Nebelweben—"at the front," June 1918
Dunkler Tropfe—Frankfurt, 17 July 1919
Melancholie—Frankfurt, 25 Dec. 1917

Sonata for Solo Viola, Opus 11.5
Completed 21 July 1919. [c. 1923, Schott]
Performance time: 22 min.

Mörder, Hoffnung der Frauen, Opus 12
(Murderers, the hope of women)
Opera in one act; libretto by Oskar Kokoschka
Completed 9 Aug. 1919. [c. 1921, Schott]
Performance time: 21 min.

Sonata for Violoncello and Piano, Opus 11.3
July–Aug. 1919
Extensively revised, Spain, Oct. 1921. [c. 1922, Schott]
Performance time: 22 min.

Three Hymns by Walt Whitman, Opus 14 (unpublished)
Baritone and piano
Der ich in Zwischenräumen an Aeonen—3 July 1919
Schlagt! Schlagt! Trommeln!—6 Aug. 1919
O, nun heb du an—6 Aug. 1919

In einer Nacht, Opus 15 (unpublished)
Fourteen short pieces for piano
Oct.–Dec. 1919

1920 (FRANKFURT)

String Quartet in C Major, Opus 16
Known as the *Second String Quartet*
Jan.–Feb. 1920. [c. 1922, Schott]
Performance time: 26 min.

Sonata for Piano, Opus 17 (only a few sketches exist)
Hindemith wrote in his work log that a scherzo movement intended for this sonata was used as no. 2 of the *Dance Pieces,* Opus 19.
Spring 1920

Eight Songs for Soprano and Piano, Opus 18
Die trunkene Tänzerin (Curt Bock)
Wie Sankt Franciscus schweb' ich in der luft (Christian Morgenstern)
Traum (Else Lasker-Schüler)
Auf der Treppe sitzen meine Oehrchen (Morgenstern)
Vor dir schein' ich aufgewacht (Morgenstern)
Du machst mich traurig—hör? (Lasker-Schüler)
Durch die abendlichen Gärten (Heinar Schilling)
Trompeten (Georg Trakl)
Mar.–Apr. 1920. [c. 1922, Schott]
Performance times: between 1 and 3 min. each.

Dance Pieces for Piano, Opus 19
A set of five
First three in June 1920, two more added early in 1922; all five were included when the set was first published by Schott in 1928.
Performance time: 12 min.

Das Nusch-Nuschi, Opus 20
Ballet opera in one act; libretto by Franz Blei
Completed 14 Aug. 1920. [c. 1921, Schott]
Performance time: 30 min.

Das Nusch-Nuschi
Dance suite for orchestra, arranged from the opera score
Fall 1920. [c. 1921, Schott]
Performance time: 8½ min.

1921 (FRANKFURT)

Sancta Susanna, Opus 21
Opera in one act; libretto by August Stramm
Jan.–Feb. 1921. [c. 1921, Schott]
Performance time: 40 min.

String Quartet, Opus 22
Known as the *Third String Quartet*
Nov.–Dec. 1921. [c. 1923, Schott]
Performance time: 24 min.

The Atonal Cabaret (refer to the preface)
A parody

1922 (FRANKFURT)

Des Todes Tod, Opus 23.1
Three songs on poems by Eduard Reinacher for female voice, two violas, and two violoncellos
Gesicht von Tod und Elend
Gottes Tod
Des Todes Tod
6–8 Jan. 1922. [c. 1953, Schott]
Performance time: 16 min.

Die junge Magd, Opus 23.2
Six songs on poems by Georg Trakl for alto, flute, clarinet, and string quartet
Oft am Brunnen
Stille schafft sie in der Kammer
Nächtens übern kahlen Anger
In der Schmiede dröht der Hammer

Schmächtig hingestreckt im Bette
Abends schweben blutige Linnen
Feb. 1922. [c. 1922, Schott]
Performance time: 20 min.

Kammermusik Nr. 1, Opus 24.1
Chamber orchestra of 12 solo instrumentalists
Jan.–Feb. 1922. [c. 1922, Schott]
Performance time: 15 min.

Sonata for Solo Viola, Opus 25.1
Mar. 1922. [c. 1923, Schott]
Performance time: 10 min.

Woodwind Quintet, Opus 24.2
May 1922. [c. 1922, Schott]
Performance time: 12 min.

Sonata for Viola d'Amore and Piano, Opus 25.2
May 1922. [c. 1929, Schott]
Performance time: 12 min.

1922—Suite for Piano, Opus 26
Between June 1921 and May 1922. [c. 1922, Schott]
Performance time: 14 min.

Sonata for Solo Violoncello, Opus 25.3
Donaueschingen, July 1922. [c. 1923, Schott]
Performance time: 7 1/2 min.

The Demon, Opus 28
Dance pantomime in two scenes; scenario by Max Krell
Fall 1922. [c. 1924, Schott]
Performance time: 34 min.

Tuttifäntchen
A Christmas play for children with song and dance; text by Hedwig Michel and Franziska Becker
Oct. 1922. [c. 1922, Schott]

Tuttifäntchen
Suite for chamber orchestra and violin, arranged from the music for the play, published by Schott in 1969. The arrangement was not made by Hindemith.
Performance time: 20 min.

Dance of the Wooden Dolls
A "fox trot" from *Tuttifäntchen,* arranged for piano
Oct. 1922. [c. 1922, Schott]
Performance time: 3 min.

Sonata for Viola and Piano, Opus 25.4
Nov. 1922. [c. 1977, Schott]

1923 (FRANKFURT)

The Demon
Orchestral suite arranged from the ballet score, Opus 28
Spring 1923. [c. 1924, Schott]
Performance time: 25 min.

Piano Concerto for the Left Hand, Opus 29 (unpublished)
Paul Wittgenstein commissioned this but he never performed it.
Feb. and May 1923
Only one copy of the score was made and it is presumed to be in the Wittgenstein estate. Efforts to obtain it have thus far been unsuccessful, but they are being continued. Unfortunately, no sketches exist.

Das Marienleben, Opus 27
(The life of Mary)
Cycle of 15 songs for soprano and piano on poems by Rainer Maria Rilke
Between June 1922 and July 1923. [c. 1924, Schott]
Performance time: 60–63 min.

Quintet for Clarinet and String Quartet, Opus 30
July 1923. [c. 1935, Schott]
Performance time: 18 min.

Minimax
Parody for string quartet
Donaueschingen, summer 1923. [c. 1978, Schott]

Sonata for Solo Viola, Opus 31.4 (unpublished)
Donaueschingen, completed 23 Aug. 1923

Canonic Sonatina for Two Flutes, Opus 31.3
Aug.–Sept. 1923. [c. 1924, Schott]
Performance time: 5 1/2 min.

String Quartet, Opus 32
Known as the *Fourth String Quartet*
Fall 1923. [c. 1924, Schott]
Performance time: 24 min.

1924 (FRANKFURT)

Lieder nach alten Texten, Opus 33
Mixed chorus, a cappella, four to six parts
Vom Hausregiment (Martin Luther)—SSATBB
Frauenklage (Burggraf zu Regensburg)—SSATB
Art lässt nicht von Art (Spervogel)—SATB
Der Liebe Schrein (Heinrich von Morungen)—SSATB
Heimliches Glück (Reinmar)—SSATBB
Landsknechtstrinklied (Anon.)—SSATBB
1923 and 1924. [c. 1925, Schott]
Performance times: 1 2/3 min., 1 1/2 min., 3/4 min., 2/3 min., 1 1/2 min., 1 1/2 min.

Sonata for Solo Violin, Opus 31.1
Mar.–Apr. 1924. [c. 1924, Schott]
Performance time: 10 min.

Sonata for Solo Violin, Opus 31.2
"On the train from Bremen to Frankfurt, one day in March or April 1924." [c. 1924, Schott]
Performance time: 7 min.

String Trio, Opus 34
Violin, viola, violoncello; known as the *First String Trio*
"On the train and in Frankfurt, Apr.–May 1924." [c. 1924, Schott]
Performance time: 15 min.

Die Serenaden, Opus 35
Small cantata on romantic texts in three parts, for solo soprano, oboe, viola, violoncello
July 1924. [c. 1925, Schott]
Performance time: 20 min.

Kammermusik Nr. 2, Opus 36.1
Obbligato piano and 12 solo strings and winds
Donaueschingen and Frankfurt, July–Sept. 1924. [c. 1924, Schott]
Performance time: 20 min.

1925 (FRANKFURT)

Kammermusik Nr. 3, Opus 36.2
Obbligato violoncello and 10 solo strings and winds
Spring 1925. [c. 1925, Schott]
Performance time: 16 min.

Piano Music, Opus 37 I
Three etudes for piano
Spring 1925. [c. 1925, Schott]
Performance time: 10 min.

Concerto for Orchestra, Opus 38
Full symphony orchestra
Spring 1925. [c. 1925, Schott]
Performance time: 17 min.

Kammermusik Nr. 4, Opus 36.3
Solo violin and large chamber orchestra
Donaueschingen and Wallis (Switzerland), summer 1925. [c. 1925, Schott]
Performance time: 23 min.

Three Pieces for Five Instruments
Clarinet, trumpet, violin, double bass, piano
Fall 1925, then called *Three Anecdotes for Radio.* [c. 1934, Schott]
Performance time: 6 min.

1926 (FRANKFURT)

Piano Music, Opus 37 II
Series of 13 short pieces
"Probably 1926." [c. 1927, Schott]
Performance time: 21 min.

Exercises for Violinists
Five etudes for violin
[c. 1958, Schott]
Performance time: 10 min.

Cardillac, Opus 39
Full-length opera in three acts; libretto by Ferdinand Lion
Between Oct. 1925 and May 1926. [c. 1926, Schott]

Toccata, Opus 40.1 (refer to the preface)
For player piano
Donaueschingen, summer 1926

Triadic Ballet, Opus 40.2 (refer to the preface)
For player organ
Donaueschingen, summer 1926

Concert Music for Wind Orchestra, Opus 41
Six variations on the song *Prince Eugen, the Noble Knight*
"Summer in three days" 1926. [c. 1926, Schott]
Performance time: 15 min.

1927 (FRANKFURT; BERLIN)

Spielmusik, Opus 43.1
String orchestra, flutes, oboes
Frankfurt, between late 1926 and early 1927. [c. 1927, Schott]
Performance time: 7 min.

Lieder für Singkreise, Opus 43.2
For SAB chorus
Ein jedes Band (von Platen)
O Herr, gib jedem seinen eignen Tod (Rilke)
Man weiss oft grade denn am meisten (Claudius)
Was meinst du, Kunz, wie gross die Sonne sei (Claudius)
Frankfurt, between late 1926 and early 1927. [c. 1927, Schott]
Performance time: 5 min.

Kammermusik Nr. 5, Opus 36.4
Solo viola and large chamber orchestra
Frankfurt, spring 1927. [c. 1927, Schott]
Performance time: 17 min.

Hin und zurück
(There and back)

Comic sketch in one act; libretto by Marcellus Schiffer
Frankfurt, "spring, 1927, in two days." [c. 1927, Schott]
Performance time: 12 min.

Eight Pieces for Solo Flute
Frankfurt, spring 1927. [c. 1958, Schott]
Performance time: 7 min.

Schulwerk für Instrumental-Zusammenspiel, Opus 44
(Educational music for instrumental ensemble playing)
I. *Nine Pieces in First Position* (beginners)
2 violins or 2 groups of violins
Performance time: 5 min.
II. *Eight Canons in First Position* (slightly more advanced players)
2 violins or 2 groups of violins, with an accompanying part for less advanced violinists or violists
Performance time: 6 min.
III. *Eight Pieces in First Position* (moderately advanced players)
2 violins, viola, violoncello, double bass, singly or in groups
Performance time: 8 min.
IV. *Five Pieces in First Position for String Orchestra* (advanced players)
Performance time: 10 min.
Frankfurt, spring 1927. [c. 1927, Schott]

Nine Pieces for Clarinet and Double Bass (unpublished)
Probably Frankfurt, 1927

Two Small Trios for Flute, Clarinet, and Double Bass (unpublished)
Probably Frankfurt, 1927

Felix the Cat at the Circus (refer to the preface)
Music for a cartoon film, scored for player piano
Donaueschingen, summer 1927

Kammermusik Nr. 6, Opus 46.1
Solo viola d'amore and chamber orchestra
St. Wolfgang [Switzerland] and Frankfurt, Aug.–Sept. 1927. [c. 1958, Schott]
Performance time: 16 min.

Kammermusik Nr. 7, Opus 46.2
Concerto for organ and chamber orchestra
Berlin, late 1927. [c. 1928, Schott]
Performance time: 17 min.

1928 (BERLIN)

Sing- und Spielmusiken für Liebhaber und Musikfreunde, Opus 45
(Music to sing and play, for amateurs and music lovers)
I. *Frau Musica* (Martin Luther)
Solo voice, chorus, audience, strings, optional winds. [c. 1928, Schott]
Performance time: 6 min.

II. *Eight Canons*
Two-part chorus, instruments optional. [c. 1928, Schott]
Hie kann nit sein ein böser Mut (Old Proverb)
Wer sich die Musik erkiest (Martin Luther)
Die wir dem Licht in Liebe dienen (Reinhard Goering)
Auf a folgt b (Christian Morgenstern)
Niemals wieder will ich eines Menschen Antlitz verlachen (Franz Werfel)
Das weiss ich und hab' ich erlebt (Jakob Kneip)
Mund und Augen wissen ihre Pflicht (Hermann Claudius)
Erde, die uns dies gebracht (Morgenstern)
Performance time: 6 1/2 min.

III. *Ein Jäger aus Kurpfaltz*
Strings and woodwinds. [c. 1928, Schott]
Performance time: 5 min.

IV. *Kleine Klaviermusik*
Twelve easy five-note piano pieces. [c. 1928, Schott]
Performance time: 5 min.

V. *Martin's Song* (Johannes Olorinus)
Solo voice (or unison chorus), instruments. [c. 1931, Schott]
Performance time: 3 1/2 min.

Trio for Heckelphone (or Tenor Saxophone), Viola, Piano, Opus 47
Mar. 1928. [c. 1929, Schott]
Performance time: 13 min.

Vormittagsspuk (refer to the preface)
(Morning Ghost)
Music for a surrealist film

Spruch eines Fahrenden
Three equal voices; anonymous 14th-century text
[c. 1950, Schott]
Performance time: 1 1/4 min.

Lügenlied
SAB, instruments optional
[Schott, n.d.]
Performance time: 1/2 min.

1929 (BERLIN)

Neues vom Tage
(News of the day)
Full-length comic opera; libretto by Marcellus Schiffer
Between spring 1928 and spring 1929. [c. 1929, Schott]

Overture to *Neues vom Tage*
Available separately as a concert piece
Performance time: 8 min.

Lehrstück
(Teaching piece)
Stage work in one scene; text by Bertolt Brecht
Three solo male voices, narrator, dancer, three clowns, audience, orchestra, band
Spring 1929. [c. 1929, Schott]
Performance time: 50 min.
(An English version by Geoffrey Skelton, called *The Lesson*, was published by Schott in 1974.)

Piano Piece (unpublished)
Prague, 27 Apr. 1929

Lindbergh's Flight
Six vocal compositions for a Bertolt Brecht radio production (3 solo voice and orchestra, 2 chorus and orchestra, 1 chorus unaccompanied)
Spring 1929. [c. 1981, Schott; in complete edition]

Ueber das Frühjahr
TTBB; text by Bertolt Brecht
Fall 1929. [c. 1930, Schott]
Performance time: 2 min.

Eine lichte Mitternacht
TTBB; text by Walt Whitman
Fall 1929. [c. 1930, Schott]
Performance time: 2 min.

Canonic Recital Piece and Canonic Variations
Two violins
[c. 1932, Schott]
Performance time: 11 min.

1930 (BERLIN)

Concert Music for Viola and Large Chamber Orchestra, Opus 48
Early 1930. [c. 1930, Schott]
Performance time: 20 min.

Wir bauen eine Stadt
(Let's build a town)
Musical play for children; libretto by Robert Seitz
Mar. 1930. [c. 1931, Schott]
Performance time: 15 min.

Wir bauen eine Stadt
Easy piano suite for children, from the music for the play
[c. 1931, Schott]
Performance time: 4 min.

Three Pieces for TTBB
Poems by Gottfried Benn
Du müsst dir alles geben
Fürst Kraft
Vision des Mannes
[c. 1930, Schott]
Performance times: 1 3/4 min., 2 1/4 min., 2 1/2 min.

Sabinchen (refer to the preface)
A piece for radio

Four Pieces for Three Trautoniums (unpublished)

Rondo for Three Guitars
[c. 1969, Schott]

Four Three-Part Choruses for Boys
Texts by Karl Schnog
Bastellied
Lied des Musterknaben
Angst vorm Schwimmunterricht
Schundromane lesen
[c. 1930, Schott]
Performance time: 7 1/2 min.

Concert Music for Piano, Ten Brass Instruments, Two Harps, Opus 49
San Bernardino (Switzerland), completed 13 Aug. 1930. [c. 1930, Schott]
Performance time: 21 min.
[This was the first commission Hindemith received from the United States, offered by Mrs. Elizabeth Sprague Coolidge.]

Concert Music for String Orchestra and Brass Instruments, Opus 50
"Berlin and Andermatt [Switzerland], Dec. 1930." [c. 1931, Schott]
Performance time: 19 min.
[NOTE: Hindemith discontinued using opus numbers after Opus 50.]

1931 (BERLIN)

Concert Piece for Trautonium and String Orchestra (unpublished)

Das Unaufhörliche
Oratorio in three parts; text by Gottfried Benn
SATB soli, chorus, boys' choir, orchestra
Jan.–June 1931. [c. 1931, Schott]
Performance time: 85 min.

Eighteen Canonic Pieces for Two Violins
Summer 1931. [c. 1932, Schott]
Published in three of a series of volumes comprising *Dofleins Geigenschule.*

Film Music (refer to the preface)
For films directed by Fischinger

1932 (BERLIN)

Philharmonic Concerto
Variations for symphony orchestra
Feb.–Mar. 1932. [c. 1932, Schott]
Performance time: 21 min.

Practice Pieces for Strings, Woodwinds, and Brass (unpublished)
Written for the students at the Berlin Hochschule für Musik.

Der Tod
TTBB; text by Friedrich Hölderlin
[c. 1932, Schott]
Performance time: 2 min.

Plöner Musiktag
(A day of music at Plön)
A. *Morning Music*
Brass choir, to be played from a tower
Performance time: 10 min.
B. *Luncheon Music*
Flute, trumpet or clarinet, strings
Performance time: 9½ min.
C. *Cantata: Advice to Youth*
Chorus, soli, orchestra; to be performed in the afternoon
Text: a statement by Martin Agricola (16th century) urging young people to become involved with music.
Performance time: 16 min.
D. *Evening Concert*
Orchestral prelude
Flute solo, with strings
Two duets for violin and clarinet
Variations for clarinet and strings
Trio for recorders
Quodlibet for orchestra
Performance time, about 30 min.
May 1932. [c. 1932, Schott]

1933 (BERLIN)

String Trio, No. 2
Violin, viola, violoncello
Feb.-Mar. 1933. [c. 1934, Schott]
Performance time: 23 min.

Concert Piece for Two Alto Saxophones
Completed 14 June 1933. [c. 1976, McGinnis and Marx, New York]

Eight Cadenzas for Mozart Violin Concertos
2 for the "Adelaide" Concerto, now known to be a spurious work, actually writ-

ten by Robert Casadesus; 4 for the *Concerto in D Major, K. 218;* 2 for the *Concerto in G Major.*
Aug.–Nov. 1933. [c. 1933, Schott]

Two Cadenzas for Mozart's Piano Concerto in G Major, K. 41
Aug.–Nov. 1933. [c. 1933, Schott]

Four Songs for Tenor and Piano
Texts by Friedrich Hölderlin
Sonnenuntergang (rewritten in 1935)
Ehmals und jetzt (rewritten in 1935)
Fragment
Abendphantasie
[c. 1965, Schott]
Cf. *Two Songs for Tenor and Piano* (1935).

Four Songs (unpublished)
Solo voice and piano; texts by Novalis

Four Songs (unpublished)
Solo voice and piano; texts by Wilhelm Busch

Three Songs (unpublished)
Solo voice and piano; texts by Matthias Claudius

Four Songs (unpublished)
Solo voice and piano; texts by Friedrich Rückert

1934 (BERLIN)

Duet for Viola and Violoncello
London, "written in 3 hours, 23 Jan. 1934." [c. 1957, Schott]
Performance time: 4 min.

Symphony: Mathis der Maler
Jan.–Feb. 1934. [c. 1934, Schott]
Performance time: 26 min.

Two Little Piano Pieces (unpublished)

Entertainment Music (unpublished)
Three clarinets; composition class project.

Cantata for an Outing (unpublished)
Solo voice, chorus, four clarinets; composition class project (the music was actually used on an outing).

1935 (BERLIN)

Mathis der Maler
Full-length opera in seven scenes; libretto by Hindemith
Mostly in Berlin, between Sept. 1933 and July 1935. [c. 1935, Schott]

Sonata in E for Violin and Piano
Frankfurt, June and Aug. 1935. [c. 1935, Schott]
Performance time: 9 min.

Slow Piece and Rondo for Trautonium (only sketches exist)
Frankfurt or Berlin, Aug. 1935

Der Schwanendreher
Concerto for viola and reduced orchestra, based on old German folksongs
Sept.–Oct. 1935. [c. 1936, Schott]
Performance time: 24 min.

Two Songs for Tenor and Piano
Texts by Friedrich Hölderlin
An die Parzen
Des Morgens
Frankfurt, Dec. 1935
These were added to the four Hölderlin songs written in 1933 and all six were published by Schott in 1965 in two editions, one for tenor and the other for baritone.

Four Songs (unpublished)
Solo voice and piano; texts by Angelus Silesius
Frankfurt or Berlin, 1935

1936 (BERLIN)

Trauermusik
(Music of Mourning)
Solo viola (or violin or violoncello) and string orchestra
London, 21 Jan. 1936. [c. 1936, Schott]
Performance time: 6 min.

Sonata in A for Piano
Known as the *First Piano Sonata*
Ankara (Turkey) and Berlin, completed 29 Jan. 1936. [c. 1936, Schott]
Performance time: 21 min.

Sonata in G for Piano
Known as the *Second Piano Sonata*
Completed 5 July 1936. [c. 1936, Schott]
Performance time: 10 min.

Sonata in B♭ for Piano
Known as the *Third Piano Sonata*
Completed 1 Aug. 1936. [c. 1936, Schott]
Performance time: 20 min.

Sonata for Flute and Piano
Dec. 1936. [c. 1937, Schott]
Performance time: 14 min.

Two Songs (unpublished)
Solo voice and piano; texts by Clemens Brentano

Das Köhlerwert (unpublished)
Solo voice and piano; text by Gottfried Keller

Five Folksongs (unpublished)
Arranged for clarinet and string orchestra

1937 (BERLIN)

Lieder nach alten Texten
In March 1937 (Berlin), Hindemith revised nos. 1, 2, 3, and 6 from his Opus 33 of 1924 for performance at the Coolidge Festival in Washington, D.C., in April 1937 (his first concert tour of the United States). They were sung in German and were so well received that AMP officials urged Schott to publish them with an English translation. For more on this, see *Five Songs on Old Texts* (1938).

Sonata for Solo Viola (unpublished)
Chicago, 20–21 Apr. 1937

Sonata for Organ, No. 1
Italy, June 1937. [c. 1937, Schott]
Performance time: 18 min.

Sonata for Organ, No. 2
Italy, June–July 1937. [c. 1937, Schott]
Performance time: 11 min.

Symphonic Dances
Full symphony orchestra.
"Composed in summer and fall of 1937—Berlin, Italy, Brussa, and Ankara."
[c. 1938, Schott]
Performance time: 32 min.

1938 (BERLIN; BLUCH, SWITZERLAND)

Nobilissima Visione
Dance legend in six scenes based on the life of St. Francis
Scenario by Hindemith and Leonide Massine
Berlin, Jan.–Feb. 1938. [c. 1938, Schott]
Performance time: 35 min.

Nobilissima Visione Suite
Orchestral suite arranged from the ballet score, with enlarged instrumentation
Bluch, Switzerland, Aug. 1938. [c. 1940, Schott and AMP]
Performance time: 20 min.

Meditation
Excerpt from *Nobilissima Visione,* arranged for violin, viola, or violoncello and piano; published separately by Schott
Performance time: 2 1/2 min.

Nine Songs for an American School Songbook
New York, Mar. 1938. [c. 1938, Silver Burdett Company, Chicago]
Only 6 of the 9 songs were used, appearing in various Silver Burdett collections.

Three Easy Pieces for Violoncello and Piano
On board the S.S. *Hamburg,* en route to Europe from New York 3–10 Apr. 1938. [c. 1938, Schott]
Performance time: 8 min.

Five Songs on Old Texts
SSATB, a cappella
True Love (Wahre Liebe)—Heinrich von Veldecke
Lady's Lament (Frauenklage)—Burggraf zu Regensburg
Of Household Rule (Vom Hausregiment)—Martin Luther
Trooper's Drinking Song (Landsknechtstrinklied)—Anon.
The Devil a Monk Would Be (Art lässt nicht von Art)—Spervogel
True Love was completed 21 Apr. 1938 in Frankfurt and added to the four pieces revised in 1937, with an English translation by Arthur Mendel. The other four were translated by William Strunk, Jr. All five were first published by AMP in 1943 under the title *Five Songs on Old Texts.*
Performance times: 1 1/3 min., 2 min., 1 2/3 min., 1 1/2 min., 3/4 min.

Quartet for Clarinet, Violin, Violoncello, Piano
S.S. *Hamburg,* Frankfurt, Wallis (Switzerland), Apr.–June 1938. [c. 1939, Schott]
Performance time: 24 min.

Sonata for Bassoon and Piano
Berlin and Chandolin (Switzerland), Jan. and June 1938. [c. 1939, Schott]
Performance time: 9 min.

Sonata for Oboe and Piano
Chandolin, June 1938. [c. 1939, Schott]
Performance time: 12 min.

Sonata for Piano, Four Hands
Berlin, Frankfurt, Aug.–Sept. 1938. [c. 1939, Schott]
Performance time: 13 min.

1939 (BLUCH, SWITZERLAND)

Sonata for Viola and Piano
Chandolin (Switzerland), Los Angeles, New York, Boston; between July 1938 and 13 Apr. 1939. [c. 1940, AMP]
Performance time: 24 min.

Three Choruses for TTBB
Das verfluchte Geld (Anon.)
Nun da der Tag (Nietzsche)
Die Stiefmutter (Anon.)
Bluch, completed 28 May 1939. [c. 1950, Schott]
Performance times: 1 min., 1 3/4 min., 1 1/2 min.

Das Marienleben
Songs Nos. 1, 5, 7, and 8, arranged for soprano and orchestra
June 1939. [c. 1939, Schott, score on rental only]

Concerto for Violin and Orchestra
June–July 1939. [c. 1939, Schott]
Performance time: 24 min.

Sonata in C for Violin and Piano
3–9 Sept. 1939. [c. 1939, Schott]
Performance time: 12 min.

Six Chansons
SATB, a cappella; on French poems by Rainer Maria Rilke
English translations by Elaine de Sinçay
The Doe — *Springtime*
A Swan — *In Winter*
Since All Is Passing — *Orchard*
10–12 Sept. 1939. [c. 1943, Schott-London and AMP]
Performance time: 8 min.

Sonata for Clarinet and Piano
21–28 Sept. 1939. [c. 1940, AMP]
Performance time: 17 min.

Sonata for Harp
Oct. 1939. [c. 1940, AMP]
Performance time: 9 min.

Two Choruses for TTBB
Erster Schnee (Keller)
Variationen über ein altes Tanzlied (Anon.)
26–27 Oct. 1939. [c. 1950, Schott]
Performance times: 3 min., 5 1/2 min.

Sonata for Horn and Piano
Oct.–Nov. 1939. [c. 1940, AMP]
Performance time: 16 min.

Sonata for Trumpet and Piano
19–25 Nov. 1939. [c. 1940, AMP]
Performance time: 12 min.

Three Songs (unpublished)
Solo voice and piano; texts by Nietzsche

1940 (BUFFALO, N.Y.; NEW HAVEN, CONN.)

A Song of Music
("As Donkeys Bray and Robins Sing")
SSA, with piano or strings; text by George Tyler
Wells College, Aurora, N.Y., Mar.–Apr. 1940. [c. 1941, AMP]

A composition class project; text later translated into German by Hindemith with the title *Lied von der Musik*; published by Schott in 1958 with both German and English texts.

Sonata for Organ, No. 3
Buffalo, between 25 May and 5 June 1940. [c. 1940, AMP]
Performance time: 11 min.

The Harp that Once thro' Tara's Halls
SATB, with piano or harp and strings
Tanglewood, Lenox, Mass., July–Aug. 1940. [c. 1941, AMP]
A composition class project; text later translated into German by Hindemith with the title *Altes irisches Lied;* published by Schott in 1958 with both German and English texts.

Concerto for Violoncello and Orchestra
Lenox, Mass., between 30 June and 9 Sept. 1940. [c. 1941, AMP]
Performance time: 28 min.

Theme with Four Variations: The Four Temperaments
Music for a ballet; solo piano and string orchestra
New Haven, completed 1 Nov. 1940. [c. 1947, Schott]
Performance time: 28 min.

Symphony in E♭
Full symphony orchestra
New Haven, between 25 Sept. and 15 Dec. 1940. [c. 1940, Schott-London, AMP]
Performance time: 32 min.

1941 (NEW HAVEN)

Cum natus esset
Soprano and piano; No. 8 of the *Thirteen Motets*
Jan. 1941. [c. 1952, Schott]
Performance time: 5 min.

In principia erat verbum (unpublished)
Soprano and piano

Sonata for English Horn and Piano
Richmond, Mass. (near Lenox), Aug. 1941. [c. 1942, AMP]
Performance time: 11 min.

Sonata for Trombone and Piano
Completed 6 Oct. 1941. [c. 1942, AMP]
Performance time: 12 min.

A Frog He Went A-Courtin'
Violoncello and piano; variations on an old English children's song
Completed 7 Nov. 1941. [c. 1951, AMP]
Performance time: 4 1/2 min.

1942 (NEW HAVEN)

Four Pieces for Violoncello and Bassoon
[c. 1969, Schott]

Little Sonata for Violoncello and Piano (unpublished)
13–14 May 1942

Sonata for Two Pianos
Completed 28 Aug. 1942. [c. 1942, AMP]
Performance time: 16 min.

La belle dame sans merci
High or middle voice and piano; text by John Keats
No. 1 of *Two Ballads*
Completed 10 Sept. 1942. [c. 1945, AMP]
Performance time: 5 min.

Ludus Tonalis
"Contrapuntal, Tonal, and Technical Exercises for the Piano."
Between 29 Aug. and 12 Oct. 1942. [c. 1943, AMP]
Performance time: 48 min.

Twenty-One Songs for Solo Voice and Piano (unpublished)
On German, French, and Latin texts
1942–44; 17 written in 1942, 1 in 1943, 3 in 1944

Songs for Soprano or Mezzo-Soprano and Piano
Part of the series *Nine English Songs*
Echo (Moore)
Envoy (Thompson)
The Moon (Shelley)
On a Fly (Oldys)
On Hearing "The Last Rose of Summer" (Wolfe)
The Wildflower's Song (Blake)
The Whistlin' Thief (Lover)
Fall 1942. [c. 1944–46, AMP]
Performance times: 1 min., 4 min., 3 min., 2 min., 3 min., 2 min., 3 min.

Echo
Flute and piano; arrangement of the first song listed immediately above
Fall 1942. [c. 1945, AMP]

1943 (NEW HAVEN)

String Quartet in E♭
Known as the *Fifth String Quartet*
Completed 16 May 1943. [c. 1944, AMP]
Performance time: 26 min.

Frau Musica
(In Praise of Music)
Solo voice, chorus, audience, strings
Extensive revision of opus 45 I (1928); English text added.
Randolph, N.H., July 1943. [c. 1945, AMP]
Performance time: 7 min.

Cupid and Psyche (Farnesina)
"Overture to a Ballet," for chamber orchestra
Randolph, N.H., 20–23 July 1943. [c. 1944, AMP]
Performance time: 6 min.

Symphonic Metamorphosis of Themes by Carl Maria von Weber
Full symphony orchestra
June and Aug. 1943. [c. 1945, AMP]
Performance time: 20 min.

Sonata for Althorn or Alto Saxophone and Piano
South Egremont, Mass., Sept. 1943. [c. 1956, Schott]
Performance time: 11 min.

Sing On There in the Swamp
Soprano and piano; text by Walt Whitman
Part of the series *Nine English Songs*
Completed 8 Nov. 1943. [c. 1945, AMP]
Performance time: 2½ min.

Monteverdi's *Orfeo*
During Nov. and Dec. of 1943 Hindemith prepared a special performance edition of Monteverdi's *Orfeo* based as closely as possible on the original score, including the use of authentic old instruments (or modern reproductions). There is some evidence that he had in mind a performance at Yale, but this never took place. Schott published the performance materials in the spring of 1954, and Hindemith conducted performances in Vienna on 25 Apr. and 3 June of that year. He also conducted it in Frankfurt in May 1960 and in Rome and Perugia in October 1963, only two months before he died.

Ascendente Jesu in naviculum
Soprano and piano; No. 13 of the *Thirteen Motets*
Dec. 1943. [c. 1959, Schott]

1944 (NEW HAVEN)

Recitativo e Aria Ranatica (unpublished)
A parody for bass and piano
Text: from the article on "Frog" in the Encyclopaedia Britannica, and Charles Dickens' *Ode to an Expiring Frog.*
April 1944

Herodiäde
Ballet score for chamber orchestra
"An orchestral recitation" based on the poem by Stéphane Mallarmé
June 1944. [c. 1955, Schott]
Performance time: 22 min.

Bal des pendus
Solo voice and piano; text by Jean Arthur Rimbaud
No. 2 of *Two Ballads.*
West Southport, Maine, completed 27 July 1944. [c. 1980, Schott]

To Music to Becalm His Fever
Soprano and piano; text by Robert Herrick
Part of the series *Nine English Songs*
[c. 1946, AMP]
Performance time: 3 min.

Pastores loquebantur
Soprano and piano; No. 2 of the *Thirteen Motets*
Dec. 1944. [c. 1952, Schott]
Performance time: 3½ min.

Nuptiae factae sunt
Soprano and piano; No. 11 of the *Thirteen Motets*
Completed 28 Dec. 1944. [c. 1952, Schott]

Ludus minor (unpublished)
Clarinet and violoncello

1945 (NEW HAVEN)

Concerto for Piano and Orchestra
Millbridge, Maine, Aug. 1945, completed in New Haven 29 Nov. 1945. [c. 1948, Schott]
Performance time: 26 min.

String Quartet
Known as the *Sixth String Quartet*
Completed 30 Dec. 1945. [c. 1949, Schott and AMP]
Performance time: 15 min.

Oh, Threats of Hell
Four-part canon for mixed voices; text by Omar Khayyam
[c. 1945, Mercury, New York; No. 7 in *Modern Canons*]

1946 (NEW HAVEN)

When Lilacs Last in the Dooryard Bloom'd: A Requiem for Those We Love
Generally known as *The Lilacs Requiem*
Baritone and mezzo-soprano soli, chorus, orchestra
Text by Walt Whitman

Between 17 Jan. and 20 Apr. 1946. [c. 1948, AMP]
Performance time: 65 min.

When Lilacs Last in the Dooryard Bloom'd
Orchestral prelude to the *Requiem*
Published separately by Schott
Performance time: 5 min.

Symphonia Serena
Full symphony orchestra
Nov.–Dec. 1946. [c. 1947, AMP]
Performance time: 30 min.

Sine musica nulla disciplina
Three-part canon on a text by Hrabanus Maurus
[c. 1951, Schott]

1947 (NEW HAVEN)

Apparebit repentina dies
Mixed chorus and ten brass instruments; on a medieval Latin text
Feb. 1947. [c. 1947, Schott-London]

Concerto for Clarinet and Orchestra
Switzerland, summer 1947, completed in New Haven 27 Sept. 1947. [c. 1950, Schott and AMP]
Performance time: 21 min.

1948 (NEW HAVEN)

Sonata for Violoncello and Piano
Feb.–Mar. 1948. [c. 1948, Schott]
Performance time: 20 min.

Suite of French Dances
Arrangement for small orchestra of dances by Claude Gervais and Estienne du Tertre from Pierre d'Attaignant's 16th-century publication *Livres de Danceries*
Spring 1948. [c. 1958, Schott]
Performance time: 8 min.

Das Marienleben [II]
(The Life of Mary)
Complete revision of the 1922–23 version, Opus 27, with an extended explanatory foreword by the composer.
Revisions made mostly in 1936 and 1937 in Berlin, and 1941, 1942, and 1945 in New Haven. [c. 1948, AMP and Schott]
Performance time: 70 min.

Septet for Wind Instruments
Flute, oboe, clarinet, bass clarinet, bassoon, horn, trumpet

Taormina, Sicily, Nov. 1948, completed in Rome, 7 Dec. 1948. [c. 1949, Schott]
Performance time: 15 min.

1949 (NEW HAVEN)

Concerto for Horn and Orchestra
Switzerland, Mar. 1949. [c. 1950, Schott and AMP]
Performance time: 15 min.

Concerto for Woodwinds, Harp, and Orchestra
Apr. 1949. [c. 1950, Schott and AMP]
Performance time: 13 min.

The Demon of the Gibbet
TBB, three to five parts; text by Fitz-James O'Brien
29 Apr. 1949. [c. 1950, Schott-London]
Published later by Schott with a German translation by Hindemith under the title *Galgenritt.*
Performance time: 3 min.

Sonata for Double Bass and Piano
Taos, N.M., 17–18 Aug. 1949. [c. 1950, Schott]
Performance time: 14 min.

Concerto for Trumpet and Bassoon with String Orchestra
Sept. 1949, first two movements only; third movement added in Nov. 1952, also written in New Haven. [c. 1954, Schott]
Performance time: 16 min.

Musica divina laudes
Three-part canon, known as the "Coolidge Canon," as it was written as a birthday greeting to Mrs. Elizabeth Sprague Coolidge
Boston, Nov. 1949. [c. 1951, Schott]

1950 (NEW HAVEN)

Sinfonietta in E
Full symphony orchestra
Dec. 1949–Jan. 1950. [c. 1950, Schott and AMP]
Performance time: 21 min.

1951 (NEW HAVEN; ZURICH)

Symphony in B♭ for Concert Band
New Haven, 7–9 Mar. 1951. [c. 1951, Schott and AMP]
Performance time: 19 min.

Symphony: Die Harmonie der Welt
Full symphony orchestra

Zurich, Nov.–Dec. 1951. [c. 1952, Schott and AMP]
Performance time: 34 min.

1952 (ZURICH; NEW HAVEN)

Cardillac [II]
Full-length opera in four acts
Completely revised and considerably extended version of the 1926 opera; new libretto by Hindemith.
Zurich, completed spring 1952. [c. 1952, Schott and AMP]

Sonata for Four Horns
New Haven, completed 29 Oct. 1952. [c. 1953, Schott and AMP]
Performance time: 8 min.

1953 (NEW HAVEN; BLONAY, SWITZERLAND)

Canticle to Hope
Mezzo-soprano solo, chorus, audience, orchestra, band
Part III of *Ite, angeli veloces,* a cantata in three parts on texts by Paul Claudel (see below under 1955)
New Haven, Apr. 1953. [c. 1955, Schott]
Performance time: 19 min.

Neues vom Tage [II]
(News of the day)
Full-length comic opera in two acts
Extensive revision (primarily textual) of the 1929 version.
Blonay, Dec. 1953. [c. 1954, Schott]

1954 (BLONAY)

During 1954 Hindemith was heavily occupied with his teaching at the University of Zurich and many conducting engagements throughout Europe and South America. Whatever time was available for writing was devoted chiefly to working on the libretto for *Die Harmonie der Welt.*

1955 (BLONAY)

Sonata for Tuba and Piano
Jan. 1955. [c. 1957, Schott and AMP]
Performance time: 11 min.

Two Songs
Soprano (or tenor) and piano; texts by Oscar Cox
Beauty Touch Me
Image
29–30 Jan. 1955. [c. 1955, Schott and AMP]
Performance times: 1 1/2 minutes each

David's Song of Triumph
Alto and tenor soli, chorus, audience, orchestra, band
Part I of *Ite, angeli veloces* (see above under 1953)
Spring 1955. [c. 1955, Schott]
Performance time: 19 min.

Custos, quid de nocte
Tenor solo, chorus, orchestra
Part II of *Ite, angeli veloces* (see under 1953)
Completed 5 Mar. 1955. [c. 1955, Schott]
Performance time: 10 min.

Max Reger's *Psalm 100,* Opus 16
Chorus and orchestra
Hindemith revised the choral and instrumental scoring, thinning it considerably to achieve greater clarity. He conducted the work several times between 1955 and 1963.
Summer 1955. [c. 1958, C. F. Peters]

1956 (BLONAY)

A heavy concert schedule again this year (including a tour of Japan as conductor of the Vienna Philharmonic Orchestra) precluded Hindemith's doing any other writing except working on the libretto and score of *Die Harmonie der Welt.*

1957 (BLONAY)

Die Harmonie der Welt
(The harmony of the universe)
Full-length opera in five acts; libretto by Hindemith
1956 and 1957, completed by June 1957. [c. 1957, Schott]
(Some of the music had been written in 1951 and used for the symphony *Die Harmonie der Welt.*)

1958 (BLONAY)

Octet
Clarinet, bassoon, horn, violin, two violas, violoncello, double bass
Dec. 1957–Feb. 1958. [c. 1958, Schott]
Performance time: 26 min.

Twelve Madrigals
SSATB, a cappella; texts by Josef Weinheber
Mitwelt (1)
Eines Narren (2)
Tauche deine Furcht (2 1/2)
An eine Tote (7)
An eine Schmetterling (1 3/4)
Judaskuss (3)
Magisches Rezept (2 1/2)
Es bleibt wohl 1(1/4)

Trink aus! (1 1/2)
Frühling (1)
Kraft fand zu Form (2)
Du Zweifel (2 1/4)

Between 20 Feb. and 29 Mar. 1958, except *Kraft fand zu Form,* written in Rome, 24 Feb. 1958. [c. 1958, Schott]
Performance times given in parentheses.

Defuncto Herode
Soprano and piano; No. 7 of the *Thirteen Motets*
Completed 11 May 1958. [c. 1959, Schott]
Performance time: 3 min.

Angelus Domini apparuit
Soprano and piano; No. 5 of the *Thirteen Motets*
Completed 15 May 1958. [c. 1959, Schott]
Performance time: 4 1/2 min.

Pittsburgh Symphony
Full symphony orchestra
Aug.–Nov. 1958. [c. 1959, Schott]
Performance time: 26 min.

1959 (BLONAY)

Dicebat Jesu scribis et pharisaeis
Soprano and piano; No. 3 of the *Thirteen Motets*
Completed 13 July 1959. [c. 1959, Schott]
Performance time: 5 min.

Dixit Jesus Petro
Soprano and piano; No. 4 of the *Thirteen Motets*
Completed 19 July 1959. [c. 1959, Schott]
Performance time: 3 1/2 min.

Das Marienleben
Songs nos. 10 and 15, arranged for soprano and orchestra
Aug. 1959. [c. 1960, Schott, on rental only]

Vidit Joannes Jesum
Soprano and piano; No. 10 of the *Thirteen Motets*
Completed 17 Oct. 1959. [c. 1960, Schott]
Performance time: 4 min.

Cum factus esset Jesus
Soprano and piano; No. 9 of the *Thirteen Motets*
Completed 21 Nov. 1959. [c. 1960, Schott]
Performance time: 3 1/2 min.

Erat Joseph et Maria
Soprano and piano; No. 6 of the *Thirteen Motets*
Completed 29 Dec. 1959. [c. 1959, Schott]
Performance time: 4 min.

1960 (BLONAY)

Exiit edictum
Soprano and piano; No. 1 of the *Thirteen Motets*
First version, New Haven, Dec. 1940; revised in Blonay, 23 Jan. 1960. [c. 1960, Schott]
Performance time: 6 min.

Marsch
Full symphony orchestra; based on a 16th-century Swiss tune
Completed 24 May 1960. [c. 1960, Schott, on rental only]
Performance time: 4 min.

Cum descendisset Jesus
Soprano and piano; No. 12 of the *Thirteen Motets*
Completed 12 June 1960. [c. 1960, Schott]
Performance time: 4½ min.

The Long Christmas Dinner
Opera in one act; libretto by Thornton Wilder, with German translation by Hindemith
Completed 23 Aug. 1960. [c. 1961, Schott]
Performance time: 60 min.

During 1960 Hindemith also made a further revision of *Neues vom Tage*, adapting it to an English translation by Don Moreland. As *News of the Day* it received its U.S. premiere by the Santa Fe Opera Company in August 1961 (a world premiere of the English version). The three performances in Santa Fe were conducted by Hindemith.

1961 (BLONAY)

Hindemith had a very heavy concert schedule this year, with 33 conducting engagements (opera as well as orchestra) in Europe and the United States. The only composition he wrote was a new duet (No. 16) for Act II of the revised version of *Cardillac*.

1962 (BLONAY)

Mainzer Umzug
(Mainz Procession)
"A theatrical scene, without costumes or sets."
Text by Carl Zuckmayer and Hindemith
Soprano, tenor, baritone soli, chorus, orchestra
Apr.–May 1962. [c. 1962, Schott, on rental only]
Performance time: 38 min.

1963 (BLONAY)

Concerto for Organ and Orchestra
Nov. 1962–Feb. 1963. [c. 1964, Schott]
Performance time: 25 min.

Mass
A liturgical Mass, for mixed chorus a cappella
Between 21 Aug. and 6 Sept. 1963. [c. 1963, Schott]
Performance time: 20 min.
This was the last composition Hindemith completed. The world premiere of the *Mass* in Vienna on November 12, which he conducted, also proved to be his last public appearance. He became seriously ill four days later and never recovered, dying on December 28, 1963.

BIBLIOGRAPHY

Note: The following contains only those works referred to in the text or notes. For other literature on Hindemith, the reader should refer to the four general bibliographies listed below.

Westphal, Elisabeth. *Paul Hindemith, eine Bibliographie des In- und Auslandes seit 1922 über ihn und sein Werk.* Cologne: Greven, 1957.

Rösner, Helmut. "Zur Hindemith-Bibliographie und Literatur." *Hindemith Jahrbuch* 1 (1971), pp. 161–96.

Zickenheiner, Otto. "Hindemith-Bibliographie: 1971–1973." *Hindemith Jahrbuch* 3 (1973), pp. 155–72.

Laubenthal, Annegrit. "Hindemith-Bibliographie: 1974–1978." *Hindemith Jahrbuch* 7 (1978), pp. 229–39.

Adorno, Theodor W. "Ad vocem Hindemith, eine Documentation." In *Impromptus.* Frankfurt: Suhrkamp, 1968.

Altwein, Erich F. W. "Zum Briefwechsel Paul Hindemith–Hans Kayser." *Hindemith Jahrbuch* 3 (1973), p. 144.

Apel, Willi, ed. *French Secular Music of the Late Fourteenth Century.* Cambridge, Mass.: Medieval Academy of America, 1950.

Baker, James. "Scriabin's Implicit Tonality." *Music Theory Spectrum* 2 (1980), p. 1.

———. "Schenkerian Analysis and Post-Tonal Music." In *Aspects of Schenkerian Theory,* edited by David Beach. New Haven: Yale University Press, 1983.

Bauer, Dietrich. "Paul Hindemith als Bratschist." *Hindemith Jahrbuch* 6 (1977), p. 142.

Benjamin, William. Review of *The Structure of Atonal Music* by Allen Forte. *Perspectives of New Music* 13 (1974), p. 170.

———. "Ideas of Order in Motivic Music." *Music Theory Spectrum* 1 (1979), p. 23.

Biber, Heinrich Ignaz Franz von. *Sonaten zur Verherrlichung von fünfzehn Mysterien aus dem Leben Mariäs und Christus.* Edited by Robert Reitz. Vienna: Universal, 1923.

Billeter, Bernhard. "Die kompositorische Entwicklung Hindemiths am Beispiel seiner Klavierwerke." *Hindemith Jahrbuch* 6 (1977), p. 104.

———, ed. *Paul Hindemith: Sämtliche Werke* V/10: *Klavierwerke II.* Mainz: Schott, 1981.

Boatwright, Howard. "Hindemith's Performances of Old Music." *Hindemith Jahrbuch* 3 (1973), p. 39.

Böhme, Franz. *Altdeutsches Liederbuch.* Leipzig: Breitkopf und Härtel, 1877.
Booth, P. J. "Hindemith's Analytical Method and an Alternative." *Soundings* 7 (1978), p. 117.
Borris, Siegfried. "Hindemiths harmonische Analysen." In *Festschrift für Max Schneider,* edited by Wilhelm Vetter. Leipzig: Deutscher Verlag für Musik, 1955.
Briner, Andres. "A New Comment on Tonality by Paul Hindemith." *Journal of Music Theory* 5 (1961), p. 109.
———. "Hindemith und Adornos Kritik des Musikanten: Oder, von sozialer und soziologischer Haltung." *Hindemith Jahrbuch* 1 (1971), p. 26.
———. *Paul Hindemith.* Mainz: Schott and Zurich: Atlantis, 1971.
———. "Paul Hindemith und Arnold Schoenberg." *Hindemith Jahrbuch* 4 (1974), p. 149.
———. "Ich und Wir: Zur Entwicklung des jungen Paul Hindemiths." In *Erprobungen und Erfahrungen: Zu Paul Hindemith's Schaffen in den Zwanziger Jahren,* edited by Dieter Rexroth. *Frankfurter Studien,* no. 2. Mainz: Schott, 1981.
Burkhart, Charles. "Schenker's 'Motivic Parallelisms'." *Journal of Music Theory* 22 (1978), p. 145.
Cahn, Peter. "Hindemiths Kadenzen." *Hindemith Jahrbuch* 1 (1971), p. 80.
———. "Hindemith aus der Sicht statistischer Analyse." *Hindemith Jahrbuch* 4 (1974), p. 140.
———. "Ein unbekanntes musikpädagogisches Dokument von 1927: Hindemiths Konzeption einer Musikhochschule." *Hindemith Jahrbuch* 6 (1977), p. 148.
Christ, William, et al. *Materials and Structure of Music.* 2 vols. 2d edition. Englewood Cliffs, N.J.: Prentice-Hall, 1973.
D'Angelo, James. "Tonality and Its Symbolic Associations in Paul Hindemith's Opera *Die Harmonie der Welt.*" Ph. D. dissertation, New York University, 1983.
Einstein, Alfred. "Paul Hindemith." *Modern Music* 5 (1927), p. 21.
Finscher, Ludwig. "Paul Hindemith: Versuch einer Neuorientierung." *Hindemith Jahrbuch* 1 (1971), p. 16.
Fischer, Kurt von, ed. *Paul Hindemith: Sämtliche Werke* VI/1: *Klavierlieder I.* Mainz: Schott, 1983.
Fischer, Kurt von, and Ludwig Finscher, gen. eds. *Paul Hindemith: Sämtliche Werke.* Mainz: Schott, 1975–.
Forte, Allen. "Sets and Nonsets in Schoenberg's Atonal Music." *Perspectives of New Music* 11 (1972), p. 43.
———. *The Structure of Atonal Music.* New Haven: Yale University Press, 1973.
———. "The Basic Interval Patterns." *Journal of Music Theory* 17 (1973), p. 234.
———. *The Harmonic Organization of "The Rite of Spring."* New Haven: Yale University Press, 1978.
———. "Schoenberg's Creative Evolution: The Path to Atonality." *Musical Quarterly* 44 (1978), p. 133.
Gay, Peter. *Freud, Jews, and Other Germans.* London: Oxford University Press, 1978.
Godwin, Joscelyn. "The Revival of Speculative Music." *Musical Quarterly* 68 (1982), p. 373.
Goebels, Franzpeter. "Interpretationsaspekte zum Ludus Tonalis." *Hindemith Jahrbuch* 2 (1972), p. 137.

Gould, Glenn. "A Tale of Two Marienlebens." Liner notes to Columbia recording M2 34597 [copyright 1978].

Green, Douglass. "Cantus Firmus Techniques in the Concertos and Operas of Alban Berg." In *Alban Berg Symposion Wien 1980: Tagungsbericht,* edited by Rudolf Klein. *Alban Berg Studien,* vol. 2. Vienna: Universal, 1981.

Grout, Donald J. *A History of Western Music.* Revised ed. New York: W. W. Norton, 1973.

Haase, Rudolf. *Paul Hindemiths harmonikale Quellen—sein Briefwechsel mit Hans Kayser.* Vienna: Elisabeth Lafite, 1973.

Halm, August. *Von Form und Sinn der Musik.* Edited by Siegfried Schmalzriedt. Wiesbaden: Breitkopf und Härtel, 1978.

Harnoncourt, Nicholas. Preface to his edition of Sonata Representativa in A by H. I. F. Biber. Vienna: Doblinger, 1977.

Hilse, Walter B. "Factors making for Coherence in the Works of Paul Hindemith, 1919–1926." Ph.D. dissertation, Columbia University, 1971.

Hindemith-Jahrbuch/Annales-Hindemith. Paul-Hindemith-Institut, Frankfurt am Main. Mainz: Schott, 1971–.

Hindemith, Paul. *Unterweisung im Tonsatz.* Vol. 1: *Theoretischer Teil.* Mainz: Schott, 1937; rev. ed., 1940. [*The Craft of Musical Composition. Theoretical Part.* Translated by Arthur Mendel. New York: Associated Music, 1942; rev. ed., 1945.] Vol. 2: *Übungsbuch für den zweistimmigen Satz.* Mainz: Schott, 1939. [*Exercises in Two-Part Writing.* Translated by Otto Ortmann. New York: Associated Music, 1941.] Vol. 3: *Übungsbuch für den dreistimmigen Satz.* Edited by Andres Briner, P. Daniel Meier, and Alfred Rubeli. Mainz: Schott, 1970. Vol. 4: *Übungsbuch für den vierstimmigen Satz.* Unpublished. Only one chapter, "Übung 21," extant. Photolithographic copy in the Yale Hindemith Collection.

———. *A Concentrated Course in Traditional Harmony.* Vol. 1: New York: Associated Music, 1943. Vol. 2: *Exercises for Advanced Students.* New York: Associated Music, 1949.

———. *Elementary Training for Musicians.* New York: Associated Music, 1946.

———. *Introductory Remarks for the New Version of "Das Marienleben."* Translated by Arthur Mendel. New York: Associated Music, 1948.

———. *A Composer's World: Horizons and Limitations.* Cambridge: Harvard University Press, 1952.

———. *Johann Sebastian Bach: Heritage and Obligation.* New Haven: Yale University Press, 1952.

———. "Sterbende Gewässer." *Reden und Gedenkworte (Orden pour le Mérite für Wissenschaften und Künste)* 6 (1963–64), p. 47.

———. "Hören und Verstehen ungewohnter Musik." *Hindemith Jahrbuch* 3 (1973), p. 173.

Holl, Karl. "Musikleben: Frankfurt a. M." *Die Musik* 16 (1924), p. 297.

Howat, Roy. *Debussy in Proportion: A Musical Analysis.* Cambridge: University of Cambridge Press, 1983.

Kaufmann, Henry W., ed. *Paul Hindemith: Sämtliche Werke* VI/5: *Sologesänge mit Orchester.* Mainz: Schott, 1983.

Kemp, Ian. *Paul Hindemith.* London: Oxford University Press, 1970.

Kidd, James C. "Aspects of Mensuration in Hindemith's Clarinet Sonata." *Music*

Review 38 (1977), p. 211.
Klein, Rudolf. "Von Hindemith zu Hindemith: Bemerkungen zu den beiden Fassungen des 'Marienlebens'." *Österreichische Musikzeitschrift* 19 (1964), p. 67.
Kurth, Ernst. *Die Grundlagen des linearen Kontrapunkts: Bachs melodische Polyphonie.* Berlin: Max Hesse, 1917.
———. *Romantische Harmonik und ihre Krise in Wagners "Tristan."* Bern: Paul Haupt, 1920.
Landau, Victor, "Paul Hindemith: A Case Study in Theory and Practice." *Music Review* 21 (1960), p. 38.
Lederer, Josef Horst. "Zu Hindemiths Idee einer Rhythmen- und Formenlehre." *Musikforschung* 29 (1976), p. 21.
Lewis, C. S. *The Pilgrim's Regress.* London: Geoffrey Bles. Repr. ed. Grand Rapids: Eerdmans, 1958.
Luntz, Erwin, ed. *Sechszehn Violinsonaten von H. I. F. Biber. Denkmäler der Tonkunst in Österreich,* vol. 25. Leipzig: Breitkopf und Härtel, 1905.
Mersmann, Hans. *Die moderne Musik seit der Romantik.* Wildspark-Potsdam: Athenaion, 1928.
———. *Die Tonsprache der neuen Musik.* Mainz: Schott, 1930.
Mersmann, Hans, Hans Schultze-Ritter, Heinrich Strobel, and Lothar Windsperger. Review of *Cardillac* by Paul Hindemith. *Melos* 7 (1928), p. 292. Quoted in Christoph Wolff, ed., *Paul Hindemith: Sämtliche Werke* IV/1: *Cardillac.* Mainz: Schott, 1978.
Metz, Günther, *Melodische Polyphonie in der Zwölftonordnung.* Baden-Baden: Valentin Körner, 1976.
Meyer, Leonard. *Music, the Arts, and Ideas: Patterns and Predictions in Twentieth-Century Culture.* Chicago: University of Chicago Press, 1967.
Milhaud, Darius. *Notes without Music.* Translated by Donal Evans. Edited by Rollo Myers. New York: Alfred A. Knopf, 1953.
Morgan, Robert. "Dissonant Prolongations: Theoretical and Compositional Precedents." *Journal of Music Theory* 20 (1976), p. 49.
Neumann, Friedrich. "Kadenz, Melodieführung und Stimmfuhrüng in den *Six Chansons* und *Five Songs on Old Texts* von Hindemith." *Hindemith Jahrbuch* 8 (1979), p. 49.
Neumeyer, David. "Counterpoint and Pitch Structure in the Early Music of Hindemith." Ph.D. dissertation, Yale University, 1976.
———. "Letter-Name Mottoes in Hindemith's 'Gute Nacht'." *Hindemith Jahrbuch* 6 (1977), p. 29.
———. "The Genesis and Structure of Hindemith's *Ludus Tonalis.*" *Hindemith Jahrbuch* 7 (1978), p. 72.
New Grove Dictionary of Music and Musicians. S. v. "Hindemith, Paul," by Ian Kemp.
Newlin, Dika. "Music Chronicle: The Case of Hindemith." *Partisan Review* 16 (1949), p. 410.
Norton, M. D. Herter. *Translations from the Poetry of Rainer Maria Rilke.* New York: W. W. Norton, 1938.
Noss, Luther. "Hindemith's Concert Tours in the United States: 1937, 1938, 1939." *Hindemith Jahrbuch* 7 (1978), p. 121.
Paul Hindemith: Die letzten Jahre. Mainz: Schott, 1965.
Paul Hindemith: Zeugnis in Bildern. 2d ed. Mainz: Schott, 1961.

Rexroth, Dieter. "Tradition und Reflexion beim frühen Hindemith." *Hindemith Jahrbuch* 2 (1972), p. 91.

———. "Von der moralischen Verantwortung des Künstlers: Zu den großen Opern von Paul Hindemith." *Hindemith Jahrbuch* 3 (1973), p. 63. [Contents page listing as "Das Künstlerproblem bei Hindemith"]

———. "Zu den Kammermusiken von Paul Hindemith." *Hindemith Jahrbuch* 6 (1977), p. 47.

———, ed. *Hindemith-Zyklus Nordrhein-Westfalen: 1980–81.* Wuppertal: Kulturamt der Stadt, 1980.

———. " 'Nun beginne ich mich zu bedeuten'—zur Biographie des jungen Hindemiths." In *Hindemith-Zyklus Nordrhein-Westfalen: 1980–81.* Edited by Dieter Rexroth. Wuppertal: Kulturamt der Stadt, 1980.

———, ed. *Erprobungen und Erfahrungen: Zu Paul Hindemith's Schaffen in den Zwanziger Jahren.* Frankfurter Studien, no. 2. Mainz: Schott, 1981.

———. "Zum Stellenwert der Oper *Cardillac* im Schaffen Hindemiths." In *Erprobungen und Erfahrungen: Zu Paul Hindemith's Schaffen in den Zwanziger Jahren,* edited by Dieter Rexroth. *Frankfurter Studien,* no. 2. Mainz: Schott, 1981.

———, ed. *Paul Hindemith: Briefe.* Frankfurt: Fischer, 1982.

Richter, Eckhart. "A Glimpse into the Workshop of Paul Hindemith." *Hindemith Jahrbuch* 6 (1977), p. 122.

Rieple, Max. "Begegnungen mit Paul Hindemith." *Hindemith Jahrbuch* 1 (1971), p. 148.

Rubeli, Alfred. *Hindemiths A Cappella Werke. Frankfurter Studien,* no. 1. Mainz: Schott, 1975.

Salzer, Felix. *Structural Hearing.* 2 vols. New York: Boni, 1952. Repr. ed., New York: Dover, 1962.

Salmen, Walter. "Alte Töne und Volksmusik in Kompositionen von Paul Hindemith." *Yearbook of the ISCM* (1969), p. 89.

Samson, Jim. *Music in Transition.* London: E. J. Dent, 1967.

Sayers, Dorothy. *Gaudy Night.* New York: Avon, 1968. [Original edition published in London: Gollancz, 1935]

Schackford, Charles. Review of *Übungsbuch für den dreistimmigen Satz.* [*Unterweisung im Tonsatz,* vol. 3] *Journal of Music Theory* 16 (1972), p. 238.

Schenker, Heinrich. *Kontrapunkt.* 2 vols. Vienna: Universal: 1910, 1922.

———. *Beethoven: Die letzten Sonaten: Sonata A Dur Op. 101.* Edited by Oswald Jonas. Vienna: Universal, 1972. [Original edition published in 1920]

———. *Der Tonwille.* Vienna: A. Gutmann and Leipzig: F. Hofmeister, 1921–1924.

———. *Das Meisterwerk in der Musik.* 3 vols. Munich: Drei Masken, 1925–1930.

———. *Free Composition.* Translated by Ernst Oster. New York: Longman, 1979. [First published as *Der freie Satz.* Vienna: Universal, 1935]

Schilling, Hans Ludwig. Paul Hindemiths "Cardillac." Würzburg: Konrad Triltsch, 1962.

Schillinger, Joseph. *The Mathematical Basis of the Arts.* New York: Philosophical Library, 1948.

Schmitz, Eugen. "Bibers Rosenkrantzsonaten." *Musica* 5 (1951), p. 235.

Schneider, Norbert. "Prinzipien der rhythmischen Gestaltung in Hindemiths Oper *Mathis der Maler.*" *Hindemith Jahrbuch* 8 (1979), p. 7.

Schubert, Giselher. "Ein Komponist in seiner Welt: Zu Hindemiths später Entwicklung." In *Hindemith-Zyklus Nordrhein-Westfalen: 1980–81,* edited by Dieter Rexroth. Wuppertal: Kulturamt der Stadt, 1980.

———. "Vorgeschichte und Entstehung der *Unterweisung im Tonsatz, Theoretischer Teil.*" *Hindemith Jahrbuch* 9 (1980), p. 16.

———. *Hindemith.* Rowohlts Bildmonographien, no. 299. Reinbek bei Hamburg: Rowohlt, 1981.

Searle, Humphrey. *Twentieth Century Counterpoint.* 2d ed. London: Ernest Benn, 1955.

Skelton, Geoffrey. *Paul Hindemith: The Man behind the Music.* New York: Crescendo, 1975.

Stephan, Rudolf. "Hindemith's *Marienleben*: An Assessment of Its Two Versions." Translated by Hans F. Redlich. *Music Review* 15 (1954), p. 275.

———. "Über Paul Hindemith." *Hindemith Jahrbuch* 4 (1974), p. 45.

———. "Adorno und Hindemith: Zum Verständnis einer schwierigen Beziehung." *Hindemith Jahrbuch* 7 (1978), p. 24.

———. "Zur Musik der Zwanzigerjahre." In *Erprobungen und Erfahrungen: Zu Paul Hindemith's Schaffen in den Zwanziger Jahren,* edited by Dieter Rexroth. *Frankfurter Studien,* no. 2. Mainz: Schott, 1981.

———. "Zum Verständnis von Hindemiths Analysen." In *Festschrift für Siegfried Borris,* edited by Richard Jakoby and Clemens Kühn. Wilhelmshaven: Heinrichshofen's Verlag, 1982.

Stuckenschmidt, Hans Heinz. *Neue Musik.* Berlin: Suhrkamp, 1951.

———. "Paul Hindemiths Aufbruch und Heimkehr." *Hindemith Jahrbuch* 4 (1974), p. 18.

———. Review of the production of *Cardillac* by the Deutsche Oper, Berlin, 1977. In the *Frankfurter Allgemeine Zeitung,* October 5, 1977. Reproduced in the *Informationen* section of the *Hindemith Jahrbuch* 6 (1977), p. 180.

Stravinsky, Igor, and Robert Craft. *Memories and Conversations.* New York: Doubleday, 1960.

Stravinsky, Igor, and Robert Craft. *Dialogues and a Diary.* London: Faber & Faber, 1968.

Strobel, Heinrich. *Paul Hindemith.* Mainz: Schott, 1930. 3d ed., 1948.

Thomson, William. "Hindemith's Contribution to Music Theory." *Journal of Music Theory* 9 (1965), p. 52.

Whittall, Arnold. *Music since the First World War.* London: J. M. Dent, 1977.

Willms, Franz. "Paul Hindemith: Ein Versuch." In *Von Neuer Musik,* edited by H. Grues, E. Kruttge, and E. Thalheimer. Cologne: F. J. Marcan, 1925.

Wöhlke, Franz. *"Mathis der Maler" von Paul Hindemith.* Berlin-Lichterfelde: Robert Lienau, 1965.

Wolff, Christoph, ed. *Paul Hindemith: Sämtliche Werke* IV/1: *Cardillac.* Mainz: Schott, 1978.

Wolff, Hellmuth Christian. Afterword to *Paul Hindemith: Cardillac (Neufassung 1952).* Leipzig: Peters, n.d.

Zwink, Eberhart. *Paul Hindemiths "Unterweisung im Tonsatz" als der Konsequenz der Entwicklung seiner Kompositionstechnik.* Göppingen: Alfred Kümmerle, 1974.

INDEX

I wish to acknowledge my gratitude to the following for permission to use the musical illustrations and quotations reprinted here:

Boosey & Hawkes, Inc., for Béla Bartók, Sixth String Quartet © Copyright 1941 by Hawkes & Son (London) Ltd.; renewed 1968. Reprinted by permission of Boosey & Hawkes, Inc.

European American Music Distributors Corporation for Sonata for Viola Solo, Op. 11, No. 5 © B. Schott's Soehne, Mainz, 1923; © renewed Schott & Co. Ltd., London, 1951. Sonata for Violoncello Solo, Op. 25, No. 3 © B. Schott's Soehne, Mainz, 1923; © renewed Schott & Co. Ltd., London, 1951. Das Marienleben (Revised Version) © Schott & Co. Ltd., London, 1948; copyright renewed. Das Marienleben, Op. 27 (Original Version) © B. Schott's Soehne, Mainz, 1924; © renewed 1951. Cardillac, Op. 39 (Revised Version) © B. Schott's Soehne, Mainz, 1926; completely revised edition © by Schott & Co. Ltd., London, 1952. Cardillac © 1926 by B. Schott's Soehne, Mainz; © renewed 1954. Kammermusik No. 4, Op. 36, No. 3 © B. Schott's Soehne, Mainz, 1925; © renewed 1953. Ludus Tonalis © Schott & Co. Ltd., London, 1943; © renewed 1971. Nobilissima Visione Suite © Schott & Co. Ltd., London, 1940; © renewed 1968. Mathis der Maler © B. Schott's Soehne, Mainz, 1935; renewed 1963. Craft of Musical Composition Vol. 1 copyright 1942 by Schott & Co. Ltd., London; copyright renewed 1970 by B. Schott's Soehne, Mainz. Der Schwanendreher © B. Schott's Soehne, Mainz, 1936; © renewed 1964. Trauermusik © B. Schott's Sohne, Mainz, 1936; © renewed 1964. Piano Sonata No. 1 in A © B. Schott's Soehne, Mainz, 1936; © renewed 1964. Piano Sonata No. 2 in G © B. Schott's Soehne, Mainz, 1936; © renewed 1964. Piano Sonata No. 3 in B Flat © B. Schott's Soehne, Mainz, 1936; © renewed 1964. Vidit Joannes Jesum Venientem © B. Schott's Soehne, 1960. Whitman Requiem ("When Lilacs Last in the Door-yard Bloom'd") copyright 1948 by B. Schott's Soehne, Mainz; copyright renewed. Messe © B. Schott's Soehne, 1963. All Rights Reserved. Used by permission of European American Music Distributors Corporation, sole U.S. agent for B. Schott's Soehne.